# Living with *HorsePower!*

# Living with *HorsePower!*

## *Personally Empowering Life Lessons Learned from the Horse*

### Rebekah Ferran Witter

TRAFALGAR SQUARE PUBLISHING
North Pomfret, Vermont

First published in 1998 by
Trafalgar Square Publishing, North Pomfret, Vermont 05053

Copyright © 1998 by Rebekah Ferran Witter

The author has made every effort to obtain a release from all persons appearing in the photographs used in this book. In some cases, however, the persons may not have been known and therefore could not be contacted.

**Disclaimer of Liability:** The author and publisher shall have neither liability nor responsibility to any person or entity with respect to any loss or damage caused or alleged to be caused directly or indirectly by the information contained in this book. While the book is as accurate as the author can make it, there may be errors, omissions, and inaccuracies.

**Library of Congress Cataloging-in-Publication Data**

Witter, Rebekah Ferran.
Living with HorsePower! : personally empowering life lessons
learned from the horse / Rebekah Ferran Witter.
p. cm.
Includes bibliographical references and index.
ISBN 1-57076-121-3 (hardcover)
1. Horses. 2. Horsemanship. 3. Human-animal relationships. I. Title.
SF285.W755 1998
636.1—dc21 98-29194
CIP

Printed in United States of America

10 9 8 7 6 5 4 3 2

# Table of Contents

# Acknowledgments

I owe a huge debt of gratitude to everyone who contributed to this work by granting an interview. For me each interview began with a "cold call" to a total stranger, but ended in the warmth of new-found friendship. During those sessions, individuals openly introduced insights and anecdotes from their own experience—some profoundly personal—in the belief that others might benefit from their lessons in *HorsePower!*

| | |
|---|---|
| Jo Abbott | Sarah Hafner |
| Adrian Arroyo | Ron Harding |
| Zaven Ayanian | Becky Hart |
| Laura Bianchi | Jill Keiser Hassler |
| James Brady | Chris Hawkins |
| Buck Brannaman | Vicki Hearne |
| Octavia Brown | Bob Henry |
| L.D. Burke III | Amy Hubbard |
| Jenny Butah | Jack Huyler |
| Bobby Christian | Allan Jamison |
| Lt. Carl Clipper | Martha Josey |
| Tracy Cole | Valerie Kanavy |
| Diana Starr Cooper | Anne Kursinski |
| Kelli Cox | Dr. Patty Latham |
| Helen K. Crabtree | Dr. Elizabeth Lawrence |
| Charlotte Dicke | Pat Lawson |
| Bev Doolittle | Doug Lietzke |
| Anonymous | Rege Ludwig |
| Bob Douglas | John Lyons |
| Phyllis A. Eifert | Larry Mahan |
| Dale Evans | Mary Mansi |
| Jimmy Fairclough | Dennis Marine |
| Mary Fenton | Dede Marx |
| Maxine Freitas | Dr. Robert Miller |
| Carol Grant | Tom Moore |

Holly Peterson Mondavi
Stagg Newman
Kelly O'Boyle
Cara O'Neill
Macella O'Neill
Rex Peterson
Irving Pettit
Mary Deringer Phelps
Michael Plumb
Monty Roberts
Roy Rogers
Sam Savitt
Jane Savoie
Tina Schuler

Richard Shrake
Penelope Smith
Curtis Steel
William Steinkraus
Genie Stewart-Spears
Susan Stovall
Carol Stratton
Sally Swift
Linda Tellington-Jones
Caroline Thompson
Diana Thompson
Camille Whitfield Vincent
René Williams
Cathy Ziffren

Love and tremendous thanks also go to my computer consultant, proof reader and wonderful husband, Kip; as well as to Gert Mazur for her transcription help; to Lynda Paffrath, the other half of my writing "group"; to William Steinkraus for his invaluable support, to Kathy Kadash Swan for the initial editing, and to Cathy Nessier, videographer.

Additional thanks to all at Trafalgar Square Publishing—especially Caroline Robbins, for taking a chance on a new writer with a new vision, and Martha Cook, who worked diligently to polish and clarify the vision. A final thank you, to Betsy Butterfield, for her magical artwork and genial rework. May you all enjoy living with *HorsePower!*

# Author's Note

LIVING WITH *HORSEPOWER!* is a conversation with seventy members of the horse world, and as such, employs a conversational format with contributors' comments set off in *italics* rather than quotation marks, allowing the reader to distinguish my voice from that of a contributor.

In light of the number of names and backgrounds to keep in mind, the page number on which a contributor's photograph and biographical information is located is cited in parentheses when that individual's name first appears in the text. Thereafter, the reader may look up the contributor's name in the index and the listing indicated in bold will reference the page to turn to for that information. And since the horse world has its own specialized vocabulary, a glossary of equine terms can be found on page 251.

As I worked directly from tapes, at times it was necessary to modify spoken phrasing to wording more conducive to written text. In doing so, I took care to preserve content; however, some quotes are no longer verbatim. I reported all conversations as closely to the original transcript as possible, and apologize if any oversights, misquotes, mistakes, misunderstandings, or errors occur in the text as they are completely unintentional.

The opinions expressed in this book were given freely and are those of the individual contributors, or mine. I attempted to reference and verify all pertinent information, however, due to the very nature of conversational anecdotes, total verification is not possible.

R. W.

Lucky

Kip on Stranger, and the author on Bay Mare

Freddie

Haji

Sable

# Dedication

This book is dedicated to all our equine teachers. Horses have sacrificed and contributed greatly to mankind's betterment, and I hope this book inspires us to open our minds, hearts and spirits to the lessons offered through them.

My personal thanks go to Freddie, Haji, Lucky, Bay Mare and Sable.

# THE ENCHANTMENT,
# EXCITEMENT
# AND EMPOWERMENT
# OF HORSES

A few years back, I was sidelined by that dastardly detour of life known as Midlife Crisis. Midlife Crisis switches perfectly sane people from logic mode to emotion mode, kidnapping sanity by blindfolding reason. During this mental disorientation people have been known to "follow their bliss" and divorce a spouse of twenty-six years, or shelve a successful career to fire ceramic pots in the redwood groves above Carmel, or sail around the world in a canoe with nothing but hook, line, and sinker (plus $100,000 worth of LORAN navigation equipment).

Me? I sold my lucrative furniture store and interior design practice for a few pieces of silver and took up the search for what-to-do-with-the-rest-of-my-life. I hadn't a clue as to what that was. My future loomed vast and empty before me—like the vision of endless blank paper that appears when one is assigned a twenty-page thesis on a topic of "your choice." Having no idea how to choose a topic for the rest of my life, I sought help. Luckily, I found a sage counselor who asked, "What is it that you always wanted to do as a young child?" The answer to that question was instantaneous: ride horses!

A child of the fifties, I used to "fantasy-canter" to and from grammar school on Dale Evans' buckskin, Buttermilk, and whenever my mind wandered in class, I found myself drawing horses in the margins of my notebook. I read all of Marguerite Henry's books, cried for Black Beauty, thrilled with the adventures of Roy, Trigger, and the gang; watched MY FRIEND FLICKA religiously, and swooned with envy over Elizabeth Taylor's incredible luck to be able to race in NATIONAL VELVET. Yes, learning to ride had been a lifelong dream of mine, yet I'd always considered it too expensive,

I

too self-indulgent, too time-consuming, too frivolous, too… too… too….

However, as so many midlife-crisis survivors discovered before me—it was do-it-now-or-never-time! Starting riding lessons at the rather advanced age of forty-two was daunting, yet afforded a mature perspective that revealed the many parallels between riding well and living well. I found that each riding lesson produced a valuable *living* lesson. In addition to riding and jumping techniques, the sessions taught me about goal-setting, facing fears, building confidence and self-esteem, relaxing, problem-solving, mental flexibility, physical coordination, balance, verbal and non-verbal communication skills, team-building, compassion, relationships, integrity, and personal accountability. I was living a more directed, determined, and dynamic life now that horses and riding were a part of it. By finally indulging my lifelong enchantment with horses, my whole being was enhanced: physically, mentally, emotionally and spiritually. I had never felt happier, stronger, or more positive.

In my quest to become a better rider I found many excellent books that explained *how* one should ride—yet none that addressed *why* one should ride. What is it that still draws people to the world of horses even though they are technologically obsolete? Few people in the horse world get a tremendous dollar return for their time and efforts, so Wall Street salaries aren't the magnet. To gain even a minor reputation in the equestrian arena takes years of doing—and doing consistently very well. In America, even Olympic riders get precious little exposure, so celebrity status isn't the big motivator.

In my search for answers, I interviewed eighty people across the horse industry: riders, farriers, trainers, veterinarians, equine artists, writers, cowboys, polo players, endurance riders, grand-prix jumpers, barrel racers, rodeo stars, western legends, and Olympic champions. Individually, each shared wonderful life lessons and inspired insights gained from his or her experiences with horses. Collectively, they answered the "why's" of riding: Why this compelling attraction to horses? Why risk being around these huge, unpredictable animals at all? Why invest the quantities of time, energy and money it takes to keep horses and learn to ride? What do people get back in return?

The compelling attraction apparently stems from an ancient

and widespread human condition that infects people with varying degrees of attraction to horses, from a mild appreciation to a driving passion, which I've termed "horse fever": the enchantment of horses.

The inherent risks of horses provide shots of adrenaline which drive some to levels of commitment that non-horse people consider crazy. This state of being "horse crazy" stems from the excitement of horses.

The time, energy and money invested is repaid with the many positive life lessons learned from working with horses—what I've termed, *HorsePower!*—the empowerment of horses.

Thus, the "why" of horses are rewards found in the personal experiences and resulting lessons that strengthen one's body, mind and spirit, and dynamically enhance one's very existence through the enchantment, excitement and empowerment of horses. People who experience this are truly living their lives with *HorsePower!*

The following chapters will usher you into the dynamic world of *HorsePower!* by exploring the attractions and passions of horse fever, the risks and rewards of being horse crazy, the basic differences between human nature and horse nature, and finally the many genuinely inspiring and insightful anecdotes that reflect the empowering life lessons learned from horses.

Within these heartfelt, personal stories, riders will discover an equestrian kinship; friends and families of "horse crazy" individuals will discover a greater understanding of the perplexing passion that consumes their loved ones; and horse lovers not yet actively involved in the world of horses, will perhaps, as I did, discover it's time to indulge their dream to mount up and begin living with *HorsePower!*

# CHAPTER ONE

# HORSE FEVER

## Getting Hooked

*Pegasus is my fantasy, but my Pegasus would be black with a blaze on his face like my wild stallion, Taj, and I would fly over the moon with him. —Chris Hawkins*

"*The kick is GOOD!* It's unbelievable! The home team has done the impossible—they've come back to win the Super Bowl in the last fifteen seconds!"

The room-full of jubilant fans explodes—leaping, high-fiving, and hugging each other. Though hoarse from screaming as their team's score had ebbed, surged, then suddenly crested in the final winning wave, their cheers nonetheless drown out the TV.

Their host, popping the cork on chilled champagne, holds the frothing bottle above his head and bellows, "Let the party begin!" But as his wife reaches for the remote control, someone yells, "Wait! Don't turn it off yet!" The hostess, instantly curious as to what has suddenly distracted the group's attention, turns back to the big screen.

Thundering across a pristine, snow-covered meadow is a band of beautiful horses; their bodies pulsing with power as they move through the glistening powder. The size, grace, and freedom of these animals suddenly strike her heart with a longing to join them and gallop away—away from the city, the job, and the bills—to run with them in nature....

There are no words with the commercial, for America needs no introduction to these magnificent mascots. They are as well known as any sports team or celebrity in the world, and for many, they thrill the soul as surely as the strains of the national anthem.

It was extraordinary. That silent commercial with just horses was mesmerizing; seizing the attention of a dozen football fans away from *partying* to watch. Those Budweiser Clydesdales distracted the revelers because they touched upon an ancient human affliction: "horse fever"—the enchantment of horses.

## Profile of Horse Fever

Horse fever is a physical, emotional, and spiritual condition that strikes people of all ages, affecting individuals to varying degrees throughout their lives. While some individuals are totally immune to the fever and never give horses a second look or thought, most people, like those in the preceding scenario, are born with a low-grade fever that simply manifests itself as a deep appreciation of the grace, beauty, and freedom of horses. This mild infection, however, can ignite into serious horse fever at any time, compelling one to take riding lessons, attend rodeos, horse shows, race meets, or even, in severe cases—to buy a horse.

The syndrome usually hits hardest in youth, occasionally goes into remission around sixteen, and can flare up again later in life—the twenties, thirties or forties—with midlife being a common time of re-infection. Those with chronic horse fever seem to require daily exposure to the very creatures that infect them and may spend their entire lives as competitive riders, trainers, breeders, cowboys, farriers, equine veterinarians or in some other horse-related vocation.

People immune to horse fever are often mystified by the actions of those seriously afflicted. To the unafflicted, riding horses seems antiquated, "why don't you buy a *Harley?*" risky, "you broke your arm jumping *what?*" ridiculously slow, "you've been riding for *that long,* and you're still taking *lessons?*" unrewarding, "you went to all those shows, and didn't win *a single ribbon?*" and horrendously expensive, "did you say chiropractic bills for a *horse?*" Others cannot understand the investment of time, money, and energy that horse fever exacts by inciting the afflicted to keep horses in their lives. They cannot understand the attraction to what appears to be a big, unpredictable, hay-burning beast that is strong as an ox one minute and in the throes of a veterinary crisis the next. "Look, if you want a pet, we could get a *dog.*" None of it makes sense—unless you have the fever.

Horses can help those with horse fever lead stronger, happier, and more dynamic lives. The lessons learned through sharing and caring for another living being hold them in great stead in their personal lives. Among the character lessons credited to their association with horses are commitment, responsibility, compassion, patience, empathy, and love. They experience competition, success and failure, sportsmanship and personal growth. They learn communication skills, goal-setting, teaching techniques, and the nature of another species. Those who successfully internalize this fever become true horsemen. Those afflicted for a lifetime usually go to their grave with a strong body, a healthy philosophy of life, and a smile on their face: all telltale manifestations of horse fever.

Not always fun and games, horse fever does have some negative side-effects: weakening of the pocket book, isolation, possible injury, and even death. These risks are readily accepted by the afflicted, for horse fever is a condition that generates strength and a passion that feeds the soul. To those with the fever, the *rewards* of horses far outweigh the *risks* of horses. This is what drives many horse people to "get back on" when bruised, battered, or bleeding. To some, that attitude is inspiring; to others, it's insane.

## What Causes Horse Fever

Mankind has shown great respect and reverence for the horse since early encounters were recorded on cave walls. *The horse is a common fetish in human culture, often deified for augmenting man's speed and strength,* points out Robert Miller, DVM, (p. 18) veterinarian and internationally recognized authority on equine behavior. *Long before man rode, when man only hunted horses for food, cave drawings showed a respect for the horse. Classical statues portray individuals on spirited horses because it enhanced their stature. In language, the terms "cavalier" and "caballero" define gentlemen as horsemen. There's an implication of aristocracy, superiority, gentility, and nobility—all stemming from man's relationship to the horse.*

From the low-grade fever of enchantment to the full-blown, life-long passion, what are the causes of various levels and symptoms of horse fever? Among the most significant are: the physical beauty of the animal, the human desire to ride, the fantasy and an inherent spiritual bond between humans and horses.

## Physical Appeal

Many people contract horse fever in their very early years. The image of the horse-crazy youngster enticed by equine beauty to spend hours dreaming and drawing horses is so common as to be stereotypical: *As a small child I used to draw horses—nothing but horses,* art historian and life-long rider Carol Stratton (p. 19), recalls. *Draw, draw, draw. It was like something flowing through me. People who saw my drawings would exclaim, "Oh, this precious child, she's going to be a great artist. She draws these horses so beautifully!" So, my parents carted me off to art school. When I drew things other than horses, you couldn't tell if it was a flower, a camel, or a house. We soon realized that it was my love of the horse that created the extraordinary drawings—not great artistic talent.*

Since artistic masterpieces are usually triggered by passion, Carol's chronic horse fever served as a singular inspiration for her exceptional horse drawings—but *only* horse drawings.

Obviously, the inspiring artistic beauty plus the dramatic action of an athletic horse are compelling, for they excite the eye and fire the imagination much the same as watching an exquisite ballet dancer: *Horses are just so beautiful. I watch my mare, Ariel, and she is so elegant and light... it's thrilling,* exclaims Cathy Ziffren (p. 39), businesswoman and avid rider.

The aesthetic attraction of horses is remarkable in that it pleases most of the senses. Sight: the image of the horse is celebrated in art, poetry, and literature, for its beauty is powerful, sensitive, romantic, and free. Touch: their warm, smooth coats and velvety muzzles invite stroking. Sound: their nickered greetings, urgent calls, and hoofbeat rhythms touch the human heart. Smell: many marvel that they find the earthy aroma of a horse as pleasing as that of home-baked bread.

## The Desire to Ride

As spiritually and physically attractive as horses may be, why do people still insist on riding these beasts when you can get around easier, faster, and cleaner in a car? This particular love of riding horses springs from many sources and circumstances: heredity, necessity, opportunity and fantasy have led to an interest in riding.

Some feel their riding fever is inherited, and riding instructor Kelli Cox (p.19) has an intriguing twist on this theory: *My parents were never interested in horses. I started drawing horses, reading about horses and getting very excited about taking lessons on my own. When I was seven, my mom took me to an English riding instructor. I started showing in my teens, rode during college, and now teach riding. I really love being around horses. What's interesting is that I am adopted and just recently got in contact with a great aunt, who told me that my birth-mother always loved horses and has a horse of her own right now. Since my adoptive parents didn't have anything to do with horses at all, my interest must be inherited in some way.*

Riding fever often grows out of necessity, from having been born on a working ranch, or farm, or in an era before automobiles were common: *Growing up on a little farm in Duck Run, Ohio, we had no car* recalls the King of the Cowboys, Roy Rogers (p. 20), star of television and feature films in the 1950's, *so riding or driving a buggy or wagon was it. I started riding when I was about seven. My first "horse" was a mule called Tom. He was crippled in one foot and didn't ride real well. Then my dad got a little span of mules, and one of them, Barney, was a terrific rider. I used him for school; I'd ride him to church. When I was eleven, Dad gave me my first horse, an ex-sulky racer named Babe. That was pretty much my riding career until I signed on as 'The Singing Cowboy' in Hollywood and partnered with Trigger in '39.*

Others who did not actually own a horse made up for this lack in unorthodox ways, as well-known horse trainer and teacher John Lyons (p. 21) relates: *When I was in fifth grade, I got to where I liked horses. At that time Phoenix, Arizona, was a relatively small town, and there were pastures with horses right around where we lived. So, a lot of times I'd ditch school, go grab a horse, climb on, take off and go riding all day. Joy riding. I didn't have any tack—no saddle, no bridle, nothing—I just rode them with a rope around the neck. I must have had some kind of control 'cause I didn't die. I'd ride in the pastures, down the streets of Phoenix, or out in the desert. There was a stable, I think it was called South Mountain Stable, and sometimes I'd ride out there. People would rent horses, and I'd ride along with them. I got in trouble for ditching school. I got caught at that, but I never got caught stealing horses...I always put them back...no worse for wear.*

Most people can identify the instant they knew they had contracted riding fever: *My family lived on a small acreage in Oregon,* says world champion bronc and bull rider Larry Mahan (p. 22). *Both of my folks really loved horses, so we always had a few around. My dad had me in the saddle before I was walking and bought me my first horse when I was about eight years old; it was instant love....*

One fascinating aspect of riding fever is that it evidently can be transmitted through animals other than horses: *The first thing I ever rode was a Jersey milk cow,* admits World Champion Saddlebred trainer, Tom Moore (p. 23), *then mules. It wasn't until I was in my teens that I saw my first gaited horse. I remember that day clearly. I was working as a groom at a riding academy at 1508 North Clark Street in Chicago in 1946. I fell in love with that first gaited horse I saw then, and I've been with them ever since....*

Like Tom, another Saddlebred trainer and equitation authority, Helen Crabtree (p. 24), was also initially infected through other animals. *The first known picture of me dates from 1918, when I was three. I was riding Jack, our old mule, going down to get the cows and turn off the windmill. After Jack, I rode everything with four legs on the farm. If I could catch a big pig or a baby calf, I'd hop on its back until I got dumped off—I loved all the animals—but I was just absolutely wild about horses.*

Occasionally horse fever begins as a related fantasy, when the past reaches forward in time and enchants a contemporary with the historic allure of the American cowboy: *The first time I saw a cowboy I was just a kid,* recalls rancher and designer of cowboy furniture and apparel, L.D. "Doc" Burke III (p. 24). *We were driving through Wyoming, and there was a guy on horseback with chaps, a lariat circling over his head, roping a cow. I'd seen movie cowboys before, but they weren't real. The real cowboy...wow! He was a presence. That image is branded on my mind.*

As with that cowboy image, many fevers begin with sheer fantasy and make-believe steeds: a pony-back ride, the mechanical "quarter horse" in front of the market, the family dog, or a trusted bicycle: *I was always drawn to horses and riding,* chef and all-around rider, Holly Peterson Mondavi (p. 37) recounts. *I starting with horsey-back rides on dad and pony rides at the fair. After prolonged begging, my parents gave my sister and me riding lessons when I was five; we got our first backyard horses when I was ten. Those were wonderful horses that we could just pile on—we actually got six kids on my horse, Roni. Life with those horses was always one of those joyful, wonderful things: I loved being outside; I loved being with horses—I just loved it all.*

Mary Deringer Phelps (p. 37), horse trainer and riding instructor recalls her feverish childhood of creative equine transformations: *When I was six, I had a J.C. Higgins bicycle I named 'Trigger' (I'm a great Roy Rogers fan). I'd put Trigger in his "stall" (an awning off of our sun porch with a snow fence around it) every night and stuff grass under his front fender so he'd have something to eat. I could jump off that bike, run beside it, and jump back on—'Trigger' stayed right with me—Roy could do it, so I could do it!*

*Our neighbors thought that I was from another world, because I also had a dog named Blackie. I'd haul Blackie around in his "trailer" (a red wagon with a cardboard box) and do jumping shows with him. I used torn sheets for his leg wraps. I longed Blackie until he jumped correctly—no paws on the jump—he'd pick his little legs up and clear a 2'6"er.* Though not from another world, Mary did have a healthy case of horse fever, complete with hallucinations that turned her dog and bike into the horses she so desperately desired.

## Romance

Nothing fans the flame of horse fever like romance. Recently a poll at the internationally "romantic" resorts of Club Med revealed that their clientele listed horseback riding as the number one activity to inspire romance. This is not new, as evidenced by this report dating back to the thirties: *In 1938, my girlfriend first came to the family ranch in Montana*, relates Jack Huyler (p. 38), English teacher and 1969 California Gymkhana Champion. *Margaret didn't know how to ride, so I'd get this old horse that was about as long as our living room sofa. We'd get on bareback and ride in the moonlight. That old horse was the means for romance. Since Margaret didn't ride very well, she had to hang on to me, or let me hold on to her. It was pretty romantic. We've been married more than fifty years now..*

As if scripted from a scene in one of their movies, Dale Evans (p. 20), Queen of the West, star of television and silver screen with her husband Roy Rogers, was a newcomer to both Hollywood and riding when she had her first heart-throbbing encounter with him on horseback. *In 1944, I was playing the part of a city girl in the picture,* THE COWBOY AND THE SENORITA. *They had me in high heels on a horse, which is ridiculous! I was just sitting there talking to Gabby Hayes, when something spooked my horse. He bolted, and I was hanging on for dear life, because my heel was caught in the saddle. Roy came after me on Trigger, caught my horse, stopped it and lifted me off.* Three years after that encounter, again on horseback, Roy proposed marriage to Dale during a personal appearance in Chicago; they've been married since 1947.

## Starting Late

As noted earlier, horse fever may lay dormant for years, so not all equestrians begin riding in their youth. Stagg Newman (p. 38), National 100 Mile Endurance Champion, was not bitten by the bug until after he married. *When I got married, I was a long-distance runner, and I tried to get my wife interested in running. She was into eventing and tried to get me interested in riding. Well, I took up competitive trail riding, and then endurance riding, but she never did take up running. Eventually, after a couple of bad eventing falls, my wife ended up in endurance too. Now we do most of our rides together. We've got over fifty one-hundred-mile rides between the two of us. We like to say, "The family that rides together endures."*

Accountant and horse owner, Mary Mansi (p. 39), tells of her later start: *A few years ago, my husband and I went trail riding with friends. I was so bad: nervous, uncomfortable, and clumsy, but I still really enjoyed the ride. I was so embarrassed by my lack of knowledge and ability that I decided to learn to ride well. My husband surprised me with a birthday gift of ten lessons, which turned out to be for English, not Western lessons as I had envisioned. My husband had been wonderful to get me riding lessons at all, so I went ahead and took the English lessons. When I got to the stables, I saw fences set up in the ring, but had no idea what they were for. When I saw students jumping I realized, "You expect me to do that?" I thought they were insane! But by the end of those ten lessons I was hooked. I've been riding and jumping for more than three years now.* Mary experienced a common side-effect of horse fever: the willingness to try things you never before thought possible, such as flying over a fence on a horse. Once you've done it, and realize how exciting it can be, soon one fear after another is surmounted, like obstacles in a jump course.

## Just for the Fun of It

*Riding is probably the utmost joy in my life—it's like icing on my life's cake,* notes Bob Henry (p. 39), recreational rider and founder of the annual Napa Valley Classic show-jumping benefit. As Bob suggests, horses remain mankind's partners because they're fun.

Veterinarian Patty Latham (p. 40) describes a few of the entertaining horse activities of her youth: *When I was a kid, growing up in the fifties, I lived in a little town—Niocia, Missouri, where it was perfectly acceptable to ride downtown, tie your pony up to a parking meter and go to the movies. On Halloween kids would go trick-or-treating on horseback. One year that was really hilarious, everybody dressed as the headless horseman—we had herds of headless horsemen out trick-or-treating.*

While legions of kids have played at being cowboys, many others are impressed with the life and exceptional equestrian abilities of Native Americans: *As a young kid I had a little gray mare I used to ride like an Indian,* René Williams (p. 40), United States Equestrian Team trainer for the Olympics and equine sculptor recollects, *just a rawhide lip-strap and one rein coming back. We'd go out on moonlit nights and gallop everywhere like that. Gosh, when I think of it, I wish I could do it today. Jump on her bareback and gallop away.*

Whether it's soaring over a jump, playing at cowboys and Indians, or the headless horseman of Sleepy Hollow, horses are a terrific source for make-believe and great times to be enjoyed and remembered for a lifetime.

## Horse Pets

Many people simply enjoy the horse as a genial companion, a pet or as a candidate for nurturing: *My sons loved the pony and the horses without having to ride them,* explains Phyllis Eifert (p. 63), painter, sculptor, pony breeder, and fox hunter. *The same with my husband— he loved being around the horses and even enjoyed mucking stalls, but he never wanted to ride. You can really have horses and love them without having to ride them.*

Another obvious example of appreciating horses without riding is the thriving miniature horse industry. No bigger than twenty-five to thirty-four inches tall, miniatures are true, complete horses and provide their owners with all elements of the equine experience, except riding. The rapid growth in this rather novel area of the horse industry indicates that a great number of people love horses for the sake of the animal—not riding.

## A Spiritual Connection

Spirituality is the connection to something beyond one's own human state. Some believe their connection to horses predates their very existence; that it is an innately spiritual part of their being. *I know it to be spiritual,* declares Mary Fenton (p. 63), 1992 Riding Instructor of the Year, *because it came to me as such a strong feeling as a tiny child—it's the first thing I remember. There were no horses where I grew up. So where else could this desire come from? All I know is that every time I saw a horse my spirit was touched and lifted.*

For others, that connection is the silent communion between horse and rider, coupled with the realization that there is a harmony connecting them not only to the horse, but to the universe beyond: *My sense is that through our connection with horses, we connect to nature, the Great Spirit, or the unseen in a way that keeps us grounded,* says Linda Tellington-Jones (p. 64), world renowned trainer and developer of innovative training methods TTEAM and Tellington-TTouch systems. *Humans today are so into the material, and logical thinking. By dancing with horses, by being with horses, by breathing with horses, by touching horses, we can get a sense of a whole other spirit that is beyond our logical comprehension. When I am with or on a horse, it's as if I feel the breath of Mother Earth coming through the horse into my body. That gives me a sense of spirit which is way beyond what I receive from being with people.*

It is understandable that such spiritual potency would motivate individuals to seek connection through horses. *This is what animals are so good at,* explains Penelope Smith (p. 66), expert on interspecies communication. *We learn from the animals to go back to the integration of body, mind, and spirit. Not just emphasize the mental, but to care for our bodies, and remember that, in essence, we are spiritual beings. The path of being with animals and understanding them is a path toward understanding who you really are. It is a basic spiritual path. Horses are tremendous spiritual teachers. I can't help giving a sigh as soon as I touch a horse, for I feel more connected to the earth. I feel they are spiritual teachers of compassion and understanding and sensitivity.*

Western trainer, popular clinician, and technical advisor to the film THE HORSE WHISPERER, Buck Brannaman (p. 65), finds his spiritual connection throughout his daily equestrian life: *Riding is such a way of life for me. Even when I have time off, I ride. I figure the horse is a special gift that God gave us in hopes that we'd respect our gift, take care of him, and learn from him. I can't help but think that when you get closer with the horse, you are closer to your Maker.* No matter how it is perceived, the spiritual rewards of working with horses are potent and compelling to those who embrace them.

## Chronic Horse Fever

Most ordinary fevers are mercifully temporary—they nearly always ignite and extinguish within a few hours' or days' time. Horse fever behaves differently. It can be short-lived, but even in its transitory state, horse fever normally lasts a year or more. As noted earlier, chronic horse fever can last a lifetime, but rather than being life-threatening, horse fever is usually life-strengthening. Chronic horse fever begets horse lovers and true horsemen and horsewomen—individuals who never, ever, tire of horses. What is it that sustains their interest over the course of a decade, a generation, or a lifetime? What makes horses so fascinating day in and day out?

What keeps me coming back for more and more equine education is the sheer breadth of experience available. Every interaction is new and exciting in some way—either a training breakthrough for me or the horse, an unexpected thrill as my horse throws a little spook or buck into the equation or the mere fun of being out in nature with a companion of a different species.

No one will ever know all there is to know about horses, riding, the horse-human relationship, or equine care. Even in competition, the mix of elements always makes for a new event no matter how many times you may repeat the same course or routine. The mindset of horse and rider, their physical states, the footing of the arena, the atmosphere that day...everything can change instantly when working with a horse. It is a constant challenge, adventure, and education full of lessons about the horse, yourself, your abilities, your goals—your life.

## Horse Fever Leads to HorsePower!

Clearly horse fever brings people to horses, but what sustains their interest and the relationship is what people get back in return: *I never tire of horses,* declares equine artist and author Sam Savitt (p. 66). *I just love watching them move. I love putting my hands on them. I love getting on them. I love the feel of them under me. I love the look of my horse's head in front of me. Sometimes I like to put my face right against his neck and just breathe him in.* Like Sam, many true horse lovers find that their initial deep attraction simply matures into love and sustains itself. Being an artist and author, however, Sam is continually studying and presenting the horse in new images and situations. He receives back an exciting, creative, and rewarding livelihood that holds his interest in all things equine.

Others analyze the relationship between horses and humans more clinically, acknowledging that the complexities of the human condition may have created an "equine codependency": *There are many different kinds of love,* retired psychology instructor Carol Grant (p. 67) explains. *In contemporary society, the horse is vulnerable and totally dependent on its human custodians. A horse that gets out on its own, in most modern settings, won't last long. Humans have made horses totally dependent, and we humans love it when things are dependent on us.*

When our own children grow up and move away, the horse can, and often does, serve as a surrogate child in need of attention, love, nurturing and training. It's hard to suddenly stop hands-on parenting just because the kids have grown and gone; a domestic horse never outgrows the need for this type of loving attention.

The feeling of freedom inherent in a horse's being is a strong magnet for those desiring to share that freedom: *Since I have cerebral palsy,* explains rider and microfilm operator Tracy Cole (p. 67), *I have a different perspective about horses. Horses allow me to do things that I could never do on my own. I can see different things: the woods, the fields. I can go over brooks and through streams—so many things I couldn't do myself. Horses give me a sense of freedom. Since I'm dependent on horses to get out into nature, I appreciate them, and I'm grateful to them.* What better way to develop a feeling of independence than with a cooperative companion that will do your bidding and share the experience. It's a sense of freedom and friendship all rolled into one.

Ultimately, the daily passion for horses may stem from the fact that horses simply make a lot of people feel good. Whenever we straddle its back, we borrow something from that horse. If we look good on that horse, it's because they make us feel good. There is a mutual understanding that riders occupy that equestrian seat of honor through the horse's generosity, gentle tolerance, trained co-operation, and trust. *The moment I put my left foot in the stirrup, step up on the horse, and settle into the saddle, I just come alive,* marvels Helen Crabtree. *That is the greatest feeling in the world. It isn't a feeling of power or superiority or even the anticipation that I'm going to do something; it's just this general feeling of being in harmony with...the whole world! That sounds very high blown, but that's just the way it is with me, and I believe, with many people. It's one of God's privileges...it's God's gift is what it is!*

From the preceding testimonials, we've seen that the journey into the world of horses is a natural progression from the enchantment of horses to the empowering lessons horses offer. In actuality, the journey is an upward spiral—a kinetic carousel of fascination, learning, mastery, spirituality, and passion. The beauty of horses draws us onto the carousel and starts the motion, but the energy necessary to sustain this carousel ride results from the many challenging experiences, rewards and insights received. Those fortunate enough to ride this carousel in life have truly grasped the brass ring and won the prize of *HorsePower!*

ROBERT MILLER, D.V.M. b. 1925, is a veterinarian with a lifetime's experience with horses and 25 years' work with mules.
An internationally recognized authority on equine behavior and author of many books, papers and videos, he is credited with popularizing the technique of imprint training foals and was the first equine practitioner to receive the Bustad Companion Animal Veterinarian-of-the-Year Award in 1995. He is shown here with Quarter Horse colt, Our Doc's Imprint.

CAROL STRATTON, b. 1929, is an art historian and avid rider who, in 1949, was Vermont State Champion in Senior Equitation. Carol is pictured at the Green Mountain Horse Association in South Woodstock, Vermont with her horse Brother, the 1996 New England Field Hunter Champion.

KELLI COX, b. 1967, is a hunter jumper riding instructor and horse trainer in Northern California. Kelli is shown with Cinnamon, a lively pony she found for this student rider; together they have claimed a number of horse show championships.

ROY ROGERS, King of the Cowboys, b. 1911 and DALE EVANS, Queen of the West, b. 1912, have been two of America's most beloved stars of television, rodeo and the silver screen. Partners on screen before becoming partners for life in 1947, they've shared a number of personal trials along with their many "Happy Trails." Currently they keep busy with their museum and amusement park in Victorville, California. Roy and Dale are pictured with their favorite equine partners from the Double R Bar Ranch: Trigger and Buttermilk.

JOHN LYONS, b. 1947, is a horse trainer who enjoys demonstrating the mutual trust and communication that is possible between human and horse. Here he enjoys an outing without constraints on his Appaloosa stallion, Bright Zip. In addition to his success as a trainer and teacher, one of the highlights of John's career was realized when Bright Zip was named to the Appaloosa Hall of Fame.

LARRY MAHAN, b. 1944, is a world champion bronc and bull rider, rodeo stockman, Western clothing retailer, host of the HORSE WORLD television program and member of the Rodeo Hall of Fame. Larry is seen giving Australian fans an exciting show of his winning style in Sydney, 1978.

TOM MOORE, b. 1934, claims consistency is an important element in training, and his record proves it—Tom is the "winningest" Saddlebred trainer of all time. A founder of the United Professional Horsemen's Association and member of that organization's Hall of Fame, two-time winner of the coveted AHSA Horseman of the Year award and trainer of many World Champion saddle and harness horses, Tom won his first World Championship at age eighteen. In this dramatic shot taken at the Kentucky State Fair in the 1960's, the exciting action of saddle seat equitation is evident as Tom rides the World Champion Five Gaited Gelding, The Contender.

HELEN CRABTREE, b. 1915, has most of the equestrian world's prestigious awards to her credit. The first female saddle horse trainer, Helen trained hundreds of world champion horses and riders over the course of her career and wrote the definitive work on saddle seat equitation. Now retired, she continues actively contributing to the horse world through writing and consulting in Kentucky. Helen is pictured here in 1971 on the Junior three-gaited horse, Gala Affair.

L.D. "DOC" BURKE III, b. 1934, may have been born a New England Yankee, but his soul is that of a cowboy philosopher. L.D. moved West and bought a ranch on which he ran cows and horses for a number of years, then began his successful career designing cowboy furniture and apparel. L.D. is pictured on his Quarter Horse gelding, Jack, searching for strays on a ranch near Aspen, Colorado during the winter of 1993.

# CHAPTER TWO

# HORSE CRAZY

## A Reality Check

*There's no good reason to have a horse.* —**Carol Grant**

*If you ain't got problems, you're most likely dead.*
—© **L.D. Burke III**

The Virginia air was warm, thick, and smoky-blue with moisture, the field shone vivid green, the course was in great shape. This was the second day of competition with the fifth contestant on course for the cross-country portion of the three-day combined training event. Both horse and rider were looking incredibly fit and handsome as they approached their third obstacle. The three-foot, zig-zag timber fence was solid, but not very high, and the two galloped toward it in a rhythmic, controlled manner.

One stride before the fence, the rider rose slightly out of the saddle in anticipation of the jump. Suddenly, at the moment of take-off, his horse balked and reversed his forward thrust. Unbalanced yet committed, the tall, good-looking rider was unable to check his momentum and was launched out of the saddle. As he flew over his startled mount's head, the rider's hands caught in the bridle and were wrenched back. He landed with crushing impact on the far side of the obstacle with nothing to break his fall. The full weight of his muscular, 6'4", two-hundred-pound frame was driven onto the vulnerable angle of his fragile neck, pulverizing two vertebrae as his face smashed into the turf.

The rider never moved. It was a cold knockout... or was it death? In an instant, a trainer was at his side, but already the competitor's face was blue from lack of oxygen.

"Get the paramedics!" "Call an ambulance!" "Radio for a helicopter!" The cries went out for help—and a miracle.

This was not possible! It wasn't that big a fence! He was wearing a helmet and protective vest—he was doing it all right! How could this innocuous fence take out Superman?!

The world was stunned that last Saturday in May, 1995 when Christopher Reeve went from being Hollywood's Superman to a quadriplegic tied to a respirator. He is still fighting his way back. He does not blame his horse, the course, or the promoters of the event. His was an accident—bad luck—a real factor in riding, as in life.

Horseback riding is a sport in which most riders take personal responsibility for their wrecks because risk is an integral part of the allure. Riders recognize the risks, accept the risks, and train to overcome the risks. Beyond that, it's up to their own competence, their horses' abilities and fickle luck. Riders who do get hurt tend not to become victims because they made the choice to accept the inherent danger. The old adage, "When you fall off, get right back on," is more than words to a rider—it's a way of life. Christopher Reeve is proving he is more Superman now in his all-too-real life than he ever was on screen.

The previous chapter explored the various enchantments of horse fever that get people hooked on horses. Now, for balance, the downside of the horse world must also be examined: the inherent risks and hard realities of dealing with horses. Riding is not always about fun, fantasy, romance and the other positive aspects we have been looking at. The reason we can learn so much from horses is because there is also pain, loss, grief and frustration, but we keep coming back anyway—because we gain so much from riding and horses.

At the time of Christopher Reeve's accident, many people wondered, "Why would someone like that even take up such a dangerous sport? He had so much going for him, why risk life, limb, and livelihood for a horse?" Again, those who are not infected cannot fathom horse fever motivations and often dismiss the afflicted as "horse crazy."

There is craziness involved here. But for the most part it's a positive craziness that gets you right back on track after things go wrong. It's being crazy *about* horses, the just-can't-get-enough-of-them-craziness. On balance, this kind of lunacy is beneficial, for it offers enlightening lessons of personal resilience, damage control, and acceptance of the bad with the good in life.

## The Horse Element

Each and every horse comes with its very own set of equine Murphy's Laws and disclaimers like, "Past performance is no guarantee of future results." *Every horse comes with a problem,* states Valerie Kanavy (p. 68), World Champion Endurance rider and trainer, *whether it's personality, training, physical, or whatever; I haven't found the perfect horse yet. So it's my job to compensate—improve it, work with it, or work around it.*

Problems are inherent in horses, as in life. There's an old Arab saying, "With sunshine every day, the world becomes a desert." *There's no way that you could do anything with horses where you wouldn't have enough 'rain' fall into your life,* assures Macella O'Neill (p. 87), owner and trainer of a successful hunter and jumper stable. *Even in the best of circumstances, horses colic and die, they blow out their tendons, they poke themselves in the eye. So, just being involved with horses provides you with plenty of 'rain.'*

Horses may bring you new problems to ponder, but they also can be a vehicle for the solution: *Usually any problem is just something that you've got to do a lot of thinking about to see what you're gonna do about it,* explains Curtis Steel (p. 68), former manager of a wild horse domestication program for the New Mexico Corrections Department. *And riding gives you a chance to do that thinking.*

Getting a horse is similar to taking on a foster child. It's a daily commitment of time, energy, expense, and emotion that affects the entire family. Unlike a foster child, however, a horse needs his very own home and yard, and the county doesn't send you a monthly support check. As the equine newcomer settles in, you get to know him and learn his likes, dislikes, abilities, quirks, and charms. Eventually you decide whether you want to adopt him full-time or pass him on to the next caretaker.

*Sacrifices? Lots. I get home from work, and I'm tired and would rather sit and watch the news and eat dinner,* Dennis Marine, farrier and cattleman (p. 87), confesses, *but the horses have to get fed. My time off usually gets used up maintaining their surroundings. A lot of money goes for necessities for them—feed or rent for pasture—that I could pleasurably spend someplace else. It's just like having kids...you are responsible for their welfare all the way around—food, shelter, shots, education, and comfort. The sacrifices are worthwhile because it's all what I enjoy. People who aren't in a situation where they take care of it all themselves are missing a good portion of the lessons to be learned.*

Responsibility and dependability are two important lessons that horses help people to learn: *I am responsible for taking care of these animals,* says Susan Stovall (p. 88), Director of Polo at the El Dorado Polo Club. *That puts the pressure on me. The more horses I have to look after, the more pressure I learn to handle because they depend on me. That's an important lesson. If I don't do a good job, they suffer; you can see it on the horse. Then I'd suffer too because I know it would be my fault.*

Sometimes the personality of the horse is an issue—not just the tough or ornery horses, but the ones you enjoy and expect to be your friend, yet are just naturally aloof. They do their job, and that's where the relationship ends for them. They don't need or want to "buddy up" with the boss. *I had one horse, Hobo, that frustrated me for the fifteen years I had him,* Jack Huyler broods. *He truly never liked me. He got to where he trusted me. I could ground tie him anywhere, go off and leave him forty-five minutes—he wouldn't have moved his own length when I came back. And boy, was he a jumper! He'd jump anything—he'd have jumped a car! When I was on him, he was a real pleasure, but gosh darn it, when I pulled the saddle off, he went off in a great hurry, whereas the other horses might hang around for a tidbit. He always acted like he'd rather be away from me—always left me with great joy. The humility that one horse kept putting into me because he really didn't like me.... Hobo was a lot like a cat in the saying, "Anyone with a dog to adore him should have a cat to ignore him."*

Personality isn't always the problem with a partnership; it can be lack of preparation that causes an "overthrow." *Roy and I were filming an episode for our show,* relates Dale Evans, *in which we had to jump a ditch—he on Trigger and me on Buttermilk. Well, I didn't take Buttermilk across it first... you know what I'm saying? We're sitting there talking, and all of a sudden they call, "Roll 'em!" and "Action!" so we start racing towards the ditch. But when Buttermilk sees it, he stops cold. That's the only time he unsat me. I went right under his belly to the ground. I wasn't hurt. And it wasn't Buttermilk's fault—it was mine. You know, horses don't like surprises.*

Talk about surprises—at one clinic it wasn't obvious whether the trainer was doing the training or being trained. *If it can happen with a horse, it has happened to me,* declares John Lyons. *One time I was doing a repetitive leading lesson with my stallion, Dream, in front of about four hundred people. Well, Dream had had enough of it, so he just reached over and ripped my shirt off. My wife was a few feet from me taking pictures, and she said all I did was to ask her, "Would you get me another shirt please?"…and I just kept on talking. Dream taught me that most anything can happen and that nit-picky leading lessons aren't the best thing to be doing when your horse has had enough.* One way or another, horses will teach you a lesson.

## *The Injury Element*

By nature horses are flighty and unpredictable, and their actions can result in injury permanently affecting a rider and his family. *My dad was thrown from a horse at age thirty-eight, broke his hip, and was crippled,* relates Ron Harding (p. 88), former Wild Horse Coordinator and Specialist for Oregon and Washington. *We lived in Oregon at the time, but after the accident Dad couldn't work in the mills any more, so we sold out and moved to Arkansas. That's how a horse affected his life—he wasn't able to work or do much of anything for years. That accident changed our whole family's life, but Dad still kept horses. We had one horse, Sunday, a narrow little paint stallion, that he could ride because it didn't spread his legs so far. Well, Dad's hip eventually got so bad that he couldn't even do that. But he still kept horses. Then, during the Vietnam War, when Dad was sixty, they developed methods for artificial joints, so he got an artificial hip. In six weeks he was walking without a cane or anything! Now what do you think was the next thing he did? He got this little filly, Baby Doll, trained her and commenced riding. He's eighty-four now, and he's always had a horse until just the last few years.… He still likes to hear about my horses.*

Veterinarian Patty Latham suffered an accident that redirected both her family and professional futures: *I've always loved equine medicine and started my career as a large animal practitioner,* explains Patty. *I could walk up to a horse that's afraid of a man and get away with treating it without having to use a twitch or some other restraint. I'm proud of that. But you cannot practice on large animals and be risk free; you've got to get in there and do what it takes. One year, my husband, Jim, and I had a two-year-old Thoroughbred in our veterinary hospital that was pretty crazy. We were working on her in the stocks in the barn when she went berserk. The weld on one of the pipes broke and hit both Jim and me. I was about five months pregnant and the pipe happened to hit an umbilical vessel and we lost the baby. I decided then that it was time to be more careful. Small animal medicine is very intellectual and very challenging. It has supported me and I love it, but it's not my passion like horse medicine is. But it was just too dangerous for my family for me continue with the horse practice. Now that the children are older I find myself gravitating back there a little bit.*

For some, a horse's unexpected reaction may take them to the very brink of destruction. *At one of my very first clinics in Scottsdale, Arizona, quite a few years ago, there was a fellah named Joe, who insisted everyone call him by his nickname, "The Polack,"* remembers Buck Brannaman. *I was a little uncomfortable with that because it seemed real disrespectful, but he wouldn't answer to "Joe." That day it was one-hundred-dred-seventeen degrees; the dust in the arena was about six inches deep and the consistency of flour. Midway through the afternoon, I gave everyone a break to get a drink. So Joe rides up next to the fence, hooks his leg over the saddle horn like the Marlboro man, tips his hat back like Hank Williams, and picks up his plastic milk jug with water and ice in it. Now the horse that Joe is on is just a "little volatile" as they say. Joe drains the jug, tips it back up, and as the ice hits the bottom of that empty jug....You can just imagine what happens....This red horse wheels around and leaves! He is heading for Los Angeles! Now, it's about three-hundred feet to the end of this steel-pipe arena. I pick up my microphone and say, "Drop the jug, Joe. Joe, please drop the jug. JOE! Drop that jug!" Well, he's so petrified, he cannot. He's holding on to that rattling jug, and this horse is running so fast he's a blur. I'm frantic by now, because I know this horse is gonna turn right or left and just make a grease spot outta this man. In desperation I yell, "POLACK!! DROP THE JUG!!" Well, that gets through to him, and he lets go of that rattle. But I know it's too late because this big dust cloud is boiling up as his horse comes to the end of the arena. When the dust clears, I look, and there's Joe—still on his horse! His leg is still hooked over the horn; his hat's still back like a country western star, and his horse has made the only perfect sliding stop of his life. The Polack looks down the arena at me, waves his hat and yells, "YAHOO!"—as if it were just another day at the office.*

Thankfully, this potential wreck ended happily, however, occasionally mishaps result in injury. *Anybody who rides horses has usually had a broken bone or two,* says Valerie Kanavy, *and if you can survive that, you can survive a lot of things. It teaches you about pain and that you'll live through it...you work back. It's the same when your horse gets injured; you let him heal up, and then you bring him back slow.*

Healing the injury may be only part of the process for many who survive a horse accident. Overcoming the resulting fears may be a tougher recuperation than mending physically. Rebuilding your strength, confidence, and trust....

*In 1988, I was working with a fun little Quarter Horse, Bentley,* Cathy Ziffren recalls. *My trainer used to say he had the body of a draft horse and the mind of a Welsh pony. He was a brat, but I was getting to the point where I was really confident on him. We were jumping in class, and as he cleared the fence, he jerked his head down and flipped his back feet up and just launched me! I don't know how far I flew up in the air, but I landed flat on my back and broke it in a number of places. That put fear back into me. A year later, when I went back to riding, every time the horse would do an unexpected move, I'd think, "If I fall, I might never walk again." I'm still wary, but I do a different type of riding now— dressage instead of jumping. And of course, I waited for this horse, too. I don't know if I would have gotten back into riding like I am now without Ariel. She's so lovely and smooth, and I trust her.*

Many accidents are just that—not the rider's fault, not the horse's fault....

*My dad was a race rider* explains Michael Plumb (p. 89), three-day event rider who has been selected to eight US Olympic teams—more than any other rider. *Timber racing is racing over solid fences, and the most awesome timber course in the world is the Maryland Hunt Cup. It consists of about twenty-five round-rail jumps over a four-and-a-half mile course. Three or four of the jumps are a good five feet high. One year Dad entered, but his horse fell at the third fence. He remounted and went on to win the race—that's a remarkable feat.*

*I began eventing in 1957, and by the late sixties Dad decided that he was going to give eventing a shot. He was so talented that he just picked up on it. He was a wonderful horseman—that was a gift that he was given. In 1969 we decided that we would both go out to Pebble Beach,*

*California, for the national championships. His horse slipped and fell at the next to last jump, and Dad was paralyzed from his neck down.*

*From then on he was in a wheelchair. He couldn't handle that at all; he'd always been such an independent person. I think he probably would have been happier if he had just died doing the thing that he liked the best. As it was, he died of a heart attack in his late eighties—fifteen years after the accident. His name was Charles Plumb. I named my son after him.*

It's a measure of the strength of *Horsepower!* that Michael Plumb acquired his father's love of horses and riding, and much of his talent, yet was not scared away by his father's injuries.

## The Excitement Element

In spite of the real threat of injury or death, many equestrians become so involved with their animals and activities that friends and family consider them a lost cause—certifiably horse-crazed or worse: addicted. As with any addictive habit, what makes the downside of horses worthwhile are the rewards of various "highs", "thrills", and "good vibrations": the excitement. Horse-crazy individuals accept and endure the tough times, long hours, dirty work, the physical and financial risks, familial alienation and possible death for the sake of the excitement horses offer: adrenalin rushes, personal accomplishments, interspecies connection, and shared love.

The adventure of being on horseback as unexpected events unfold around you can provide exciting hits of adrenalin. No matter how smart or powerful you may be, as a rider you have only limited control of a horse. That fragile balance between control and disaster makes every outing a potential thrill ride. *Endurance riding often takes you where it's very wild and away from civilization,* Stagg Newman explains. *One of my favorite rides is the Virginia City Hundred in Nevada. At one point in the early morning desert light, three of us were galloping along with a dozen wild horses leading us down the trail. Later in that same ride, we were out in front alone; I looked up and there was a bright red wild horse just ahead. All of a sudden he charged across the trail and whirled around facing us. I saw three other horses behind him. I assume that was a stallion who thought we were about to get between him and his mares. He wasn't going to have any part of that. Fortunately, my horse just kept booking down the trail, and the wild band took off. That whole ride was pretty fantastic!*

In addition to adrenalin rushes, riding offers romantic adventures that can be shared with loved ones: *My wife Cheryl's first hundred-mile ride was the Swan Endurance Ride in Davenport, California,* Stagg Newman continues. *We started out in a redwood grove and rode through Big Basin National Forest in the morning mist—beautiful! About ninety-five miles out, we hit a narrow trail cut out of the side of the hill with a drop of about five hundred feet to the valley below—that got our adrenaline pumping! At the end of that trail, the landscape fell away to the ocean. We happened to arrive right as the sun was melting into the Pacific with a full moon rising in the East. It was then we knew that Cheryl was going to finish her first hundred-mile ride. We completed that ride together, crossing the finish line hand in hand. Those are very special times for us.*

Since each situation and animal present new opportunities for work or pleasure, horses offer mental excitement. *I like all phases of horses,* declares John Lyons. *I enjoy taking the horse as an athlete and learning how to get a better performance out of him. I also enjoy the companionship of the horse. As we're riding down trails, I have a great imagination of what it was like a hundred years ago.... It is always fun to be out with a horse.*

Training horses is an on-going process that sustains interest for many working to make a horse their responsive partner. *I love taking a green horse and polishing him,* says Jack Huyler. *When I'm on the back of a polished horse that I've trained—he knows my every cue, and we're in tune with each other—it's just one of the wonderful sensations. To be on a good horse is a privilege; to be on a polished horse, that I have polished, is the ultimate.* The rewards of a working partnership that you have designed and developed are deeply satisfying, yet rare even in the human arena. It is particularly exciting to achieve a polished partnership through interspecies communication—without the benefit of a shared, spoken language.

Recognizing the value of interspecies communication invites a spectrum of new perspectives. *I was never interested in team athletics—baseball or football,* says Sam Savitt, *but when I found horses, boy it was all there. That's what I wanted! When you're working with horses, it's a whole other dimension. You have to try and think like a horse and visualize what he is like, then cope with that. Instead of trying to work the way I am, I know enough to be able to go his way. It's a whole other dimension in living.*

Additionally, the challenge and excitement of besting one's own record is a daily incentive for many trainers and riders. *My oldest brother taught all eight of us kids (six boys and two girls) to "trick" ride and "Roman" ride. It was great family fun,* admits Rex Peterson (p. 90), horse trainer for the movie industry, *but we competed, believe me! When one of us learned a new trick, we'd all try to learn something better. Those early days got me interested in the specialty horses I train now. But nowadays I keep myself busy trying to better my own bag of tricks. Studying the horses to figure how to do something that's not been done before, or to improve on something that has, fills my day up pretty fast.*

The miracle of the horse and human relationship itself is reward enough for some: *To me horses are the most beautiful creatures on the planet, both inside and outside,* claims Caroline Thompson (p. 90), screenwriter and director of BLACK BEAUTY. *They're like watching a piece of poetry in action. It's miraculous to me that they not only tolerate us, but actually want to work and play with us. It's also miraculous when we are working well together. It's like the most perfect dance that ever was. And we are always trying to get to that perfect dance.*

Dance is an appropriate and recurring metaphor within the horse world. When two beings meld flawlessly and move in fluid synchronization like Astaire and Rogers, or Torville and Dean, it is spectacular. To achieve that high level of communication and partnership between species is nothing short of miraculous: *It is magical,* exclaims Olympic silver medalist show jumper Anne Kursinski (p. 91), *to be able to fly when you're on a horse—that's what I do.*

Author and trainer Jill Hassler (p. 92) proclaims, *For me, the highest level of beauty is to be in harmony with a horse.* Magic, beauty and harmony; this is powerful sustenance for any relationship. In the alliance between horse and rider that perfect combination does exist, yet as with anything of great value, it is rare. No rider ever achieves such harmony continuously, and some riders never experience it.

However, once experienced, such equestrian magic fuels motivation, becoming the challenge and the goal of every ride. Riding magic is akin to the runner's high with the added advantage of being accomplished in unison with another independent being. *If I didn't have a horse to ride, honey, I wouldn't want to be here,* declares Chris Hawkins (p. 92), Quarter Horse breeder and promoter of the Wild Horse and Burro Protection Act of 1971. *There's such rhythm with riding—not just the rhythm of the beat of the horse's hooves, but the rhythm of the blood surging between you. The oneness....* A shared unity reached through mutual desire, communication, and partnership.

Not only is that oneness thrilling to experience, it is soulfully energizing: *There is no other source of energy that revitalizes me as much as being with a horse,* claims Jill Hassler. *I can teach lessons for thirteen hours and have more energy at the end of that day than when I started—just because I'm around the horses. Their power energizes me.*

Psychotherapist and horse owner Jenny Butah (p. 122) relates the following exchange about her own, self-diagnosed "horse-craziness": *I bought my first horse shortly after my divorce. A friend of mine, who'd been supportively listening to all my new-horse-enthusiasms on a daily basis for months, finally turned to me and said, "Now I understand why they call heroin 'horse'...It's addictive; it's risky; it's expensive; it gives you a helluva rush, and you'll do anything to keep it in your life!"*

Yes, horses definitely can be addicting, but a "real horse" delivers a natural, healthy high: *At the end of a real good day of training,* says James Fairclough (p. 121), Winner of a Gold medal in the 1991 World Pair Driving Championships, *I do get a natural high. I've had my horses in a dead run in tight turns, up banks and down through streams...a real team effort. That's a rush like you can't believe; your adrenaline gets going; your heart's pounding...everybody comes back pumped. You cannot buy that. You cannot put a dollar value on that. It's something that you have to go out and work for to achieve. I'm not one to try drugs to get euphoria...a day like that is something you could never buy.*

## The Life Lessons

The mental stimulation, physical challenge, and spiritual energizing gained through working with horses, can create a feeling of integrated wholeness. For horse-crazy individuals, such balanced wholeness, coupled with the exciting highs that punctuate a life with horses, more than compensates for the risks, drudgery, disappointments and inherent dangers of the horse world.

Although perhaps not always enjoyed, the downside of horses is endured and even valued as an educational proving ground and *im*proving ground for lessons of character, compromise and coping. By accepting the bad with the good, equestrians find that hard work can lead to commitment, imposed sacrifices can lead to chosen priorities, problems can lead to solutions, injury can lead to resilience, losing can lead to improvement, and highs and lows can lead to balanced unity.

HOLLY PETERSON MONDAVI, b. 1959, is an accomplished chef who began riding as a child and enjoys many of the aspects of equestrian life: jumping, trail, cross-country, hunting, and competing. Most important to her are the friendships, laughter and wonder horses and riding have provided. Holly and her handsome Thoroughbred gelding, Bacchus, clear an oxer at the Calistoga Horse Show in 1994.

MARY DERINGER PHELPS, b. 1940, is a hunter/jumper and equitation instructor who has trained a number of champion horses and riders in Texas and in Maryland. Mary is shown aboard the Hanoverian gelding, Ikarus, in 1989 at the Willow Bend Polo Club, Plano, Texas.

JACK HUYLER, b. 1920, has been a mainstay at the Thacher School in Ojai, California, for more than fifty years teaching English, coaching sports and imparting horsemanship. He was the 1969 California State All-Around Gymkhana Champion and has served on the American Horse Show Association rules committee and as President of the National Horse and Pony Youth Activities Council. Now retired, he and his wife Margaret split their time between Ojai and their home in Wyoming where this shot was taken.

STAGG NEWMAN, b. 1948, is an engineering technologist and record-setting endurance rider. In 1992, he was the National 100 Mile Champion and went on to claim the individual bronze and a team gold medal at the FEI North American Championship in 1993. He was selected for the 1994 USET World Championship Team and in 1997 completed his 25th one-day 100 mile ride. Stagg is shown on his champion Arabian gelding, Ramegwa Drubin in 1993.

MARY MANSI, b. 1954, is a
certified public accountant who
took up riding at the age of 37
and was hooked. She soon
became a horse owner, then a
multiple horse owner, and
learned to jump. Mary credits
horses with enlivening her life
and teaching her many wonderful
lessons. Mary is shown with
her Thoroughbred mare, Caprice,
after a chilly morning lesson.

BOB HENRY b. 1936, and CATHY ZIFFREN, b. 1943, retail business
partners, are pictured with two of their equine partners: Cathy's
Oldenburg mare, Ariel, and Bob's 17.1 hand Selle Français gelding,
Bubba. Cathy has ridden most of her life, enjoying hunter jumpers for
twenty years before turning to dressage. A Western rider in his youth,
Bob took up English riding at the age of 50 and went on to compete
over fences in hunters and jumpers. In 1991 he founded the annual
Napa Valley Classic show-jumping benefit for local youth projects.

PATTY LATHAM DVM, b. 1947, runs a successful veterinary hospital with her veterinarian husband in California. Patty's equine experience predates her veterinary exams—she's been raising, showing, barrel racing and cutting with Quarter Horses since she was eight. In this prophetic shot, 12-year-old Patty gets acquainted with a Quarter Horse foal that became her personal charge when its dam's milk production proved deficient. When Patty's family had to move, she was heartbroken about leaving "Lillie Too," but the filly's owner—perhaps recognizing a perfect match—gave her to Patty.

RENÉ WILLIAMS, b. 1916, grew up in a famous horse-training family and has seen tremendous success throughout his career in a variety of disciplines: jumping, hunting, showing, racing and breeding. He was a trainer for the US Olympic teams for many years at Gladstone, New Jersey. After his retirement, he became a self-taught equine sculptor of international acclaim. This charming portrait shows 11-year-old René with his pony, Sunbeam, at the Far Hills [New Jersey] Horse Show, where they took first prize in jumping.

# CHAPTER THREE

# HORSE NATURE

## Understanding Horse Vs. Human Nature

*Life on earth is a mosaic. We must respect even the weakest, most minimal of all of our creatures for they are part of that mosaic. When pieces are cracked, or crumbled, or missing out of that mosaic, it makes less of a piece of art than nature meant it to be.*
—*Monty Roberts*

A lone horse and rider carefully pick their way through the traffic and turmoil of New York City. Suddenly, a band of youngsters appear, forcing the rider to halt. Their leader, a skinny nine-year-old, asks, "Can I pet your horse?" Lt. Carl Clipper (p. 122), on patrol out of the U.S. Park Service Mounted Division Substation in Brooklyn, smiles, "Sure, you can pet him."

The youngster reaches out, touches the warm, polished-copper shoulder and pulls his hand back instantly, as if he'd hit a live wire. His eyes widen in amazement as he exclaims, "He's made out of skin!"

Surprised at his reaction, Lt. Clipper asks, "What did you think he was made of?" The boy didn't have an answer—he just didn't know.

Today's inner-city kids are exposed to a lot in life, but rarely a flesh-and-blood horse. Most likely the only horses they've seen are celluloid images on television where factual knowledge of the species may be sorely distorted. Equine portrayals such as television's talking horse, Mr. Ed, or the Hollywood steed of old-time westerns that manages to toss a rope to his cowboy master mired in quicksand, then pull him to safety, are entertaining fiction, but nothing more.

Yet urban dwellers are not the only ones operating under misconceptions of horse nature. After a recent seminar, veterinarian Dr. Robert Miller was approached by a man who said, "I want to thank you because you've given me a whole new viewpoint about horses."

Since he knew this man to be an experienced horseman, Dr. Miller was pleased and curious, "What was that?" he asked.

"Well, I never, ever thought of horses as a prey animal before," the man replied, "But you're right; they are a prey animal. So, even though they're big and powerful, they really are timid creatures."

Dr. Miller was amazed that a rancher who'd been around horses most of his life had never thought of them in that way.

With industrialization, urbanization, legislation and domination, modern man has set a regrettable course of alienation from the natural world. We don't even refer to our species as the human animal—but rather as human "beings"—separate and superior to animals. The fact remains that man is an animal: a mammal, a carnivore, a predator, a naked ape.

Horses are animals, too—sentient beings with independent thinking capabilities, sensitive awarenesses, individual natures, physical abilities and limitations. The more one learns about equine nature, the more one can relate appropriately to horses.

Insightful trainers point to the ability to "think like a horse" as a hallmark of success in training, communicating, and riding horses, and in predicting and evaluating equine behaviors. The more I learn of equine physiology and behavior, the more I understand the *why* of their actions, reactions, and state of being. Not yet able to think like a horse, or predict actions, I'm at least able to answer the "Why'd he do that?" question more often. Learning how a horse interprets the world has given me heightened sensitivity and greater tolerance for what used to appear to be silly, puzzling, or stupid behaviors. The smarter I become about horses, the more sensible equine behavior appears, merely because I now understand.

This chapter will consider man's perception of the horse; explain inherent distinctions between predator and prey; examine some of the physical, mental, temperamental, and social factors that define the true nature of the horse; and discuss the importance of staying connected to the animal kingdom through equine relationships.

## Predator vs. Prey

A knowledge of the basic distinctions between predator and prey is paramount to interpreting equine actions and reactions as well as understanding differences in human and horse natures. A prey animal is stalked, caught and consumed by a predator.

A prey animal's life depends on being continually on guard against cunning, camouflaged carnivores that may spring out of hiding to attack anytime, anywhere. Thus, horses are constantly wary and suspicious of unidentified objects, sounds, smells, and touches.

This vital vigilance requires that equine senses be highly tuned; hence horses are vastly more sensitive and reactive to environmental stimuli than are humans.

## Herd Security

As with most prey species, horses in the wild find safety in numbers. By living in small herds, or bands, comprised of a stallion, his harem of mares, their foals and some adolescents, horses have developed organized social behaviors. There is a distinct social hierarchy, or pecking order, which is determined by the more dominant animals winning disputes over the more submissive herd members. There are also specific duties taken on by herd members which necessitate cooperation, such as being a sentry so others may sleep, or "babysitting" foals.

Surprisingly, the herd leader is not the stallion, but rather a senior (alpha) mare, whose longevity speaks to being a "street smart" successful survivor. This leader decides when and where the herd goes to find food, water, shelter, or to escape a threat. The stallion follows behind, herding stragglers, keeping the band together yet moving fast enough to stay out of harm's way.

Interdependent group living leads to unquestioned trust in the reactions of others. If the leader suddenly bolts, the rest of the herd follows suit. *I had a horse that got frightened and panicked one day recounts Jimmy Fairclough. It was like a sudden virus hit the team—it went from that horse to the second horse; then the third horse got scared, and the fourth horse. Instantly, that one horse had the whole team in a*

*dead run, and I couldn't stop them; all I could do was pray! I did finally
stop them, and no real harm was done, but it's amazing how that feeling
spread from horse to horse to horse.*

This seemingly mindless panic behavior highlights another
distinction between predators and prey. If a predator misjudges an
attack, he forfeits his dinner, but lives to hunt again. If a prey animal misjudges an attack, he *is* dinner. Thus, in order to survive,
prey animals must react instantly to alarm, while predators must
quietly plan the stalk, time their attack, and be able to analyze errors in order to succeed and survive. The hair-trigger "sense and
escape" mentality of prey species is inherently simple and explo-
sive, while a predator's more complex mental process of planning
and executing an attack requires considered strategy, careful timing, and a cool head.

As a predator, it is to man's advantage to be considered "innocent until proven guilty." As a prey animal, vulnerable to attack at
any time, it is to the horse's advantage to consider everything "guilty
until proven innocent." This explains why, when confronted with
an unfamiliar object, sound, or motion, horses prick their ears, snort,
tighten muscles, cock their heads to study the object, and dance
about. They are focusing their senses to collect the data needed
for identification, while staying light on their feet ready to run if
necessary.

## Individual Defense

Horses have two instinctive responses to threat—flight or
fight—with flight being their first and foremost line of defense.
Their life force dictates "run now; question later." True to that creed,
a frightened horse will run a sufficient distance, then turn, and
focus on the threat from a safe vantage point.

Despite impressive size and power, horses are not naturally
aggressive, since serious fighting exposes them to injuries that may
jeopardize their ability to run. However, if flight is not possible, a
panicked horse will fight, and stallions habitually clash when challenged over mares or territory.

## Sleep

In the wild, horses are always on the move and on alert, sleep-
ing an aggregate of only about four hours in twenty-four. Horses

can nod off for three- to five-minute naps of short-wave sleep (SWS) while standing. This shallow sleep, coupled with special locking mechanisms in their fore- and hindlimbs, allows them to awaken and gallop off at the slightest alarm. When fully relaxed, assured of security by herd sentries, horses will lie down for more substantial, deep, rapid eye movement (REM) sleep; though rarely spending more than half-an-hour at a time in this vulnerable prone position (McBane 24).

## Procreation

For horses, "being caught in the act" could be fatal, so even the act of mating is allowed precious little time, taking less than a minute from start to finish (Morris 60). Similarly, a foaling mare is vulnerable prey and can control the timing of the birthing process until she feels it is safe to lie down. The birth itself takes only a few minutes, and the newborn foal is on its feet in less than an hour (Morris 67).

## Feed

Plains horses feed as much as sixteen hours a day (Morris 45); comparatively sparse but continuous feedings afford a consistent energy level and avoid enervating gluttony. Horses cannot regurgitate, so ingesting poisonous, spoiled or very rich feed can lead to life-threatening situations. Contrary to what one might expect of such large, healthy-looking beasts, the equine digestive tract is a delicate system.

## Smell

A horse's olfactory system can locate water, food, receptive mates, and predators at great distances. In close proximity, their sense of smell also serves as nose to nose identification of friend, foe, and foal (Morris 36). Horses also detect the specific scent humans give off when fearful (McBane 31). These invisible indicators add to equine vigilance and anxiety.

## Touch

Only in the fingertips does a human being have the tactile sense that a horse has all over its body surface. A horse can literally feel a fly land on a hair, then shrug it off with a pin point shimmy of his hide. Under saddle, a horse can feel the subtlest changes; if the rider is tense or nervous, the horse feels it, even through a leather saddle and fleece pad. That is exceptional tactile sensitivity.

## Hearing

Like continuous tracking satellite dishes, equine ears are always tuned in, actively searching, locating, and identifying sounds. Since each ear operates independently and can rotate 180 degrees (Morris 13), horses are able to pick up on everything going on around them. Due to this superior hearing, a horse is often alerted to a sound before any human is aware of it.

## Sight

Perhaps the most fascinating difference between human and horse is sight. Human sight is based on stereoscopic binocular vision—two synchronized eyeballs, set into the front of the head, allowing depth perception and varying degrees of focus, contrast and color.

Twice the size of a human's, equine eyeballs are set on the sides of the head and can work independently (monocular vision) as well as in synchronization (binocular vision). Usually, a horse is in monocular mode—with each eye able to scan about 170 degrees, allowing for a generalized view of 340 degrees (Morris 40) around the animal. This wide-range scanning, coupled with the ability to detect action, general shapes, and light intensity, makes monocular vision very effective for area surveillance.

Although highly sensitive to motion, monocular vision does not provide sharply focused details or depth perception; these functions require binocular vision. Unlike the human eye, the equine lens cannot change shape to focus on objects. A horse must position his eye so that the image hits an area of the retina that is "pre-focused" to certain distances in order to bring the image into focus (Hillenbrand 74). Thus, when monocular scanning detects an alarming motion or object, the horse must turn his head toward the concern and employ frontal binocular vision for focused identification.

This information explains why something like a blowing plastic bag can make a horse explode in terror. The horse picks up that action in its indistinct, flat, monocular vision and sees only a sizeable object flying at him. If the horse's head is restricted by bridle and reins in the hands of a rider, he may not be able to turn his head quickly enough to focus on the bag for clear identification. Hence, he is instantly anxious to get away from the large flying object that appears to be leaping at him while making a crinkling, hissing sound like a cat. Now his "silly"skittishness makes sense.

Two triangular blind spots occur in the range of equine vision—a short triangle directly in front of the horse and a longer triangular blind spot directly behind the animal (Morris 40).These areas of blindness explain why a horse may strike out when approached from behind, or pull away when a person raises a hand to stroke his face. What a horse can't see well, it fears. The blind spot also explains why fingers get bitten when a tidbit is offered in a closed hand. Since a horse literally can't see what's in front of his nose, he relies on his sense of smell and touch to identify the tidbit; i.e., he smells carrot and feels carrot, but since the finger wrapped around the carrot is round and firm like the carrot, before you know it—"that 'stupid horse' bit my finger!" Hence, when hand-feeding a horse, always offer the food from an open, flat palm.

Some other interesting facts about equine sight are: the pupil is horizontal so as to scan the horizon panoramically (Morris 41). Although their color spectrum may be limited, recent experiments show horses can discern red, blue, bright yellow and bright green (Timney 36).

They have evolved as prey that is hunted day and night, so horses are nocturnal as well as diurnal, so their night vision is far superior to a human's, and with eyes placed high on the head, horses can survey their surroundings over grass while still grazing.

## Memory

Horses have extremely good memories—particularly for instances of pain or harm. *When my horse was five years old,* relates Amy Hubbard (p. 123), member of the U.S. Pony Club Show Jumping Championship team, *he was in a movie where donkeys knocked him down and scrambled all over him. Just recently, he saw one of the donkeys from that movie experience and went for him. It took my Dad, a couple of instructors, and me to hold my horse and get him calmed down. My horse is twenty-five now and that happened when he was only five, but he still remembered that particular donkey—twenty years later!*

Such a memory can make re-training difficult Rex Peterson notes: *From the first day man puts a hand on him, writing goes on that blank chalkboard of a mind. Can you erase it? Sure, but you're going to have to scrub that blackboard, because if you just brush it off, you're going to leave the tell-tale signs of that writing. Then the first accident that happens, that writing comes right back through as readable as ever. So, if you have a problem, you must spend the necessary hours to erase it.*

In spite of their terrific memories, horses do not seem to generalize well. Generalization is the ability to categorize similar, though not identical objects. Humans are good at creating and labeling sets and subsets of objects through generalizing. For instance, mailboxes vary a great deal, yet humans recognize a wide set of containers to be mailboxes. Horses are much more visually literal in their interpretation of objects, so dissimilar mailboxes may not be recognized as related. Also, location is important, so a horse may readily accept an old, familiar mailbox on the street as non-threatening, while an identical mailbox in a new location may set him off, or a brightly painted mailbox may cause a problem. Horses simply do not generalize as broadly as humans (Saslow 20).

## Homing Instinct

Equine homing instincts are truly remarkable. Whether horses' ability to find their way back is based on their acute senses of smell, hearing, visual memory, or some relation to the earth's magnetic field is not yet known, but equestrians have long recognized and relied upon this uncanny equine gift: *When I first came to California I was cowboying up in Middletown,* Dennis Marine relates. *One night we had to trailer our horses to a remote part of the ranch. It got dark—black dark—and none of us could see anything. One guy had been there before and was supposed to know his way back. As it turned out, this guy couldn't find the way back either. So I just gave my horse, Sundown, the reins, and he led us all back to the trailer where we had unloaded.* Pretty handy radar to have!

Another striking example of equine homing radar was evidenced at the Wild Horse Sanctuary in California's Northern Sierras. The Sanctuary had received a band of feral horses from the government range in Burns, Oregon, since they were deemed "unadoptable". The band eventually escaped through a break in the Sanctuary's fence, and the stallion managed to drive his harem back to Burns—more than 300 miles away! (Sappington 10).

## Independent Learning

Horses have an interesting way of assimilating training, which makes it important to train them on both sides of their bodies—not only for balanced muscle development and coordination, but because they learn visual cues independently on each side. As Rex Peterson has observed: *I work liberty horses. I have no strings attached to them of any kind. They work off of eyesight. If you teach a horse something on one side, it means nothing until you teach it on the other side. I can teach a horse something on the left eye, go to the right eye, and it means absolutely nothing to him. That's why I say that they are very independent left and right. But the more you educate a horse, the more you balance a horse. By balance I mean, if you teach it on the right you must teach it on the left; then they'll get equal left and right. That is what you must strive for in horses—constant balancing. Now in the balancing, my belief is that you put interconnectors between the left side and the right side of the brain. My chestnut horse, I can teach him something on the left side, walk around the right side and in three minutes have it happen on the right side. He wasn't that way when I started him. He was very difficult to go from left to right with things. Now it's no problem. I believe the more you balance him, you get more interconnectors between the left and right lobes of the brain, and you make him easier to train.* This need for right-left balancing may be related to equine monocular vision and could account for horses showing no fear as they pass an object on one side, yet shying when they approach it from the other side.

The need for training on both sides of a horse was dramatically demonstrated by veterinarian Dr. Robert Miller in an episode of Larry Mahan's television program, HorseWorld (Mahan 04-92). Dr. Miller desensitized the right side of a young foal's body by manipulating its right ear, stroking its right eye, and so forth. A little while later, the foal stood calmly while being handled on its desensitized right side, but fought Dr. Miller's advances on its as yet untrained left side.

## Imprinting

A newborn foal identifies and bonds with the first object it sees moving after its birth—normally its mother—then follows and accepts that animal's ministrations without fear. Proper handling by educated human trainers within that critical time immediately after birth adds human handling to a foal's experience of accepted actions. Thus a properly imprint-trained foal accepts human interaction *naturally* and as a result is calmer and more submissive.

## Comparing Horses and Humans

This brief equine primer illustrates that horses are very different physically, mentally, and temperamentally from humans. In general, horses are fast, strong, sensitive, wary, alert, timid, submissive, cooperative and instinctive animals of flight. Humans are slower, weaker, less sensitive, more calculating, controlling, complex, cerebral animals who will stand their ground and fight or kill for many reasons: food, religion, politics, sport, revenge....

*Humans are much more in their heads, and horses are more in their bodies,* explains Diana Thompson (p. 123), horse trainer and founder of THE WHOLE HORSE JOURNAL, *and a wonderful part of educating one another is that humans train the horse to be more of a thinking, considering individual and not let his fright reflex override him all the time. Horses challenge humans to get out of their heads more and to listen to their instincts, feelings and intuitions. It is an incredible blending of two species that are on the opposite end of the spectrum. When people realize that what a horse is seeing and feeling is immediately reflected in his body, and how instantly his adrenaline flows from his deep survival instincts, we can better understand why he does what he does. Then we can begin to teach the horse not to be afraid; we can educate him past what he was born to know. Just as a human being can learn to get out of his head, a horse can learn to consider dangerous situations in a different way and become desensitized to naturally frightening stimuli.* By understanding the innate differences between human nature and horse nature, knowledgeable horsemen are able to devise methods of training to achieve more successful partnerships.

Just as the discipline of "sociology" was developed to better understand human social order, I believe animal behaviorists need to develop "equinology," as the specific study of equine social behaviors. Only through research initiated from the perspective of "the other" can humans comprehend the true nature of different species.

## In Man's Image?

When observing a being outside of ourselves, humans often begin the process by trying to relate that "otherness" to themselves. Thus, when we see a horse yawn or sigh, we identify with those expressions and assign to that animal the feelings that we experience when we yawn or sigh. Such interspecies parallels aid the process of relating, which is a step toward empathy and understanding. This practice of assigning human emotions or characteristics to a nonhuman is called anthropomorphism. Throughout history, mankind has anthropomorphized everything from God to pet rocks.

The assumption that horses yawn and sigh for the same physical or emotional reasons as humans may be valid, or it may be invalid. Within our own species, we have the advantage of a common verbal language that allows us to discuss and determine that a yawn indicates a common stimulus. Between species, however, we are limited to hypothesizing and extrapolating a conclusion based on observation. Additionally, man's verbal language promotes "linguistic anthropomorphism" since most words have sprung from human experience and reference.

Anthropomorphism is helpful to the degree that it establishes common ground, allowing us to identify with something outside of ourselves and possibly bond with it. Yet it can be very misleading when taken to the extreme of a Mr. Ed where anthropomorphism creates false impressions and false expectations that mask and even deny the true nature of the other being.

Horses are distinct and different from human beings, and they are also unique within their own species. Horse owner Bob Henry points out, *Horses share obvious physical similarities, but horses are individuals; they all behave differently, have different temperaments, and different ways of going. They don't have personalities since that term refers to a very convoluted overview of a person. It's an easy word to use in reference to a horse, but it is inherently misleading.* Thus, as each person has a "personality," each individual horse has what I would like to call a "horsenality". This new term is a more important distinction than mere semantics, for using the word "personality" sets up a reference point of expectations, behaviors, or traits of a *person*—which a horse is not.

Acknowledging similarities and respecting differences between species create an open-minded awareness that is necessary to understand and realize what other species have to teach us. Respect and curiosity motivate us to want to learn *about* others, while perception and understanding allow us to learn *from* others.

*Native Americans learned to survive by studying and emulating animals,* explains Bev Doolittle (p. 124), internationally renowned watercolorist. *By observing how animals hunted or lived through the winter, then passing that knowledge on to the next generation, Native Americans learned to live successfully in their environment. They would don the fur of the wolf, or the feathers of the eagle, and become those animals—taking on the animal's power and characteristics. It was a spiritual process. Almost everything they did had a religious tie to it because they lived in nature, and the wilderness was their church. To me, that's about as pure an existence as one can have. Sure, I like my creature comforts, but through civilization and urbanization we cut ourselves off from living close to the earth. We've got our washing machines and all the things that make our life easier, but those things keep taking us farther away from our relationship to the earth. How many people today regularly go out in nature and really reconnect? There's a solitude and a refreshing connection with nature that you can't get in a city with other people around. We need to realize that we're not above nature, we're simply one part of it.*

The more time and energy spent getting to know true animal nature, the less human projection is needed and the more you come to appreciate the animal's inherent uniqueness.

## Celebrating "Horsenality"

Even though horses cannot be "personalities," they can be wonderfully unusual characters. *What's the sign for March 15th?* Asked Genie Stewart-Spears (p. 125), endurance rider and equine photographer. *It's gotta be a fish! My horse, Z Heatzon, I raised from a baby and he is just crazy about water. I don't know why; personally, I don't like water. But every time Heatzon goes into water he goes for the deepest spot. He puts his whole head in and opens his eyes under water—he just loves it! On one ride, we'd stopped in a river and Heatzon had his head down fooling around when a school of fish went by. Well, he went after them, plowing through the water like a submarine! I don't swim, so it was a little scary for me...but everybody watching was laughing hysterically.*

*Heatzon is a real comedian; if he were a human, he'd give David Letterman a run for his money.*

*When a horse is full of energy,* says Larry Mahan, *I love to get on, and instead of just thinking, "I'm gonna go lope this horse for 30 minutes until we get rid of this energy," I go ahead and channel that energy in a different way. I'll put him on a cow when he's real fresh, and it's like he says, "You think you can get past me, cow, to get back to the rest of the herd? Well, come on and just try it!" He just loves it. And I love it, too, because I get to experience what he's feeling. I don't run the feeling out of him; I go ahead and enjoy it with him. There's a lot of satisfaction in letting a horse be a horse.*

By allowing horses to act like horses, a person acknowledges their intrinsic qualities. This is a valuable lesson to be learned within our species as well. Not everyone needs to, or should, conform to a standard. Unorthodox styles can add flair to most any program: *Suddenly is a horse that had a rough time of it when he was on the racetrack,* explains Anne Kursinski. *When we go to the jumps, he gets excited and erratic, yet he's a great jumper. Some people say he looks crazy, the way he throws his head and gallops to the jumps. But I know he's not crazy; that's just some of his old baggage, his childhood stuff from the track, so I ignore it. He doesn't have to go the same way Star Man or Top Seed go. I trust him, so I let him go his own way, instead of trying to control and hold him back. That's the way he goes, and it works fine for us. He really isn't a nut; he tries hard for me, and he's actually very kind in the barn. But he is a very, very smart horse who takes in everything that happens. It took a long time for him to trust me, but now I believe he'd jump anything for me.*

By allowing Suddenly his own style of jumping, Anne has constructively channeled his energetic spirit. Why fix something that's not broken? Or, more to the point, why break a successful jumping style simply because it's different?

Unique characters often develop unique talents as Laura Bianchi (p. 125), first female officer of the San Francisco Police Department Mounted Unit discovered. *In 1985, Monserrat Caballe was the featured singer for the annual Opera Day at the Golden Gate Park band shell. I was assigned to crowd control and was riding Doc, a 16.2-hand bruiser with a blaze on his face in the shape of the Washington Monument. It was a beautiful day, and the crowd was enormous. I'm sitting there on Doc, off to the side, surrounded by people, enjoying Monserrat*

*Caballe's aria when she starts hitting some real high notes. All of a sudden, Doc starts trumpeting—not nickering, but trumpeting whenever Monserrat Caballe was singing. Well, she finished, but Doc kept going. Everyone was applauding and laughing. It was Doc's finest moment, but I got so embarrassed that we left. Doc always was a riot; he had a real sense of humor.*

The ability to allow idiosyncracies in our horses can lead to human acceptance, as Mary Fenton discovered: *Why can't we just recognize individuals as different characters instead of trying to change everybody? I know my wonderful Morgan, Cappy, always moves a little off, but that's just Cappy...horses are individual beings—as humans are. This realization has helped me relate to my mother, who is now living with us. I've only recently accepted that my mother is truly fine just the way she is—a real character. She really is an interesting old lady, and I don't want to change her because she's okay just the way she is! It's a hard thing at times, but a big ability to accept people as they are.* That recent acceptance of her mother is a direct result of Mary's work with horses, perhaps slow in coming, yet thankfully not too late to enrich her relationships.

Even if you do not enjoy another's acknowledged differences, working with them can foster personal growth: *One of the best lessons I've learned is to ride different horses,* states Jenny Butah. *Not just the one that suits me, but horses that are difficult as well. Even though I may not want to ride the difficult horse again, I think, "What can I learn from him while I'm on him?" It's taught me to have a much more open mind. Doing that has taught me I can get along in lots of different situations without forcing others to be a certain way.* That expanded attitude of tolerance can produce additional opportunities for learning. Not only can you tolerate more diversity, but you can learn from the very attributes that are difficult for you to embrace.

Like people, no horse is perfect. Attorney Pat Lawson (p. 126), founder of Ebony Horsewomen a non-profit troupe of African-American riders who support urban youth has had her beautiful palomino, Star, for years and is still reminded that he can be a handful when he wants to be: *Star tends to be spooky,* explains Pat. *I've had him for a long time, and I understand him, but I can't relax on him because there are times when he gets too strong. I've learned that some things you can change and some things you can't. I'll never be able to change Star; his behavior is just too deeply ingrained in him. Age is not mellowing him either; he's about 17 now, strong as a bull and just as athletic as ever. I can't change him, and I've realized that the same holds true for some people. Sometimes you can help change them; sometimes you can modify them; sometimes you can't do anything at all. You have to come to appreciate that there are some things that you just can't do, but that which you can do, do it to whatever extent you can. Beyond that, if you can't do anymore, accept it. It's not a matter of how much Star loves me or doesn't love me; he's just that way.* Over the years, Pat has learned to cope with Star's less-than-perfect behavior because his good points outweigh his bad. She accepts his spookiness as inevitable given who she knows Star to be. Accepting this flaw, though not always fun, is a challenge for a rider and has made her a more competent equestrienne in the long run, as well as a more open-minded person.

Acceptance can also defuse judgmental first impressions. Rather than having idealized expectations for a new horse, I now try to discern its individual traits and work from there. This process works with people as well. I used to size people up from an initial impression, which often led to improper judgments and unfounded expectations. Now I make an effort to find out more about who the individual really is and what's inside them—as I do with horses.

When horses meet, they gently blow in each other's nostrils. That is how they come to recognize individuals—by their breath. To me, there's something wonderfully gentle, honest, and accepting about that behavior—breathing in another's essence, getting to know them from the inside out.

## Domestication

The vast majority of horses are domesticated and survive at the pleasure of man. The only true "wild equines" remaining in the world are African zebras and a few ancient breeds in Russia, Mongolia, and China—including or related to the Przewalski horse. All other "wild" horses in the world, notably the mustangs of the American West, are feral—animals that broke away or were released from domestic herds. The fact that even today domestic horses continue to join feral bands and successfully revert to the wild indicates that although domestication does take the horse out of nature, it does not take the nature out of the horse.

Since a domesticated mare or stallion has the same survival instincts as its feral counterparts, it is nothing short of a behavioral miracle that any horse ever allows its most formidable and persistent predator, man, upon its back. For a freedom-craving flight animal to be isolated from his herd, captured, bound by leather and metal restraints, then mounted by a predator, definitely qualifies as a life-threatening situation worth going to the mat over.

For a number of years, the US Government's Bureau of Land Management (BLM) contracted with the New Mexico Department of Corrections, for selected inmates to be trained to ready feral horses for adoption by getting them used to handling, haltering, and being led. For many inmates, this program was initiation by fire; they hadn't been with horses before, and these wild, adult horses hadn't been with humans before. *The inmates used to call the feral horses "crazy,"* relates Curtis Steel, *but I always told them, "These horses are wild and scared, but they are not crazy. I've never seen a crazy horse. I don't even like to hear that term applied to a horse. There are horses that are not near as smart as others, just like people, but none of them's crazy."* Much like outlaws, these animals had been hunted, captured, and shipped to prison. Needless to say, many inmates came to identify with these desperately frightened, incarcerated beasts. Through that program, both horses and inmates received valuable rehabilitation in preparation for new roles in life and society.

Equine fear is often confused with "being crazy." Fright is not insanity—it is a normal catalyst to flight. Since flight is the best line of defense for horses, restraint can be potentially fatal. Thus, when a frightened horse is prevented from running by ropes, fences, or a rider, its fear may turn to panic, resulting in a fight for its life. In such a fight, a horse may actually kill itself—not a result of insanity, but rather a result of its desperate combat against the unnatural enemy of restraint.

For centuries, traditional methods of "breaking" horses were based on physical domination. The animal would be roped, thrown to the ground, haltered, then tied to a "snubbing" post and left there to fight it out. If the man's rope was stronger than the horse's will, he would eventually submit to the restraint. If the horse did not submit, he very often died from panic, injury, or exhaustion.

This tradition of physical domination does relate to the natural equine order of dominant hierarchy (deference to a stronger leader), in this case, man and his restraints. Obviously this traditional method worked, but it created a lot of negative energy ending in submission rather than cooperation. In a working relationship, cooperation is much more valuable than submission, for it promotes willing contribution rather than mere deference.

As a result of experience, observation, and experimentation, new techniques of working horses are being devised: *Over the years, we've developed special handling methods that use horses' nature and psychology to our advantage,* explains wild horse management specialist, Ron Harding. *We used to think in order to vaccinate, determine age and worm a wild horse, we had to halter him and tie his head up, but we found out the less restraint you use the better wild horses react to you. So, we now use a padded chute and very little restraint. We don't put halters on them at all. We just run them into this padded chute, flip a rope around their neck and kind of ease them over to the back side of the padded chute, so we can work with them. That's all the restraint they have, and there's a lot less fight.* Without the restraint, the animal does not feel as threatened and is more willing to tolerate handling. This illustrates the point that the more you know about horse nature, the more you can "think like a horse," the more successful you can be in dealing with the horse. This is true in human relations as well—getting to know others well allows for more effective communication, more realistic expectations, and mutual cooperation.

Considering the natural equine behavior described earlier, it is evident that humans impose many unnatural routines on horses under their care. Horses are confined for our convenience. They are given rich feed two or three times a day as opposed to occupying their time with lighter, more frequent grazing. They are often socially isolated by virtue of being in a one-horse situation, or being restricted to a single stall where physical and mental stimulation are sacrificed to boredom. Exercise is controlled, so spontaneous romps and runs are not possible.

Frequently humans climb on horses' backs and work them until the horses do their bidding. Bit and bridle not only direct horses, but also restrain their heads, making it difficult to turn and focus on frightening objects or motions. Thus, a horse must place his trust in the person on his back to act as "surrogate sentry," even though equine senses are much more perceptive to danger signals than humans'. Occasionally, horses are loaded into a tiny, dark, mobile space and hauled to unfamiliar places with many unknown, anxious equines, snapping flags, raucous humans, loud speakers, and bright lights. Is it any wonder that these timid creatures become nervous? Or that they eventually exhibit neurotic behaviors such as cribbing, chewing, weaving, shying, or bucking?

I've often compared having a horse with keeping a deer. Would you expect much cooperation if you saddled up a large buck? As another prey animal, a deer is very close to having the nature of a horse, yet humans expect and accept timidity and wildness in deer while expecting "courage" and cooperation in a horse. Why? Because horses are big, strong wizards at adjusting and they honestly try to do as we ask, so we continue asking more and expecting more of them. *I think the horse was especially beloved by The Grandfather, (that's what we Comanche call the Lord), explains Chris Hawkins, because He gave them the ability to give of themselves. The horse has given so much to mankind.... A horse that's treated right will give you everything. He'll run himself to death for you—if he's treated right.*

Even owners with the best intentions demand much of horses with little regard for their inherent needs. Understanding those inherent needs may at times necessitate taking a chance with a valuable asset in order to "treat him right." *I see expensive horses that are never, never turned out with another horse because they might get kicked, bit, or pawed,* observes Rex Peterson. *I know people who own show horses who think I am the craziest man that ever walked the face of the earth because Justin, my black stallion that was featured in the movie,* BLACK BEAUTY, *runs outside with the geldings all the time. But you know something? When I keep Justin in the barn, he goes to losing weight and gets depressed. I put him out, and he's three times happier a horse. He's a nicer horse to be around. Horses are herd animals. Even though we've bred some horses that have adjusted to it, I still disagree with people that isolate their horses—horses are and always will be herd animals.*

Unnatural though it may be for a migratory range animal, domestication is also equine salvation—responsible for the preservation, propagation, diversification, and enhancement of the species. With burgeoning human populations and shrinking habitat, it is obvious that if horses are to continue on this earth, it will be through human management and domestication. Even America's wild herds, though not tamed to the point of domestication, are confined to preserves and managed by man. Their numbers are controlled by adoption and contraception programs as well as natural attrition, and they are occasionally aided with feed in severe winters and water during drought. Basically, the BLM is protecting and maintaining America's wild horses on a few very large government "ranches."

## From Domination to Dominion

"And man shall have dominion over all the creatures of the earth." This passage from Genesis is often cited by individuals advocating total domination of the animal world by man. As with the entire Bible, this excerpt is open to interpretation. Although the terms dominion (sovereign authority) and domination (power to control) can be synonymous, "dominion" implies responsible, enlightened rule in which a wise sovereign seeks to understand and provide for his subjects' needs, keeping them content and productive by creating a mutually beneficial symbiotic relationship. Dominion recognizes the power in honoring and harnessing spirit, whereas domination seeks to crush spirit in order to control.

As domesticator, it behooves man to study equine nature and apply that knowledge to training methods that work with natural instincts and behaviors. This is the commonsense "New Age" philosophy espoused by trainers such as Buck Brannaman, Richard Shrake, Monty Roberts, John Lyons, Rex Peterson, Linda Tellington-Jones, and many more. "Work *with* the horse, not *against* him." "*Make* a horse; don't *break* a horse." Slogans such as these indicate the goal of educated cooperation over the tradition of forced domination.

The more one knows of each equine subject, the easier it is to establish individually effective schooling. As a trainer for the movie industry, Rex Peterson is often called upon to teach his horses stunts that are diametrically opposed to their natural instincts: *A number of years ago, a producer called around looking for a horse to use in a rock 'n roll video. She'd called every trainer in Hollywood including the very best: Glenn Randall.* [Rex Peterson's mentor and trainer of Roy Rogers' famous horse, Trigger, Glenn Randall enjoyed an illustrious career training horses for movies such as BEN HUR and THE BLACK STALLION.] *Three of them gave her my name saying, "If this boy can't do it with his horse, it can't be done." She called me and told me what they wanted: to have a horse burst out of the ground on cue—meaning he'd first have to be buried alive. She also said she needed it done by Saturday. Well, I told her I'd call her back, and I went out and tried it with my little black stud.*

*I called her back and told her this is what it's going to cost and this is what I must have. She said, "No, no, we can't do that!" So I said, "Thank you very much," and hung up. She called me right back and said we must have been cut off. But I told her, "No, I hung up." She asked, "Why?" And I explained, "Because I have the greatest of patience with horses; I do not have any with people. When I tell you how I work, I'm not just wanting to hear myself talk. This is what I do for a living. This is the only way I'll do it. If we cannot do it that way, you can get somebody else." She said, "But everybody else said it was impossible!" "Well, lady, let me explain it again. I told you I would come out and do three takes and guarantee my work. If we do not get it in three takes, you do not pay me." She asked, "But how do we know you can do it?" I said, "Lady, I just guaranteed you! I will lay the horse down three times and bury him. I guarantee you, he's gonna lay down; he's gonna be totally covered up, and he's gonna bust outta the ground!" And we did it.*

*The moment we were done with the shoot, I went to my best friend, Glenn Randall, the man who taught me most of what I know about training liberty horses. I couldn't help myself. I said, "Glenn, I got a call to do this…how would you do it?" He said, "Well, I don't know; you'll have to bring your horse down, and we'd have to try it." I got to laughing, and he said, "You already went and did it, didn't you?" "Yeah, I did." He smiled and asked, "Well, how'd you do it?" We sat all afternoon and talked about it then.*

Obviously such a "buried-alive stunt" requires a great deal of understanding and trust between horse and trainer. However, even such extreme training stems from the same source as general equine adaptability and tractability: a horse's tendency to defer to, cooperate with, and trust in a dominant leader. Working with equine nature in the way that Rex did by utilizing trust allows for greater advances in training and the horse-human relationship.

## *From Dominion to Affiliation*

Through the study of others, there is the added advantage of mutual edification and personal expansion: *The more we learn about the animals, the more we learn about ourselves and our own relationship to the world around us,* claims Bev Doolittle. *There's a quote by a Na-*

tive American chief, *"If you know the animal and he comes to know you, you will have no more fear." You don't fear what you know; you only fear what you don't know. But you have to want to take the time and the effort to get to know the animals. That applies to people as well; strangers are not that far from being friends.... If we took the time to get to know other human beings, there might be less fear and prejudice of different ethnic groups. That's why all animals are really important—that relationship between all living things.*

One of the America's most successful equestrians (six-time Olympian show jumper), and accomplished citizens, William Steinkraus (p. 143), holds a refreshingly modest and egalitarian perception of the relationship between all living things: *I view life all together. We're all here on this earth, and I think my relationship is animal to animal rather than a divinely inspired product of God's only son to all of these lesser creatures. I'm simply a part of the same continuum.* By acknowledging our own place in the living continuum, we admit to our inherent relationship to all others: a relationship based not on domination, but on informed understanding and compassionate dominion: a shared trust for another's well-being, a relationship based on mutual affiliation.

## Life Lessons

Learning about others refocuses the egocentric "I" to consider "you" and "we." Not as "I" *imagine* you to be, but as "you" *truly are*—your essence—so that we might accept each other as individuals. By getting to know the rare qualities of others, (personality, horsenality, individual traits) we are able to share a respect, appreciation, and enthusiasm for each being's singular talents, limitations, and idiosyncracies. Getting to know and appreciate others in this way is the foundation for connection, brotherhood, and love.

Even if we do not find all their various traits attractive or endearing, we do learn from each individual. Such knowledge elicits familiarity and tolerance, breaking down the prejudice and fear of difference, that harbor disconnection and bigotry. There is an old adage, "A good horse cannot be of a bad color" (Vernon 454). If only mankind would accept that a good human cannot be of a bad color....

By recognizing each species' group dynamics through the study of sociology and "equinology," we expand our understanding of interspecies relationship (such as predator to prey). Such knowledge fosters more realistic expectations and effective training methods for successful coexistence. As Bill Wyman, Headmaster of Thacher School in Ojai, California notes: "It's not what you learn about horses that makes them important; it's what they teach you about people" (Huyler 339).

It is crucial to know the true nature of others in our world in order to relate and exist in greater harmony. Monty Roberts (p. 144), ASPCA Man of the Year in 1998 and specialist in horse communication, says, *Horses are but one piece in life's mosaic, as are human beings. All animate objects on the face of the earth are connected spiritually through that mosaic. That's how nature works. The spiritual connection is as big as all outdoors, and it is crying out to us. We just have to understand it better.*

By studying other species we learn about individual pieces of nature's mosaic, our connection to them, and the shared relationships to the whole. In this particular instance understanding, working with, and learning from true equine nature contributes to the dynamic balance and harmony of nature's living continuum.

PHYLLIS EIFERT, b. 1929, is a painter, sculptor and avid rider since the age of six. As a youngster she foxhunted and showed hunters. She has raised crossbred ponies, was a horse-show mother for nine years, and currently rides with the Tryon Hounds in North Carolina. Phyllis is shown in this 1967 snapshot with her husband and children and their beloved family pony, Yankee Doodle.

MARY FENTON, b. 1938, has been riding and teaching most of her life, from Pony Club instruction to directing a large riding school. After studying with Sally Swift, Mary became a certified Centered Riding Instructor. She has been mentor/instructor for Becky Hart (see page 174) and was named 1992 Riding Instructor of the Year by the American Riding Instructor Certification Program. She is pictured with her homebred Thoroughbred gelding, Egyptian Hemp, aka Tempo, on his maiden camping trip to California's Pt. Reyes National Seashore.

LINDA TELLINGTON-JONES, b. 1937, is an innovative trainer and master teacher who achieved international acclaim for creating TTEAM Training (Tellington TTouch Equine Awareness Method) and TTOUCH (Tellington TTouch techniques): holistic methods for training, healing and interacting with animals. A record-setting equestrian in many disciplines, Linda has worked with a variety of international Olympic teams, basing her success on aiding both horse and rider to maximize their potential. In addition to her clinics, many articles, books and videos chronicle her techniques. A receptive Arabian mare receives the TTouch from Linda in Galisteo, New Mexico.

BUCK BRANNAMAN, b. 1961, is a cowboy whose colorful career has included being a child roping star, which won him rodeo credits as well as a stint with his brother as the rope-twirling "Sugar Pops kids" in the sixties. Since then Buck has turned his talents to horses, where his abilities at starting colts and training horses developed into a very successful clinic practice and led to his becoming the technical advisor for Robert Redford's production of THE HORSE WHISPERER. Buck is pictured working with a horse at one of his popular clinics.

PENELOPE SMITH, b. 1946, is a recognized pioneer in the field of animal communication. A popular speaker and author of books and audio tapes on interspecies communication, Penelope holds workshops and seminars through-out the United States and the world. Penelope is shown with her companion llama, Raindance.

In addition to being one of America's most admired equine artists and the official artist of the United States Equestrian Team, SAM SAVITT is also an award-winning author, illustrator of more than 150 books, acclaimed teacher, and a devoted equestrian who still appreciates the excitement of riding cross-country near his home in New York state. Sam is pictured with companions, Randy the cat and McClaurey the horse.

CAROL GRANT, b. 1933, is a college Sociology and Psychology instructor whose articles on horse behavior have appeared in QUARTER HORSE JOURNAL. Her lifelong love of horses blossomed with her first horse at age eight, and flourished over the years as she rode, bred and trained more than twenty pleasure horses of her own. The highlight of her experience with horses is her palomino Quarter Horse mare, Skips Snow White, better known as Rosie, shown with Carol at a Quarter Horse Show.

TRACY COLE, b. 1965, is a principal microfilm machine operator who began riding with the Somerset Hills Handicapped Riders Club in 1972 as therapy to combat the effects of cerebral palsy. She competed in a national horse show for disabled riders in 1989 and in the Victory Games in 1991. Tracy is pictured on her beloved riding partner, Freckles, warming up before their equitation class at the 1992 Somerset Hills Handicapped Riders Club show.

VALERIE KANAVY, b. 1946, is a horse trainer and world champion endurance rider who has competed since 1972. After claiming six major wins in 1994, including a gold medal at the World Equestrian Games in Holland, Valerie came in second at the subsequent 1996 World Games, crossing the line an instant behind the victor— her 25-year-old daughter, Danielle. Valerie is shown with her Arabian, Pieraz, better known as Cash, enjoying the Race of Champions in the Black Hills of South Dakota in 1993.

CURTIS STEEL, b. 1942, is a ranch manager and former horse training supervisor for the New Mexico Corrections Department, where he managed the wild horse domestication program within the prison system. Curtis and his wife enjoy raising, riding and competing on the registered Quarter Horses and mustangs they train. Curtis and his Mustang, Jake, are shown during a roping demonstration at the state prison training arena in Las Cruces, New Mexico in 1991.

# CHAPTER FOUR

# HORSE SENSE & HONESTY

## Intelligence and Integrity

*Horses are direct reflections of the people that handle them.*
*—John Lyons*

*Horses see through us like we're lucite. —Macella O'Neill*

Dust hadn't even had a chance to settle on the shiny new sign proclaiming Diamond Mountain Stables: Hunter/Jumper Lessons, Boarding, Training, before the tall, husky man and his slender wife walked their dapple gray gelding up the driveway. At the barn the eager new proprietors, Macella O'Neill and Charlie White, greeted them warmly.

"Hi! I spoke with you yesterday." the man said as he shook Macella's hand. "This is my wife, and *this* is Jaqeem," he said, indicating the gelding with almost parental pride.

Charlie took the lead rope as Macella gently rubbed the gelding's neck, then watched as the four-year-old Arab walked calmly about the parking area.

"He leads well and seems gentle enough," said Charlie.

"Yeah, he's a real pet," the man replied. "Like I mentioned on the phone, he was born at our place, and we've raised him from day one, but now he needs professional training so we can ride him on the trails around our property."

"That shouldn't be any problem," said Macella confidently. "Just leave him with us, and we'll let you know how he's doing in a few weeks. Feel free to stop by any time."

When the couple left, Macella and Charlie put the horse in a stall near the arena and congratulated themselves on their first training client. The barn was off to an auspicious start. This particular couple was well known in the area. A success with their young horse would lead to recommendations for a lot more work.

Jaqeem took to schooling enthusiastically and was soon going well under saddle. After one training session, however, as Macella was leading him to the stall, Jaqeem suddenly reared and lunged toward Charlie who was walking past nonchalantly swinging a bucket of grain and whistling to himself. Macella was able to steer the horse away and get him down, but both she and Charlie had been surprised and a bit shaken by the incident.

The next day, Jaqeem went up again—this time punching the air with his front legs and marching towards Macella like a huge, crazed, boxing kangaroo. "Man, he's fast on those hind legs!" said Macella as she ducked back into the feed room to escape his assault. "I've never seen anything like this before—I swear he was trying to box my ears!" Over the next few days, Jaqeem went up a number of times and won a solid reputation among the stable hands as an insane rogue bent on homicide. No one but Macella and Charlie were allowed near him as they discussed how best to proceed.

Both knew that a failure with this client could be devastating to their fledgling business. However, as a public stable, Diamond Mountain could not afford the liability of a dangerous horse on the grounds. Charlie and Macella scoured their minds to figure out what set off Jaqeem's behavior and how to correct it.

Since his owners had mentioned no history of assaults, and this would certainly be something they'd want corrected in training, Macella and Charlie concluded the problem had started since Jaqeem came to Diamond Mountain. But why? They consulted their vet, their farrier, and a few of their more experienced training buddies. No one had any explanation except that crazy rogues do exist, and Jaqeem seemed to fit the profile.

Macella refused to accept that. "He's gentle and kind other-wise," she thought. "It just doesn't make sense. I just can't accept that he's crazy." She and Charlie agreed they'd have to tell Jaqeem's owners, since they weren't having great success breaking him of what was now a distressingly frequent habit. Rather than discuss it over the phone, Macella decided to have the owners come to the barn, so that they could see Jaqeem in action.

The afternoon was warm and bright. Jaqeem was already saddled and in the arena when the couple arrived. Macella wanted to deliver the good news first. An impressive equitation exhibition followed, with Jaqeem showing off his newly honed skills: a rhythmic walk, trot, canter, halt, backing up, leg yields. Macella even took him over a couple of low jumps. Through it all Jaqeem was quiet, attentive, and obviously enjoying his performance. After twenty minutes, Macella slid lightly from the saddle and proudly led her young student up the hill to his delighted owners.

As soon as Jaqeem saw his master standing there with a hand-ful of carrots, he reared up and raced toward him—fully tacked up with legs flailing!

"Damn!" thought Macella. "I knew the bad news was next, but I didn't think he'd attack *them*!" She thought ironically, "Ah well, that's the horse business!" Luckily, Charlie was at hand and got Jaqeem down before he made contact with his owner.

"He seems to have a bit of a bad habit..." Charlie said slowly, trying to feel out the owners' reaction.

"Oh...yeah...he does that. We were hoping you could train it out of him," the man replied.

"You *knew about this?*" asked Charlie incredulously, at once re-lieved that Jaqeem had not picked up the behavior at their facility, but at the same time, upset that the owners had failed to mention such a dangerous habit when they turned Jaqeem over to them.

"Why didn't you tell us about this when you brought him over?" asked Charlie with an obvious edge to his normally affable voice.

The couple looked at each other as if they held a shameful secret that they could not bring themselves to share.

"We were embarrassed.... You see, Jaqeem is the first foal we've ever raised." began the man.

"He was such a precious little one!" interrupted his wife. "We now know it was stupid of us, but at the time we didn't give it a thought," she hesitated. They looked at each other and then down at the ground.

"You see, when Jaqeem was little—I mean, *really tiny* and cute and cuddly..." the man continued, "I would kneel down in front of him, place his spindly front legs on my shoulders, hug him, and give him a treat. Well, he's such a smart guy, pretty soon all I had to do was show him some grain or a carrot, and he'd place his little hooves on my shoulders. He was such a teddy bear."

"Honestly, we never gave a thought to his doing it full grown." added the wife apologetically.

"When we realized he was getting too big for that, we tried everything we could think of to break him of the habit, but nothing's worked. We heard that you're terrific with horses, so we brought him here," the man said hopefully.

"Jesus!" exclaimed Charlie. "No wonder we've made so little headway—you practically imprinted him from birth! Then you rewarded him for it with affection and treats! You did everything right to train that behavior into him! It's real hard to *un*train a horse under those circumstances. I sincerely doubt that he will ever stop completely."

"But we'll do our best," said Macella, still trying to be pleasant and positive. "Pick him up next month as planned, and we'll work on retraining him until then."

The following weeks brought impressive advancement for Jaqeem under saddle, yet painfully little improvement on curbing his life-threatening attempts at "hugging." The barn staff became particularly alert around Jaqeem and had strict orders to keep all treats out of his sight. When the training contract lapsed, Macella returned Jaqeem to his owners, satisfied that he was now a lovely trail horse, though still a potentially lethal "teddy bear."

## Man-Made Misconceptions

Horses are dumb; they cannot speak. The above situation underscores how easily horses' mute behaviors can be misread and motives misconstrued. Jaqeem was not bent on homicide, he was bent on "hugging" for rewards of attention, affection, and a tidbit. Far from being a "rogue," Jaqeem was simply a well-trained animal responding correctly to the visual cue of treats. Once his history was revealed, Jaqeem's actions demonstrated real "horse sense" in that he knew when and what to do to get rewards, and "honesty" in that he was performing exactly as he'd been taught.

Given that incident, which animal is smarter? The humans who didn't think ahead to "full-grown trouble" or the horse that was doing what he knew should earn him a reward? Which animal was more honest? The humans who withheld important information due to embarrassment, or the horse that performed as trained each time the visual cue was presented?

Had the actual facts never been revealed, Jaqeem might well have been branded a dangerous rogue and severely punished for performing as he'd been trained. The sudden change from reward to punishment for the identical cue would definitely confuse Jaqeem and could lead to defensive counterstrikes against the punishment. It is easy to imagine this scenario escalating to the point of someone getting hurt and demanding that the homicidal rogue be destroyed.

Interpreting for mute animals is not an easy job. It takes knowledge, experience, sensitivity, and an open, inquisitive mind to fathom some of the puzzling behaviors presented. Even when the behavior is as outrageous and seemingly straightforward as Jaqeem's "attacks," there are often those subtle clues of timing, physical stimulus, or past history that must be uncovered for remedial training to succeed: *When I bought my Quarter Horse stud, Dream, he was in a major fight with everyone around him,* relates John Lyons. *He was real aggressive over the stall, biting people; he was real aggressive towards other horses. He'd been beat up a whole lot and was just fighting back and was real serious about it. When I finally got through to him I found what he wanted was attention. He was like a little boy. He just wanted to be handled all the time; he loved being petted and rubbed on. Initially that had got him into trouble because people took it as aggressiveness, so they started beating him back.... There are a few horses like Dream, that no matter how bad you beat on them, they'll come back and fight harder and harder. Pretty soon, they're winning the battle, and then they're labeled as rogue horses, or bad horses. Then they're left alone, which is the opposite of what Dream needed so he just got worse and worse.... Dream taught me that some really, really aggressive horses just get off to a wrong start with people and they're actually special horses inside.*

Incidents such as Jaqeem's and Dream's are all too common. Misconceptions, mistreatment, and poor training techniques have created many confused, scared, and dangerously defensive animals, leading to a belief in crazy or rogue horses. Among most of the experienced horsemen I interviewed, however, the widespread contention is that 99.9% of bad, crazy, or rogue horses are man-made: *When I was working with Glenn Randall, people used to bring him a lot of bad horses,* says Rex Peterson. *Glenn called them "lions and tigers." And believe me, they were man-made; every one of them.* Along the same line, Chris Hawkins observes: *I don't think the good Lord ever made a bad horse—it takes mankind to make bad horses.* Certainly through genetics or hormonal imbalance the possibility of mentally defective animals exists. However, genetic insanity is exceedingly rare; the vast majority of rogue horses are man-made and can usually be man-cured—if the horse gets to the proper handler and home— luckily, Jaqeem and Dream both did.

## Is "Horse Sense" Intelligence?

In the preceding chapter the horse is described as a prey animal with simple, mainly physically oriented needs: protection, propagation, socialization, subsistence, and survival. Hence equine mental functions are geared to physical activity. Humans, as cognitive predators, need to think creatively, strategize, and initiate hunting scenarios. Add to those needs the wide range of human emotions, cerebral recreations, imagination, and linguistic demands, and it is clear that humans engage in much more complicated mental functions. Thus the human brain is considerably larger, more complex and advanced than a horse's.

Additionally, equine monocular vision, limited generalization, right/left balancing, and imprint-training make it evident that horses perceive and learn very differently from humans and other species. Each and every species develops unique intellectual talents to survive in specific ecological niches. Therefore, commonly heard statements such as that pigs, dogs, or turtles are smarter than horses are totally meaningless, for each species has its own measure of intelligence. Equine intelligence enables horses not only to survive and flourish around the globe, but also to adapt successfully to incredibly artificial environments and varied labors thrust upon them by man: from pulling a cart to performing in a circus and from competing in the Olympics to charging into artillery fire, horses have learned and performed admirably. That is why I say, "Horses may be 'dumb,' but they are not stupid."

As with humans, there are gradations of intelligence among horses. Within the species, it may be possible to measure levels of equine intelligence just as man attempts to do with human IQ tests. However, even the measurement and comparison of human intelligence has become extremely controversial in recent years. If intelligence tests within one species are not accurate or valid, what possible hope can there be for intelligence comparisons between species?

Dr. Temple Grandin has a Ph.D. in animal behavior, yet she has autism, an often–debilitating mental disorder. In her fascinating book, THINKING IN PICTURES, she reports that she is unable to think in a verbal, linear, sequential reasoning way that many people do; instead she thinks in pictures, by association.

"...I would be denied the ability to think by scientists who maintain that language is essential for thinking.

"When a well-respected animal scientist told me that animals do not think, I replied if this were true, then I would have to conclude that I was unable to think. He could not imagine thinking in pictures, nor assign it any validity of real thought. Mine is a world of thinking that many language-based thinkers do not comprehend. I have observed that the people who are most likely to deny animals thought are often highly verbal thinkers who have poor visualization skills. They excel at verbal or sequential thinking activities, but are unable to read blueprints.

"It is very likely that animals think in pictures and memories of smell, light, and sound patterns. In fact, my visual thinking patterns probably resemble animal thinking more closely than those of verbal thinkers. It seems silly to debate whether or not animals can think. To me it has always been obvious that they do.... Differences between language-based thought and picture-based thought may explain why artists and accountants fail to understand each other. They are like apples and oranges" (Grandin 160).

"As Elizabeth Marshall Thomas, author of THE HIDDEN LIFE OF DOGS, would say, 'Dogs have dog thoughts.' I would apply that to farm animals, too. One of my students remarked that horses don't think, they just make associations. If making associations is not considered thought, then I would have to conclude that I am unable to think. Thinking in visual pictures

and making associations is simply a different form of thinking from ver-
bal-based linear thought. There are advantages and disadvantages to both
kinds of thinking" (Grandin 173).

Even the term "intelligence" refers to the cognitive, abstract
reasoning powers of humans. Equine "intelligence" should be measured by specifically equine standards. Horses have varying degrees
of intellect or "horse sense," combining unique, effective talents,
attributes, and awareness that permits them to learn, adapt, and survive. Diana Thompson comments: *Moshe Feldenkrais has a saying
that horses exemplify: "The ability to adapt is a sign of intelligence." From
an evolutionary standpoint, if a species didn't adapt, they became extinct.*

Although ego-based human nature seeks to compare one's position on an IQ measuring stick, Mother Nature has simpler, more
pragmatic methods of measurement: adaptation and survival. Hence
a savvy, senior, lead mare would be the "Rhodes scholar" of the
equine set.

Through the ages horses have proven themselves to be masters at adaptation and survival: *The horse is a moldable, changeable animal with an amazing ability to adapt to its environment and training,*
declares John Lyons. *No matter what the horse has done in the past, as
that horse is passed to a new owner, it can become a completely different
horse. That's what's so neat about them. Any person who makes the state-
ment that a horse is stupid is a person who doesn't know horses very well.
The last thing that a horse is is stupid. In fact, as I become a better teacher,
I work with "smarter" horses. As I get better at explaining the subject
matter to the horses, the horses seem smarter and smarter and smarter. That
has nothing to do with the horse at all. I'm better at explaining to the
horse what I want, so the horse seems more intelligent, but he's always
been intelligent. We need to become better teachers and explainers and then
build better lesson plans.* When they combine realistic expectations,
clear and proper lesson plans, appropriate training time, and
"equine-friendly" methods, human handlers discover their horses
are suddenly much smarter.

What most people mean when they say a horse is "smart" is
that he's easily trained, or well-trained, and able to override his
natural "flight or fight" response. That definition places the onus
of "smart" on the trainer and an abiding equine trust in handlers,
not just on horse sense. Since innate horse sense usually demands
very different responses than what most humans consider "smart"

(shying from blowing paper, or giving wide berth to a mailbox), the basic foundation for smart horses—training and trust—depends on the talents of their human handlers. It is up to all a horse's handlers to consistently reinforce that desired training and trust: *Bill Steinkraus gave me some very good advice,* Sam Savitt recalls. *He said, "Never lie to your horse. If you tell the horse this is okay, you can do that; you'd better be sure that he can do it. Because if he can't, and he starts getting hurt every time he does it, he's going to start losing confidence in you and in himself at the same time."*

## Naturally Smart Horses

Equine instincts and physical sensitivities are impressive and bear consideration: *Horses are so perceptive. They pick up messages that we miss, or are unaware that we are giving,* explains Dr. Robert Miller. *I've had people tell me, "If I come out to groom him, I can catch him, but I can't catch him if I'm going to go ride." I ask, "Do you wear different boots?" "Yeah…" "Don't you think the horse can see that?" "But they can't tell…." "You bet they can tell! They make those associations. They're extremely perceptive, and they have an infallible memory."*

Equine perception goes beyond reading the obvious such as boots; they can read fear and moods as well. Scientists theorize that horses pick up on hormonal or "emotional odors" emitted, such as anxiety-induced perspiration. However they do it, they are terrific judges of people's states of mind. *All those old wives' tales and cowboys' phrases about how horses can tell you're scared, it is completely true,* says Macella O'Neill. *Horses see through us like we're lucite. You gotta mean what you say and say what you mean to horses. Without total integrity, there's no hope of ever forging a bond with any horse. If you watch somebody that's false with a horse, you can almost watch the horse get agitated. They're fabulous barometers that way.*

To be able to read those equine barometers accurately is a real asset. Since the horse is aware of menace before the rider is, it would be tremendously helpful to be able to interpret what the horse's behavior is actually indicating: *I often ride in Griffith Park, which is smack dab in the middle of the city of Los Angeles,* says Caroline Thompson. *One day my horse, Chester, and I were heading up one of our most familiar routes that winds into the hills. When we reached this sharp corner where you can't see the continuation of the trail, Chester stopped and refused to go on. Since we'd ridden this trail many times before, we had a conversation about it, and I finally convinced him to continue. We got around that corner, and here is a guy with his pants down around his ankles, masturbating. I had no idea he was there, but Chester knew. And Chester knew that person was someone we should not be near. We'd passed hikers on that trail many times, but Chester didn't want to get near this guy. And he was right! Who is the more intelligent creature in that context? Horses are only "stupid" when we don't understand what they're reacting to. They are much more sensitive and instinctual than humans.*

Horses often appear much smarter in knowledgeable human hindsight than they are in oblivious human foresight. If we could correctly interpret all that horses are aware of ahead of time, we would have greater respect for their abilities, concerns, and horse sense in general.

## Man-Made Smart Horses

Roy Rogers' palomino stallion, Trigger, was billed as "The Smartest Horse in the Movies." That was not empty Hollywood hype—Trigger earned that billing. Not only athletically accomplished at natural equine talents such as racing and rearing on cue, Trigger also had a repertoire of over one hundred tricks, many never before asked of a horse (Rogers 144): In 1954, in the movie, SON OF PALEFACE, Trigger—complete with dealer's shade—sat in on a hand of poker with Roy, Bob Hope, and Jane Russell. Trigger signed in to the Hotel Dixie in New York City by writing his X on the registry (Rogers 145). Special rubber boots were made so Trigger could accompany Roy safely and quietly on his many visits into children's hospital wards and orphanages. While in the wards, Trigger would perform by holding one end of a jump-rope with Roy for the more able children to jump. Trigger often rode in public elevators, and once, when both Roy and Dale were hospitalized in Liverpool, England, with a serious bout of flu, Trigger climbed up seven flights of stairs to deliver flowers and get-well cards. Since Trigger went with Roy on most of his public appearances, he was often indoors—not necessarily in sawdust-covered arenas—but in lobbies or on theater stages. It was his many indoor appearances that prompted Trigger's most unusual training: *I had Trigger broke to go to the toilet, you know,* explains Roy Rogers. *We'd poke him in the ribs right in front of his hind legs about the time he should want to go. And we'd keep poking him, keep poking him, keep poking him—just with your thumb, you know. He'd flinch every time, but pretty soon he'd spread out his legs and let go. Finally he got to where you could just do that and he'd go.* It took his trainer, Glenn Randall, two years of persistence and patience, but Glenn succeeded where no horse trainer had before.

*Trigger taught me that horses can learn a lot of things,* Roy continues. *Basically it depends on how much time you've got to spend with them. You practically have to live with them teaching some of those things.*

Given proper training, it's astounding what some horses learn to do: *We were in Europe working on* [the movie] BLACK BEAUTY *when Caroline Thompson told me, "There's a horse opera in France you must go and see," recalls* Rex Peterson. *Now, I thought, "Horse opera! What would I want to go and see a horse opera for?" But Caroline's the director, so I went...I saw a horse canter backwards! I'd heard about it from Glenn— he had seen it once in his life time—I didn't think I'd ever see it. There was a black Andalusian that cantered backwards: he did not run backwards; he did not shuffle backwards; he cantered backwards! It's probably the greatest thing I've seen a horse do, bar none. I've seen horses levade, capriole...you name it. But I think that was the greatest move I've ever seen a horse do. I would give anything to be able to teach a horse to do it.*

There's an old saying, "Whether a horse turns out to be a good cow horse or a poor one pretty much depends on the intelligence of the handler" (Montana 2). Trigger had an exceptional trainer in Glenn Randall and an exceptional partner in Roy Rogers; as a result, he became the exceptional horse loved and remembered by millions of "buckaroos."

*Super horses are few and far between and should be,* declares Helen Crabtree. *If you're smart enough to train them, the sky's the limit. That's where we get the Seattle Slews, the Secretariats, and the Wing Commanders. They are exceptions, but of course, everybody in the senior class in college isn't a Phi Beta Kappa either—wouldn't be any fun if they were!*

*There was one little horse, Fancy Stonewall, that was almost an outlaw—he'd run into the ring and do all kinds of unacceptable things because his trainers weren't using him right. They were trying to force him into things instead of working with him. I bought him because I could just see intelligence oozing out of that horse's head. He was one of the smartest horses I ever trained and became a World Champion.* So one person's rogue can become another's champion.

When a super horse knows what is expected of him and enjoys doing it, often the best strategy is to just let him do his thing: *In the sixties I had a horse that I swore watched everybody else run, and then he ran just as fast as he knew he had to do,* marvels Martha Josey (p. 145), World Champion Barrel Racer and National Finals Rodeo contestant in four consecutive decades. *He was Cede Reed, one of my first great horses. I won fifty-two barrel races in a row with him. He was so automatic and did things so easily, people thought that I just wound him up!* A number of the top competitors I spoke with indicated that one of the most difficult judgments of their horse-and-rider partnership was to know when to stay out of the way of an exceptional horse.

## Honesty

One of the aspects I like most about horses is their simple honesty—in the sense of complete genuineness. Horses let you know how they are feeling, what they like, what they don't like, what they can do, and where they come up short—just by watching them. Of course you have to be tuned in and savvy enough to know how to interpret all the signals correctly: *Glenn Randall always said, "No matter what a horse does: rears, bucks, strikes, kicks, rears over backward, you name it, whatever it is, he forewarns you,* remarks Rex Peterson, *A horse will tell you what he's gonna do before he does it." Glenn could be sitting in his chair and read a horse from the ground and say, "Look out, that horse is gonna do this." And it did! How did he know? Goes back to being able to read horses in an instant. I try to learn to read them better everyday. I hope some day to be one tenth as good as Glenn was at it; he was excellent at it. How did he do it? Was mental telepathy a part of it? I don't know.... That's what made him a great trainer. He could read those horses and tell exactly what they were going to do next. Some of them are hard to read; some are easy to read, but none of them lie to you. So when I sit and read one, everything is true fact. Everything's honest.*

*When I take a horse in the round pen and spend an hour with him,* says Monty Roberts, *I will know just about all the important things that happened in his life—things important to him. I'll know that a groom kicked him in the belly; I'll know that a guy bashed him over the head; I'll know that the horse dentist used a twitch on him; I'll know that there was a nice groom too—that there were people who did respect him. I'll know a whole lot about him in one hour's time in my round pen. Maybe it is deducing, but it's certainly being told straight from the horse's mouth, and they can't lie. Horses cannot lie.*

Humans can play intricate mind games on themselves as well as others, where horses cannot. Integrity is a human choice to be honest; horses do not *choose* honesty; they just are what they are each moment. Horses lack the imagination, ego, and full range of emotional masks that humans employ to dupe, deny, delude, defraud, and deceive.

*Look deep into a horse's eye,* Chris Hawkins suggests. *It's beautiful; their soul really shines through. I trust horses because their eyes don't lie to you; a human being's eyes can lie to you—and do, frequently.* It may be difficult to look someone in the eye and lie, but we all know it's been done throughout human history ("Check's in the mail." "Read my lips: No new taxes!" "For better, for worse; for richer, for poorer...").

*John Steinbeck wrote that he was curious why royalty have always seemed so drawn to working with horses when anything they ever desired was available to them,* Buck Brannaman recounts. *His theory was, the horse in its honesty would buck off the prince as quickly as he would his groom. That sort of honesty is something that a prince would value, considering that everyone else would agree with whatever he said no matter what.... The horse is noble in his honesty.*

## "Dishonest" Horses

If horses are so "nobly honest," where does the term "dishonest horse" come from? When I asked about dishonest horses, most trainers denied the very existence of such an animal: *There is no such thing as a dishonest horse,* Monty Roberts replied emphatically. *There's just no such thing. What there is, is a person who's not willing to accept what the horse is telling him. The most often incident to use the term, "dishonest horse" is when a horse works well for you at home, and then works badly in the show ring. Now think about that for a minute....Why is he working badly in the show ring? It's because of the anxiety level of the rider being heightened, or the confusion of a new place, or the distractions of the arena, or the difference in show equipment from training equipment. Things are different; the horse doesn't act the same, so he becomes a dishonest horse—something which does not exist.*

Buck Brannaman concurs: *I don't believe there's such a thing as a dishonest horse. Horses just don't have some of the things that people have in terms of spite and hate and jealousy and that sort of stuff. That's not how a horse is.*

A horse is totally honest, declares Carol Grant. *I don't think horses have the ability to be dishonest. I hear people say, "That's a dishonest horse." I think that horse has just learned to live with behavior that's so erratic that the horse doesn't know what to expect next. When I was a little kid I had a "dishonest horse" given to me: a big bay named Beauty. The people who raised her must have done something really bad to her because she'd actually run people out of the barn—she'd attack—so they gave her to me. To this day, I don't know how my folks let me have her. But within a month I could do anything with that horse, and I didn't even work hard at it. She was the horse that I used to jump. She just trusted me. And I trusted her because she'd never done anything bad to me. She was a real gift horse.*

Larry Mahan agrees: *If a horse is dishonest, it's probably because man made him that way. I've heard them called dishonest, but a horse will not cheat you if they're trained properly. You have to develop consistent control yourself: soft hands, a good seat, soft legs, precise aids. And spend the time with them, let them develop the confidence in us as humans and the trust to help them reach their maximum potential. However, if we take them beyond their abilities, to reach what we feel should be their maximum potential, that's not fair to the horse. When we do that, all of a sudden you've created a dishonest horse, or a no good horse, or a treacherous horse.*

A notable exception to the faction denying the existence of dishonest equines is William Steinkraus, who explains his position this way: *Someone told me once, "There are people who will climb a tree to steal apples when you could pick them up off the ground." In the securities business I found some terribly gifted people who have a little larceny in their soul, and horses are the same way. Some horses just have a little dishonest something and when you give them a chance to duck out, they will duck out. The expression that is commonly used with jumpers is that "he cheated." He gets to a good spot and refuses. Not due to a technical flaw, but a temperament flaw. This kind of horse, when he gets to the point where he has to make that really big effort, says, "No, I'm not going to make that effort." Not because he's afraid of being hurt, he just says "No! I'm not doing this!" That comes under the general heading of dishonesty because the physical capability is there, but there is a mental, psychological refusal.*

Not wanting to stack the deck on this issue, I would, however, question whether this isn't more an example of lack of heart to make "that really big effort" rather than dishonesty. Given a chance to duck out and taking it seems very honest to me. Yet, in the same vein: *A horse cannot lie, but I think that a horse can play a trick on you*, states Diana Cooper (p. 146), trainer and author of a book on circus life. *Some horses canter to a fence and damned if anybody can see three strides out if he's going to stop or not. That's what we call a dirty stopper. That is very true of some horses—that they will find a way to "getcha." But I don't think that they're dishonest about their intentions the way a person might be—they don't plot against you.*

Horses that have the ability, but not the desire to pass other horses in a race are called "common" by jockeys (Helm 89). They're not considered "dishonest" or "cheaters"; they just don't have the bold "heart" of a champion.

At any rate, the majority opinion is that a dishonest horse is more likely to be confused and not understanding what is being asked of him, misread by the rider, or reacting to stimuli not perceived or understood by the human observer. When a rider asks a horse for one move and gets something else, the first place to look for correction is the rider's communication skills—not the horse's ulterior motives.

I'm not trying to make horses out to be perfect—they certainly are not. But by and large they are genuine in their needs, presentation, and reactions. By not reading them accurately, human handlers can and do misinterpret actions and then assign intentions or ulterior motives to them unjustly. There are lazy, stubborn, and resistant horses, but not plotting, scheming, inherently dishonest ones.

## Ulterior Motive, Revenge, and Grudges

The basis of equine "reasoning" power is stimulus and response or reward. Hence, there are valid reasons for horses' actions and behaviors, but not strategic motives. Ulterior motive, revenge, and grudges, like dishonesty and scheming, require a level of reasoning that horses simply do not possess: *Horses don't plot*, explains Dr. Robert Miller. *Sometimes people will swear they do, "He was out to get me...." Horses have enormous intelligence when it comes to speed of learning, desensitization, and memory retention, but they have zero reasoning power. People think they see horses reasoning, but what horses do is put things together. They learn that by nibbling on this chain, I can unlatch this gate. Then they unlatch the gate, and go and unlatch everybody else's gate. Well, there's a reward—the horses come out. It's all a question of stimulus and reward, but people interpret that as a reasoning process.*

In most situations, horses are an honest sounding board. If there is an ongoing problem, a horse's behavior will continue indicating the problem until you realize the source is mostly likely with you: *Last year a young girl brought her horse to me,* recounts Jane Savoie (p. 146), reserve rider for the 1992 US Olympic Dressage Squad, trainer, and author. *She was a green rider on a four-year-old green horse. Every time she went to sit the trot, the horse would pick up the canter. She was okay on a rising trot, but when she'd sit, she'd get the canter. This girl complained, "You see? She keeps doing this to me!" She was looking for a scapegoat, blaming the horse as if it was purposely trying to embarrass her or to get her.... I watched them for a while and then said, "The horse isn't doing anything to you. When you sit the trot, you keep pulling on one rein and make it impossible for the horse to trot in an even rhythm. It's easier for the horse to hop into the canter because you're blocking that hind leg when you sit." "OOOHHH!" she said. I made her put her hands down and just keep them still and then she realized that the horse would stay in the trot for her. But her immediate reaction was that the horse was doing it to her, at her, to get her. Horses don't have that kind of motivation. They just don't!*

*A team, a riding partnership, comes because the horse wants to do for you—not because he wants to go out and get a 72% at training level test three—that might be the rider's motivation, but it's certainly not the horse's motivation. The horse has to want to please you because there's reward in that. They don't have the same kind of motivations that human beings do. I think sometimes people forget that.* This is a good example of a horse forcing a rider to evaluate critically and then accept responsibility for correcting the problem.

Experienced horse people recognize that most "horse problems" are in fact "people problems": *When a horse and rider have had a bad experience and the horse continues to act out, for instance, in the same corner of the ring where the incident occurred,* explains Jill Hassler, *I don't believe it's the horse causing the ongoing problem, but rather the rider's anxiety that causes the horse to continue to misbehave. On many occasions, I've gotten on the horse and can get the horse past the spot or through the bad behavior, but the rider can't. That makes me know that it's the rider causing the problem. I am absolutely as certain as my name that a horse does not calculate revenge.*

In order to plan revenge, or hold a grudge, one must blame something outside oneself. Blame is a human concept. Horses understand cause and effect, stimulus and response, but they do not comprehend blame. In order to plan revenge, one must have strategic reasoning ability, which horses do not possess. Grudges and revenge are human, not horse, behaviors.

*The most important lesson I learned from horses is: don't hold grudges,* states Mary Deringer Phelps. *Horses like you one way or the other because they don't hold a grudge. They don't stop talking to you for four years, or backstab you. They don't care; they just want you to show up at six to feed.*

*If you abuse a horse, it will remember,* says Octavia Brown (p. 147), Assistant Professor of Equine Studies at Centenary College, and founding board member of the North American Riding for the Handicapped Association. *I wouldn't call it a grudge; they won't necessarily get you, but they will want to keep away from you. And if that necessitates lifting a foot and pinning ears when the abuser comes near, they definitely will do that. Who wouldn't try to get rid of a stimulus that hurts? They don't seek out the abuser to do harm; they don't hold grudges or plan revenge like that.* And aren't we lucky that they don't! If horses were capable of holding grudges and executing revenge, mankind would probably have been trampled into oblivion eons ago.

## Lessons Learned

Horse sense and honesty offer many lessons for those willing to risk some introspection: *People are an easy read for a horse,* claims Buck Brannaman. *There are times when the horse, in the way he operates, may be telling you that you're no good at all. Now a person should listen to that because there's no reason he would make that up. There's nothing in it for him to lie. At the same rate, there are times when the horse, through the way you both work together, might be telling you that you're the best person in the whole world that day too, and you can believe that as well. A horse will only offer you what you deserve, and it's hard to look in that glass sometimes.*

About three months after I got my mare, Freddie, she made me look in that glass, and I learned an enlightening lesson about motive. By that time, I was totally in love with this beautiful animal, who rubbed my cheek with her lips and gave me "kisses." As I was grooming her one morning, Freddie suddenly reached back and bit me on the shoulder—really hard! My immediate reaction was, "How could she do that to me?! She must *hate* me!" I brooded about Freddie hating me for the rest of the morning.

When I got home, I realized, "I am being ridiculous! Freddie doesn't know the emotions I've assigned to her actions. When she feels me with her lips, she's not *kissing* me! And that bite was probably because my industrious grooming hurt her sensitive skin—not because she hates me!" I started to laugh at myself for assigning human motives to a horse's actions.

This realization of assigning motives made me recognize that I do the very same thing to people. When someone does something that hurts me, I start searching for the motive behind the action and often end up creating one.

Through that lesson with Freddie, I realized the importance of identifying the true motive for an action, which can only be determined by the instigator. I've learned not to jump to judgment. Now, if I feel slighted, I speak to the individual instead of resentfully assigning a motive to them. (Most of the time, the person is unaware that there was ever an offense to begin with!) I now give others—horse and human—the benefit of the doubt, which I call "the benefit of love" since love is usually what's in doubt. Thanks, Freddie, for handing me that looking glass.

DENNIS MARINE, b. 1951, is a farrier and cattleman who grew up on a Nebraska ranch helping his dad with a boarding barn and starting colts. Since getting his degree from Oregon State University in horse shoeing, Dennis has logged more than 20 years in the trade. He has recently returned to the cattle business, where he is able to apply all his knowledge and skills doing jobs that he truly enjoys. Dennis and Sage, his Quarter Horse gelding, take a break after gathering cows in Napa, California in 1994.

MACELLA O'NEILL, b. 1963, began her riding career on Sultan, the donkey she received from her parents on her third birthday. Years in the saddle ensued, and after graduating from the University of California at San Diego, she and partner Charlie White founded Diamond Mountain Stables, a successful hunter and jumper training stable, in 1983. Since then she has devoted her time to teaching, training, and riding the California Grand Prix Circuit. In 1997 she was the leading Northern California Jumper rider. Here she is shown aboard Gizmo at the Napa Valley Classic Grand Prix Jumping Benefit.

SUSAN STOVALL, b. 1945, is Director of Polo at the El Dorado Polo Club in Indio, California. She has won the United States Polo Association Governor's Cup twice—in 1984 and 1989, when her team won against 26 competing teams. In 1997 she was on the winning team for the Women's International Polo Event in England. She is pictured with her Thoroughbred mare, Gratia, (the Best Playing Pony in the ladies tournament) and tournament sponsor, Mike Conant.

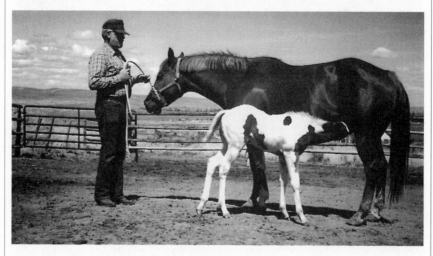

RON HARDING, b. 1938, is a horse trainer, breeder, and wild horse management specialist. He started with the Bureau of Land Management (BLM) in 1974 and became Wild Horse Coordinator and Specialist for Oregon and Washington from 1982 through 1996. In 1977 he gathered the Kiger Mustang herd and helped establish the Kiger Mesteño Association. Ron proudly shows off two of his favorite horses: Foxy, a registered Quarter Horse, and her registered Paint filly, Checotah Fox, near Burns, Oregon in 1994.

J. Michael Plumb, b. 1940, is a trainer, editor-in-chief of Michael Plumb's Horse Journal, and three-day eventing champion. He holds the US record for selection to the most Olympic teams: 1960 in Rome with his horse, Markham; 1964 in Tokyo on Bold Minstrel; 1968 in Mexico City on Plain Sailing; 1972 in Munich with Free & Easy; 1976 in Montreal, where he won an individual silver medal and a team gold on Better and Better; 1980 in Fontainebleau (alternate games) on Laurenson; 1984 in Los Angeles with Blue Stone; and 1992 with Adonis in Barcelona. Michael is pictured on the handsome Count Trey, sailing easily over an oxer.

Rex Peterson, b. 1954, raised in the Sand Hills of Nebraska, is an award-winning trainer for the movie industry specializing in liberty horses. Equestrian entertainment has been Rex's life's blood since he learned to trick- and Roman-ride as part of his family's rodeo act, thrilling crowds at Wild West Shows. For years Rex worked with legendary Hollywood trainer Glenn Randall, Sr. With many exciting movie credits to his name, Rex asks one of his equine partners, Quarter Horse stallion, Doc's Keepin' Time, or "Justin," star of the 1994 production of BLACK BEAUTY, to take a bow.

CAROLINE THOMPSON, b. 1956, is a film writer and director with many major films to her credit. She directed the beautiful 1994 production of Anna Sewell's story of BLACK BEAUTY, working with Rex Peterson and his horse, Justin (Doc's Keepin' Time), the equine star of the movie. Caroline lives in Southern California, where she keeps her own horses and enjoys riding in the hills near her home. She is shown with Justin in England during the production of BLACK BEAUTY.

ANNE KURSINSKI, b. 1959, has competed on more than thirty United States Equestrian Team (USET) Nations' Cup teams, nine World Cup Finals, and four Olympic Games from which she returned home with silver medals in 1988 and 1996. Her stellar record also includes gold (team and individual) medals from the 1983 Pan American Games plus other prestigious awards: 1988 American Horse Shows Association (AHSA) Horsewoman of the Year; 1991 US Olympic Committee Female Equestrian of the Year; 1996 USET Whitney Stone Cup and more. In this 1968 photo, nine-year-old Anne hones her winning style as she clears an obstacle aboard a Flintridge Riding Club school horse at La Cañada, California.

JILL KEISER HASSLER, b. 1944, is manager of Maryland's Hilltop Farm, a comprehensive sporthorse and educational facility. For almost twenty years Jill offered an Easter Seals Handicapped Riding Program and was a director for the North American Riding for the Handicapped Association. A devoted instructor, Jill loves helping pony clubbers prepare and achieve their "ratings" and has served on the Board of Governors of the US Pony Club. Author of two popular training books, Jill has shared the pride of training dressage and eventing riders to national titles. Jill is shown here with 5-year-old Thoroughbred gelding, Night Hawk, at Hilltop Farm.

CHRIS HAWKINS, b. 1931, is a passionate horsewoman of Comanche heritage who breeds and trains Quarter Horses at her Washington State ranch. Chris was instrumental in the fight for the Wild Horse and Burro Protection Act of 1971 that legislated the preservation and control of America's feral horse herds. She is pictured with her beloved mustang stallion, Tajhe Maneche, the first horse adopted out of Oregon's Ochoco National Forest in the early 1970's under the provisions of the newly instituted federal program.

# CHAPTER FIVE

# COMMUNICATION TO COMMUNION

## From Aids to Telepathy

*It's so simple, it's difficult.* —**Anonymous**

*When I train my horse, I'm not talking at the horse; there is always a conversation going on.* —**Jane Savoie**

In the 1890's, Wilhelm von Osten, a retired German teacher, decided to teach basic arithmetic to his horse, Hans. Before long, Hans was solving double-digit addition and subtraction problems by stamping the answers with his foot. The incredibly consistent accuracy of Hans' math tests soon spread his fame throughout Europe. Even skeptics were impressed when Hans was able to perform without his trainer present—Hans stamped the correct answer regardless of who posed the problem.

It wasn't until an experiment was held in which no one in Hans's presence knew the answers to the problems posed that Hans's responses degenerated to a level of chance. Only then was Hans's true ability revealed: "Clever" Hans was no equine mathematician, he was just keenly observant. The horse responded to cues unwittingly supplied by people in the audience as they anticipated—and thus unconsciously telegraphed—the correct answer through their own body language (Hart 20–21). With Hans's ability at math thus debunked, the idea of horse-human communication returned to the realm of disbelief.

What no one working with Hans seemed to realize, however, was that Hans was actually demonstrating exceptional communication skills by accurately reading such subtle physical cues. True, Hans did not posses the abilities originally assigned to him: comprehending verbal language and abstract reasoning of arithmetic, but he did interpret human body language correctly and was able to apply what he had learned from his trainer to other individuals. The significance of this was lost on his audience. Unfortunately most human societies do not allow for communication through means other than human-based methods—we always attempt to teach others our language, while spending little energy trying to learn theirs. As biologist Stephen Hart notes: "A tendency to see human verbal language as all important shows up in the story of Clever Hans.... People of the time stood ready to believe that Hans could understand human speech and carry out verbal commands to add and subtract—accomplishments observers could identify with. But they declared Hans a fraud and lost interest when skeptics revealed that the horse was 'only' exquisitely sensitive to human body language—a means of communication of which we are only vaguely aware" (Hart 118).

## Human to Horse Communication

To accurately explore inter-species communication, we must suspend our dependence on verbal methods and open our minds to explore other vehicles of communication: body language, physical cueing, visual and sensory imaging, communion, and telepathy.

So, what is communication between man and horse? It is a dialogue comprised of two body languages and conditioned-response requests made through vocal and physical cues as well as artificial aids to which man has trained the horse to respond. Such commands, coupled with interpreting the nuances of equine feedback, create a conversation that for some truly fluent individuals can develop into "communion."

As with any living language, the human-horse exchange is evolving. As equine nature becomes better understood, the language of domination and submission used in traditional training methods is currently being amended and augmented to utilize natural horse behaviors for more effective, cooperative responses: *I've been training [horses] since I was fifteen,* Ron Harding relates. *From fifteen to twenty-five, I still used a lot of the old ways—rope 'em, choke 'em down, sack 'em out, throw a saddle on 'em, get on and hang on. Those horses...they were broke. That's all we knew. But then, all of a sudden, we started asking questions, "How do these horses really think? Maybe I'll try this...maybe if I touch this horse in certain places, he'll do certain things...and maybe if I watch how other horses treat him...maybe if I act like a horse...you know? Maybe they'll respond to me better if I act like them." Pretty soon you're into this communication process....* So what used to be a dictatorial human monologue—human demands put on a submissive horse—is now being recognized as an interspecies dialogue enriched by deciphering feedback from the horse. This change of attitude from dictatorial monologue to interactive dialogue is what allows for the intriguing human-horse conversations we enjoy today.

*Since humans are the species capable of reason and communication, the easiest way to achieve communication between horse and human is for people to learn to communicate with horses,* Dr. Robert Miller explains. *As we learn how other animals communicate, we can utilize that information to communicate with them. That's what these new masters of training teach: how to communicate with the horse in horse language. The secret of communicating with horses is controlling motion, since movement is survival. When you cause or prevent a horse's motion, and it's your idea, not the horse's, you go up the hierarchy in the horse's mind. This is how we achieve "dominance" over the horse in horse language, not human language.* This "equine-based dominance" differs from traditional "human dominance" established through pain, restraints, fear, or exhaustion. Once established, it allows the horse to cooperate out of hierarchical respect rather than forced submission. It allows a conversation based on cooperative compliance rather than fearful resignation.

There is no mysterious "magic code" to deciphering horse language. As with any language, communication isn't difficult once you've mastered the alphabet, vocabulary, pronunciation, and grammar. However, gaining these fundamentals takes study, ability, practice, and patience—you must be willing to make the investment. The reward comes with ensuing dialogues—simple phrases of requests and response at first, then more and more complex conversations as you and your horse build a vocabulary of experience, ability, and mutual understanding: *I love the process of not only developing communication with a nonverbal being, but then being able to have a conversation,* states Jane Savoie. *When I train my horse, I'm not talking at the horse; there is always a conversation going on. I am saying things, and I'm getting feedback. I'm making a request, and I'm getting a response like "Yeah, yeah, got it," or "This makes me nervous." Then I respond to that. I like having that kind of conversation.*

The beauty of language is only experienced in the sharing of it and the development of more complex, yet subtle nuances— soon you are creating not only conversation, but poetry. *Communication with a horse through riding is complicated by having to converse with your body through feel, in order to direct the horse's energy,* explains Jill Hassler. *You have to learn a lot more about yourself, and you have to give up a lot more of yourself to horses to be able to communicate—if you want to do it successfully. A horse can be a dangerous pet if you can't communicate successfully with him. Riding is more complex than most any other form of competition or sport, since you are not just dealing with yourself and another human; you're dealing with a creature that you've got to communicate with mainly without words. It makes for an intricate language as well as an art.*

As demands of competition increase, more complicated moves are required, and clear communication becomes more critical. To be an effective communicator, a rider must give precise communiqués: *I find that when people honestly communicate, horses are extremely cooperative beings,* says Penelope Smith. *They are patient with people for the most part if you show them what it is that you expect. If you are clear with them, they generally will cooperate. Horses listen so well, and they love it when you are clear with them.*

Short of abuse, the worst thing you can do with a horse is to be confused or ambivalent. As a rider, you need to decide what it is you want and then be able to communicate your request to the horse in a distinct and precise manner. After that, you must be able to interpret the response; so you need to be open to listening as well as asking. *To be a better rider, you need to be a better communicator,* says Rege Ludwig (p. 147), master polo coach and instructor. *That horse does not have to jump a fence, run around a track, or play polo. You have to get the horse to give that to you. And the more you can get the horse to give it to you willingly, the better chance you have of performing well. Therefore, you are the one that really has to communicate clearly as well as understand the horse. In order to communicate you have to make sure the one you're talking to understood you. Communication then becomes a two-way street.*

Human-horse communication is a wonderful vehicle for learning the importance of definitive, clear communication and sensitive listening. A successful rider must be decisive, explicit, controlled, consistent, sensitive, and responsive—sounds like presidential material! These qualities, applied to everyday discussions with people, would certainly enhance one's personal communication skills as well.

## Verbal Cues and Emotional Overtones

For a horse, communicating with a human requires learning a foreign verbal language, a foreign sign language, and a foreign body language. As difficult as it is for us to communicate with them, at least we have the luxury of creating all those languages. Horses have those languages imposed upon them; they must figure out what all the new sound cues, physical aids, and human body language mean and then interpret it all from one very different rider to the next.

*I've heard a lot of people say, "You can't communicate with a horse."* Ron Harding claims. *The heck you don't! If you're a horse trainer, you communicate. My horse, Flash, in thirty days' training, she knew seventeen voice commands. Knew them! It's kind of like a child: once they learn the first two or three, then they begin to listen to you. So the next time you give a command and show them, by the fourth or fifth time you've told that horse, he understands what you want of him. From then on, it's just a matter of repetition, repetition, repetition….*

Special words become very important to certain horses as James Brady (p. 148), Press Secretary to President Ronald Reagan, who was shot in the head during an attempted assassination, discovered with his therapeutic riding buddy, Bernie. *To give you an example of how well horses know English…. It was a little scary to say the word "carrot" around Bernie, because I had a pocket on the back of my wheelchair, and he'd stick his whole head right in there. He could pick the whole chair up! He wasn't trying to hurt me; he was just looking for his carrot. So I learned to say, "Bernie, let's go in now to get you some of those 'orange things.'" Bernie also knew colors—if it was orange, that was a carrot, and it was good....*

Not only the word itself, but tone of voice is also very important. *An obvious example is "whoa" which should never mean "slow down,"* warns Jack Huyler. *It should always mean "stop" because that's your safety brake.*

So "whoa" is pretty universal for "stop," but how do you tell a horse to move out? There's more verbal leeway here: *I had a filly born on Palm Sunday, I named Palm Reward,* recalls Irving Pettit (p. 171), harness racer, breeder, and trainer. *I could smack her with the lines or tap her with the whip, and she'd just keep going along the same; but if I blew her a kiss, she'd take off just like a Cadillac. I sold her to a man for $3,000 when she was just over two years old and said, "I hope you make a million with her." Well, she did very well; she made a quarter of a million.* That's a lot of smackers for blowin' a few kisses!

*Because I drive and do not sit on the horses,* explains Jimmy Fairclough, *I have to use my voice much more than the other aids. When I call my team, they all know my voice, and each of them knows his own name. Somebody else can be driving my team, and I can whistle to them— not even touch them—and they would take off. I've been in hazards or in marathons, where we've had to make very tight, little turns that I didn't think we could make. I'd need one horse to move up to get out of the way; I can call his name, and he literally jumps forward and knows his job. No use of the whip, nothing with the reins, just voice and they know what to do and they get there—somehow.*

One of the refreshing aspects of equine voice training is that pumping up the volume is not the measure of success—quite the opposite: *Katja Schumann, horse trainer at the Big Apple Circus in New York City, is infinitely quiet around her horses,* declares Diana Cooper. *Katja stands in the middle of the circus ring with eight Arabian stallions going a mile a minute around her—that's a lot of action, right? Yet she never speaks any louder than a low conversational tone. I asked, "If you speak to them so quietly in training, how do you get their attention when there's all the noise of a circus performance going on...a band playing, clowns running, and a crowd of 1,500 people yelling and cheering? Katja said, "That's why I am so quiet, because when things are that loud, I need to go under the music." She explained, "If I'm talking to you LIKE THIS (yelling), you back away, right? But if I'm talking LIKE THIS (whispering),* then you lean forward; you come closer and pay more attention so you can hear me. So, that's what I do, and I get their close attention."

*Well, I was enchanted with that,* Diana continues. *So, when I got home, I took out my nice old grey horse, Terralot, and put him on a longe line and instead of calling, "TERRALOT!" when I wanted his attention, I said, "*TERRALOT*." At the end of fifteen minutes he was just working off my body—I was whispering to him.*

Thus, the voice can be very important in human-horse conversations, yet it is not essential. Voice commands are actually frowned upon in many show rings, so other means of non-verbal communication must be explored for those situations.

## Body Language: Ours and Theirs

A horse is naturally responsive to weight on its back because it must adjust under that weight to maintain proper balance at all times. Hence it monitors the slightest shifts in the rider's position. *Horses read movements,* explains Roy Rogers. *When I leaned forward and went "sssssssssttt", boy, Trigger just flew wide open, and if I'd just start to lean back, ole Trigger would come to a screeching halt.* Trigger was well tuned in to Roy's cues on the ground as well: *When I'd want Trigger to count and tell people how old he was, I'd put my foot down and turn it to the right toward him, and he'd start counting. Then, when I wanted him to stop, I'd just pull my toe back, and he'd stop instantly. We'd have fun with that trick; I'd have Trigger tell people how many days in the week, and he'd count to seven, and I'd say, "One more, Trigger," and he'd shake his head, "No." You could make jokes out of a lot of things he could do by being the dummy yourself, you know.*

The equine ability to read subtle cues often appears magical, as with Trigger's counting trick. *I had a little buckskin horse named "Jeep" who I could ride anywhere—into your house or any place else—without a string on him,* Jack Huyler proclaims. *Jeep trusted me, and we communicated with no visible signals. It was marvelous fun! One of my teaching colleagues was convinced the communication was telepathic. But it wasn't—it was leg pressures—it was fluent body language. Communication between horse and rider is: the rider's mind transmits his body language, and then the horse communicates back to us in body language— the ears probably more than any other single thing. What riders tend to overlook most are the ears—true horsemen watch a horse's ears all the time.*

Liberty horses are masters at body language and visual cues—they must be, for there are no reins or restraints between them and their trainers; they work freely, truly "at liberty." *I don't think people realize how responsive horses are,* Rex Peterson declares. *I'll tell you when I really realize it: when I turn my liberty horses loose. I've got nothin' between them and me but confidence. Their confidence in me; my confidence in them. When my confidence gets shook, they get shook. When I get nervous, they get nervous. When I get relaxed, they get relaxed. Why? Because I naturally transmit those feelings to them with my body language.*

Body language: that magical, mystical mystery of motion and emotion. It is often difficult to discern and can be difficult to comprehend even though we are exposed to it every minute of our lives: *There was a lady in Phoenix at the Arabian show where I'd been talking about the difference between eliciting a response through pressure and contact,* recounts John Lyons. *As an English rider, she couldn't understand how you could have pressure without actual rein contact on your horse. We were standing in a trade booth with a whole bunch of people, and there was this one fellah who was looking at different video tapes. I had her walk over by him and stand within just a couple of inches from him. Now he didn't know what we were talking about; he didn't know the lady; he was just a stranger who didn't have a clue what was going on. Pretty soon she was moving him all over that booth—like a lamb at a sheep dog trial—just by standing too close to him where he felt uncomfortable. He never looked at her, but he kept moving away—he was responding to pressure from her with no physical contact. There's all kinds of things you can do with body language to pressure horses and people without physical contact.*

The language lab for body language is always open—it's everywhere life is. Body language conversations are going on constantly: on buses, at the office, on the street, in bars, on the dance floor, whether or not the participants are conscious of it. Becoming fluent in this language gives you an edge in every living relationship.

## Physical Cues: Different Dialects, Different Needs

In my search for a new jumper, I have ridden a lot of horses. Each one has an individual way of going, and I am not a quick study—it takes me time to relax into the rhythm of a horse I don't know. Yet, as riders, we expect horses to be able to read physical cues from each of us immediately no matter how differently we're built. My trainer is 5'10," 135 lbs, supple as a willow, and all leg. I'm 5'3," lots of pounds, and ride a bit like Humpty Dumpty sitting on his wall, with just about as much leg. Yet when I ask for a right-lead canter, my mare, Freddie, gives it to me, just as she does for my long-legged trainer. It never ceases to amaze me. I thought the different "physical dialects" from one rider to another would be more confusing for a horse. After all, I speak the same language as my countrymen in "N'Orleans, Loosana," but I can't always understand what it is that they are saying. Yet, if a rider is at all close to a recognizable cue, a well-trained horse will respond.

*We did a piece on my television program,* HORSE WORLD, *on dressage,* relates rodeo champion Larry Mahan. *They put me on a 21-year-old gelding—the only Appaloosa that had ever qualified for the US Dressage team. I had no idea what I was doing, and I made a lot of mistakes on this horse. At one point, the lady asked me to do something while she explained the cue: "Move one foot this way, and do this and that...." Well, I didn't do it correctly, but in attempting, I managed to give the horse a cue he recognized; he went into this little canter where he changed leads every stride. He did what he thought he was being asked to do. She said, "No, that's not right," but I let him go ahead for thirty or forty feet just to experience it. For each of the mistakes I made that day, this horse always had a reaction to my action. So many different cues and gears and moves! I felt like a Cessna pilot dropped into the cockpit of an F-14 playing with the control panel to find out what happens if I push this button, or twist this dial, or pull this lever? It was quite an experience for me to be able to play with something like that.*

As discussed earlier, being decisive in communication is important, and so is clarity. Precise physical cues allow for the clarity in which many horses find security: *One of the horses I've written a lot about was a mare named Drummer Girl,* relates Vicki Hearne (p. 171), award-winning author and trainer of horses and dogs. *She was a chestnut Thoroughbred off the track and as flawlessly built as any horse I've ever seen in my life. She was a horse who went bonkers, really bonkers, if you just got on and let the ride evolve freely. However, if you gave her very, very precise instruction—this hoof here, that hoof there, then she settled and was happy. Most horses would be saying, "Nag, nag, nag, leave me alone!" But Drummer Girl needed that precise direction from* the rider. I loved that horse, and I learned a lot from her. She taught me about the beauty of clarity because she was so responsive to clarity. Clarity is important in many situations. To have instructions spelled out in detail and then have instant feedback that you're performing as expected can be very reassuring—especially when trying to please, as Drummer Girl was.

## Listening: Horse to Human Communication

Monty Roberts assigns the name "Equus" to the language of horses he has come to know. He describes it as a true language which is "predictable, discernible, and effective. First and foremost a silent language. Body language is not confined to humans nor to horses: it constitutes the most often used form of communication between animate objects on dry land.

"I learned the [dominant] mare was constantly schooling the foals and yearlings without the need for sound, [and] they were reacting without the need for sound.

"The stallion was operating his security system with the distinct need for silence...nothing was done by accident. Every small degree of a horse's movement occurs for a reason. Nothing is trivial.

I discovered that the key ingredient to the language 'Equus' is the positioning of the body and its direction of travel.

"These were precise messages, whole phrases and sentences which always meant the same thing, always had the same effect. They happened over and over again." (Roberts 87–89)

"Listening" to a horse means recognizing and interpreting their emotional and physical postures, by reading their signals, their state of being, as well as the way they are going: *Horses always are aware and tuned in, and many humans can be,* says Buck Brannaman. *I refer to "feel" in lots of different ways; that word takes on lots of different meanings. It's not just the physical touch when it comes to "feel." Some people who have none of this working for them; they're not into horses or animals at all...that kind of a person really lacks "feel." I'm not talking about it from the "mystical" approach; it's just plain old common sense—you feel it in your guts. It's sometimes hardly no more than a thought—so subtle it appears nothing happened, yet causing something to happen with the horse—that's "feel." What price do you pay for "feel?" I've given my whole life to it.*

Being a good equine listener helps keep the dialogue calmly conversational. If you are able to read signals early on, you can respond to the conversation before it escalates to a shouting match: *"A good trainer can hear a horse speak to him, a great trainer can hear him whisper,"* quotes Monty Roberts. *When we listen to the whisper and act on it, we're a better communicator with the horse than if we wait to hear him speak.* Once again, the subtle sensitivity of horses encourages whispers of communication and communion.

*Horses are great communicators,* declares Stagg Newman. *The challenge is our learning to listen and understand their language because they're never going to speak ours. Listening to all their different signs: feeling the way the horse is going under you, looking for the expression in eyes and ears.... This communication is so much a right-brain function that some of it's very difficult to explain. It's almost like trying to explain why some music sounds great and others not. By being attuned to horses, anyone can learn to listen, but some people have a God-given ability that's beyond most of us: some sort of sixth sense. Communication that I can't quantify and explain. You can't use logic alone to communicate. When there are non-verbal and non-logical messages going back and forth, you need to be attuned to them and address them.* This exceptional ability enhances the purely logical interpretations of feedback by incorporating facts and feelings into a comprehensive realization.

## Interpreting to Comprehension

One of the trickiest aspects of communication is interpretation. We have all experienced that state of surprise when a conversation we thought was crystal clear was misheard or misconstrued by the other participant. If conversations in a common verbal language are so easily mistaken, accurate interpretation of nonverbal interspecies conversations seems nigh impossible. It's not. But it does take an open, knowledgeable, empathetic, and aware individual who is "simpatico" with the other being to interpret correctly.

Individuals who have this facility appear to be blessed with a special genius: *Really good riders are gifted,* declares Mary Deringer Phelps. *People like Olympians Anne Kursinski, Michael Matz, and Hugh Wiley—they're gifted. It's an instinct that you are not even aware of—it's "The Gift." You can teach a person to ride, and a person can be extremely coordinated, but there's something in a person that has the gift that just reacts instinctively. I rode with Hugh Wiley at his barn for a week one year. He would ask, "Why did you do that?" and I'd say, "Do what?" and he'd say, "Why did you move your horse over here to approach this jump?" and I'd say, "I don't know." And he said, "It's because you have the gift." Well I could feel my helmet get tight as my head swelled with that remark—I was so proud!*

"The gift," "feel," "sixth sense"…whatever you call this ability, it is an intuitive sensitivity that receives and interprets nonverbal input instantaneously and accurately, triggering an appropriate response. Developing such an ability to understand what is going on with another being and interpret their unspoken communications can be advantageous in interpersonal relationships: *My partner, Charlie, tells me that what he hates about living with me is that he can never lie,* states Macella O'Neill. *I can read people and animals instantly, and I'm rarely wrong. I must do it on a pretty subconscious or unconscious level 'cause I couldn't tell you what I'm doing.*

*An animal communicator once told me that people would be more competent at communicating if they could get "other-centered" rather than being "ego-centered," or "self-centered." It's just that simple. Instead, people go around thinking their own thoughts—about their clothes, or their work, or their schedules, and not thinking about their horse and truly tuning in to that other entity. That's one of the most therapeutic things about horses is that they really do encourage you to tune in to others—and that can aid you tremendously in life.*

I believe that we all have the capacity for nonverbal communication and its ensuing interpretation. The problem is that in contemporary society we tend to discount our own intuition because it may not be tangible or provable. Interpretation of non-verbal communication is not just consideration of logical facts; it must take into account body language, emotions, as well as other intangible, intuitive indicators. The stronger we become in all these skills, the more astute, balanced, and complete comprehension will result.

## Visual Imaging

The study of psychocybernetics, or imaging, is a fascinating theory exemplified by the story of Major Nesmeth, an American who was prisoner of war for seven years in Vietnam. The Major occupied his mind by mentally replaying every swing, from every conceivable angle, through every hole, on every golf course he'd ever played—in a cell too tiny to even stand erect and even mimic a chip shot. After being liberated, Major Nesmeth returned to the golf links. Amazingly, his handicap had improved by twenty strokes—even though he'd not played golf for more than seven years except in his mind's eye (Savoie 15). The theory is that the human mind does not distinguish between actual memory of physical events and vivid imagination. This allows for the possibility of training one's mind and body for an action without actually rehearsing it physically.

*Imaging is extremely important,* Doug Lietzke (p. 172), sports psychologist and endurance competitor, claims. *Because the most subtle images and thoughts of the rider become translated into barely perceptible bodily movements, which the horse is sensitive enough to pick up. An easy demonstration of this is to tie a foot-long piece of string to a metal nut. With the tip of the string between your forefinger and thumb, hold it out in front of you so the nut hangs free and still in the air. Now imagine the nut swinging backwards and forward. Think to yourself: away and toward, away and toward. Usually within five or ten seconds it will be swinging. Do the same thing imaging the nut swinging in a circle. At first it's just a small circle, barely perceptible, then it gets larger and larger as the swinging increases. It doesn't happen with everybody, but for about 90% of the people it works. This is a dramatic demonstration of "I know my hand isn't moving, but this nut at the end of the string is moving, so why is it happening? Am I wishing it to happen?" Well, since I can't wish this hat off of my head, I believe there's a whole bunch of subtle body movements.*

Of course people were "imaging" long before the theory of psychocybernetics was recognized scientifically: *I do believe in picturing a performance,* William Steinkraus concurs. *I've done that all my life—visualizing what I'm trying to do. I don't think I could compete, ride, play golf or the violin—any of those things—without imaging.*

Method acting is a form of psychocybernetics; most sports coaches employ imaging, and I believe imaging is the force behind the realization of dreams. As Jane Savoie asserts, "If you can dream it, you can do it." Jane's book, THAT WINNING FEELING, is a great resource for imaging techniques applied to riding.

One of the techniques used in imaging is to be completely relaxed and run a vividly detailed "mental movie" in your head: *Before a competition,* Jack Huyler elaborates, *I used to lie in bed and plan out how I was going to ride certain events. I'd run the event in my head before I went to sleep; then I'd know exactly what it is I want to do—exactly. It's thought through and rehearsed in my head until I do it right without having to think it. Then the horse does it right because my cues to him are just right. We work better because it's conditioned reflex. Now my stud, El Paso Doc, was maybe the best gymkhana horse that ever was. He set records in 1969 that are still standing today. But I think we won some of those events in bed—with me lying there thinking about them—I really do.* Preparation for a big event doesn't get much simpler than lying in bed and training your muscle memory to winning form through imaging—it's so easy, it almost sounds illegal.

## Sensory Imaging

Effective imaging actually goes beyond the "mental movie" of what I refer to as "visual imagery." It should also include what I call "sensory imagery": smells, touch, rhythm, pressure, emotions, feelings, "vibes," shared energy...any and all positive, pertinent sensations. The more details and impressions you embrace, the more complete your image becomes, until you're recreating a "mental experience," not just a "mental movie" limited to sight and sound. Thus, imaging is comprised of "visual imagery" and "sensory imagery"—both contributing to the powerful psychocybernetic process.

*When people learn to use imagery correctly, they are able to recreate inner feelings,* trainer and author Jill Hassler elaborates *I teach imagery that doesn't replay the thought, but rather replays the good feeling that the rider experienced on the horse at a given time* [sensory imagery]. *This way feeling is governing your riding, for feeling is the ability through which you successfully communicate with your horse. Some people think of "feeling" as meaning when I touch you, you feel my touch. I'm referring to a deeper level of feeling—your inner sense of rhythm, and straightness, and balance resulting from sensing the movements of the horse under you and your connection to him. Those feelings are the basis of your ability to listen to the ride. With that basic sensing-listening, you can stay in conversation with your horse. So imagery works this way: first you get the feeling; then you hold the feeling; then you replay the feeling; so that the next time you get on the horse, you don't even think about the feeling, it's just there because you've done this sensory imaging. It becomes an unconscious awareness that helps in communication.* Visual and sensory imagery eventually resides in the subconscious, bypassing the conscious thought process, which may be slower and more mechanical.

*I have some older students who are terribly, terribly bright and I'm sure have IQ's in high numbers,* reports Michael Plumb. *I find that people who are that bright sometimes aren't able to communicate with horses very easily. They think first; they internalize; they mull it over, and by the time they finish having a conversation with themselves about what I asked them to do, or to feel, it's all gone. The hardest thing to do in riding is to teach feeling.* This is where imaging can be so valuable, for it helps to get people out of the conscious process of thought in their heads and into a subconscious state of "being" with the experience.

Psychocybernetics, especially in the world of sports, has produced convincing evidence that imaging can and does alter personal performance. In riding, improvement in the rider would, most likely, enhance the horse's performance through more effective body movements. But can imaging also affect the horse's skill independent of a rider? This is where things get very interesting and controversial. We are now inquiring into the existence of that emotionally laden concept: telepathy.

## About Telepathy

After interviewing interspecies communication expert, Penelope Smith, I was so intrigued with her work that I asked her to come to our ranch for further discussion. We had a lively talk around the luncheon table then she offered to demonstrate her ability by communicating with our animals. As we approached the barn, Penelope asked me, "What do you want to ask them?"

I suddenly realized that I had never actually thought about what questions to ask our horses; I pondered a minute, then said, "Just ask them if they like it here and if there's anything they need."

Penelope and her husband, Michel; my husband, Kip; our niece, Jacquie; and our friend Michael watched as she composed herself and began her work.

Haji, our gray Anglo-Arab, and Lucky, a bay Quarter Horse, were in adjacent stalls. Our two dogs, Zeppo and Baxter, bounded excitedly into the shady interior of the barn with the entourage. Penelope asked everyone to cease talking while she quieted herself in order to communicate with the horses. She approached Haji first. After a short silence, she began matter-of-factly, "He says he likes it here...he likes the people...everything is good.... He says sometimes Lucky is "pushy," but when he gets too pushy, then he,

Haji, takes over until things settle down. If Haji gets overbearing, Lucky is back in charge." I began to laugh. Penelope held her finger up to her lips, once again requesting silence. "He says he would like to have the radio in here all the time. He likes it when there's music."

She then turned her attention to Lucky. As she entered his stall, the caretakers' cat, Boots, leapt down from the hayloft, sauntered along the beam over the sliding stall doors, stopped above Penelope, sat down, wrapping her tail about her, and watched. The dogs below began to whine and jump as they saw their elusive prey tauntingly out of reach. Penelope turned to Lucky and said aloud, "Lucky likes it here...the people are nice...but he says he wants to be in the house, with the people, like a dog." With that, Kip shot me a cynical look. Penelope continued, "Lucky says he'd like to have a ball to play with—a big blue one." Everyone laughed with that pronouncement.

Penelope's attention turned to the cat. She said, "The cat thinks this is very interesting. She's pleased that you care enough to talk with them. She says she moved to the barn because the horses will talk to her. She's tried talking to the dogs, but she thinks they're stupid because they want to chase her, not talk. But what can you expect—they are after all, *dogs!*" With that, Boots got up and climbed back to her perch up in the hayloft while our Brittany Spaniel, Baxter, followed her from below; then sat, looking up at her quietly. It appeared as if they were now having that long-awaited conversation.

Penelope turned to us and said, "Baxter's stomach upsets are because he doesn't think he has enough love to give everyone. He worries about that so much he makes himself ill. And Zeppo...," Penelope continued, referring to our McNab Shepherd stock dog, "You've pretty much dismissed him as merely a chaser of tennis balls, but he's really very bright. He's got a lot of excess energy and has created a job for himself and Baxter: making this place quiet for you by keeping the other animals away. They patrol a big circle, except for that area," she said, pointing to the north corner of the property. "They're pretty successful except for one coyote who tells Zeppo to 'Bug Off!'. This coyote isn't quite right in his brain due to ingesting poison some time ago." Kip shot me another puzzled glare.

Penelope reached down and tousled Zeppo's head, saying to him, "It's all right; just chill out." Again we laughed, for getting Zeppo to "chill out" was nearly impossible—he never relaxed— even neutering hadn't slowed him up. He simply had no "off" switch that we'd been able to find in the six years we'd had him.

That ended the demonstration, and Penelope asked, "Did any of that make sense to you?" I looked at Kip, for I didn't want to be the only one deciphering these communications. He was hesitant to respond, but finally said, "Yes. Just about all of it." He then added suspiciously, "How much had Becky told you before?" Annoyed that he would think we were in cahoots, I answered defiantly, "None of it!"

Now it was Penelope's turn to laugh. "Hold it! I don't want to destroy a marriage here. This happens a lot: not believing. That's the biggest problem. People don't believe it's possible even after they see it occur! Kip, we are not plotting against you. If what I've related makes sense, it's because the animals have told me of things you have experienced with them, or of them. But it all comes from them, not me."

With that, Jacquie interrupted, "Some of that seems like pretty strange stuff. Why would Lucky want to be in the house? What does Haji mean about music in the barn? Is Baxter sick? And where's this crazy coyote?"

"Yeah," said Michael, "Fill us in on what this all means."

"Okay, okay," said Kip, "But first let's go inside and get comfortable—I need fortification after this—can I interest any of you in a hot shot of caffeine?" While Kip got the coffee, I began explaining the animals' comments, starting with Haji:

"Haji's been here since August of 1989; we got Lucky in November of that year. When Lucky arrived, I assumed Haji would be the lead horse in the hierarchy since this was his territory. And he was for the first few weeks, but then it became evident that Lucky had exerted his dominance and was the lead horse. I was surprised, but didn't think much of it until about a year later when suddenly Haji was in charge again. Then, eighteen months after that, Lucky was head honcho in the paddock. Not knowing a lot about equine social order, I asked our vet and trainer about these role reversals. Both thought such constant trade-offs were unusual since normally the pecking order stands until a new horse is introduced into the group. Lucky is pushy, by the way. He shepherds me around the paddock with his head, and watch out if you ever get between him and an open gate to the grass!

The music comment refers to our caretaker, Tony, who often brings his boom-box into the barn when he's working in there. I guess Haji really likes it.

Lucky's comment about being in the house is a really odd one for a horse, but makes perfect sense in his case. Lucky was born on our family's cattle ranch, Lone Pine, and three days after he was foaled his dam was killed in a freak accident. He was hand-raised by the foreman's daughter, Ardis, in the fenced-in yard of their house. Lucky's playmates were ranch dogs, and soon baby Lucky was chasing trucks along the driveway fence, just like his pals. Whenever the kitchen door was left open, Lucky would let himself into the house along with his canine companions. He got to like it inside so much that Ardis had to halter him and physically drag him out. Ardis told us how cute he was—hiding in the corner trying to be invisible—only he was a rapidly growing horse colt and pretty hard to miss.

The blue ball also makes sense in that all of Lucky's grooming tools are color-coded blue, and Haji's are red; so it's interesting that Lucky asked for a *blue* ball.

It's remarkable that Boots showed up at all. We see her so seldom, I forget there's a cat on the property. She stays hidden when the dogs are about. The comment that she moved to the barn is intriguing because she's lived in the caretakers' apartment the past five years, until six months ago, when she relocated to the barn after they got a new kitten she seems to detest.

Baxter's vomiting has been a fairly consistent part of his history. I'd asked the vet about it early on, and she said it was nothing serious, unless it became chronic. It only happens every couple of months, and he doesn't seem any worse for it, so I didn't follow it up after that.

The coyote is another really weird situation. We do, in fact, have a crazy coyote. Tony first heard it at 3:00 in the morning when it was chasing the horses around the paddock. It sounded just like a laughing hyena, and when it ran, it would often run into a fence post, fall down, only to scramble up and run into another one.

Tony thought it was rabid and tried to shoot it, but when he couldn't see where dark-bay Lucky was in the tar-black night, he didn't dare shoot in the direction of the paddock. He shot in the air instead, and the coyote ran off—cackling like a madman. We figured he was so sick with rabies that he'd die soon, but that didn't happen. He returned three weeks later, then six months, and a year. So he wasn't rabid, but we had no idea what caused his insane behaviors.

As for other animals—we rarely see any. Kip and I joke that we must have built on a toxic-waste dump, because even with more than 300 acres of forest around us, we hardly ever see wildlife—nary a squirrel or a raccoon. The few times in the last five years that we had spotted anything—wild turkey and deer—they were in that north quadrant Penelope said the dogs overlook.

I have to hand it to you, Penelope; you have certainly batted a thousand today. If you have anywhere near that success regularly, you could *prove* the validity of telepathy."

Were there not witnesses for all that took place that Sunday late in '94, it would be difficult for me to include this testimonial, for I recognize that it is hard to believe. It did happen as reported, however, and has set me on a fascinating inquiry into animal communication.

What struck me most about Penelope's report of the animals' accounts is that it was such unusual information. If someone were a charlatan, I would expect them to play it safe and stick to more typical equine topics such as feed, work, or body aches, for example. Why take a chance of being exposed by calling attention to abnormal behaviors like trading off hierarchical order, wanting a radio, or being in the house? Why bring up an insane coyote at all? These are very strange and specific descriptions that would be million-to-one-shots. Yet, even though they sounded preposterous, Penelope reported them.

Although it is not necessary to be in the presence of the animal to communicate, (she can tune in at great distances, and even over a phone) Penelope has revisited and reported additional information from Haji and my mare, Freddie, which was also atypical, yet accurate. Call me naive, but I think she's onto something—hers is a communication of communion.

Is it possible to communicate telepathically (direct extra-sensory mind communication) from one being to another? Of the individuals I interviewed, almost sixty percent stated an opinion on telepathy: 46% of respondents believe in it, 33% do not believe in it, and 21% are not sure. Of the believers: 70% are female and 30% male. Of non-believers: 80% are male and 20% female. Of those not sure: 70% are male and 30% female.

Let's address the non-believers first. They stand on pretty firm ground, for clinical telepathic trials have yet to produce any consistent positive results. For many, that's definitive: no scientific proof—no telepathy. Jimmy Fairclough refers to it as voodoo. Richard Shrake thinks it's trickery. William Steinkraus believes it's simply deductive behavior on an extremely subtle level. And John Lyons calls it ESPN: Extra Sensory Perception Nonsense. John elaborates, *The horse is such a special animal just the way he is. I think that over-playing him to make him like some super-intelligent animal with extra senses actually degrades the horse. They're not more intelligent than people; they're an animal who's capable of doing certain things and has acute physical perception—but not extra-sensory perception.*

Fair enough. However, proponents of telepathy do not limit that extra sense to the horse; they believe it is a universal sixth sense, which animals use and which mankind possesses, yet has let atrophy.

Modern man has become insulated from instinctive sensory communications by "civilization." We live in secure houses, locked away from messages sent on the winds, or through the vibrations of the ground. We no longer depend on our senses to warn of intruders or events; we have motion sensors, burglar alarms, and smoke detectors instead. Communication is either direct or hardwired. If the facility for telepathy has been, and still is, part of the human condition, perhaps telepathic rehabilitation is possible.

Buck Brannaman is representative of the group who is ambivalent about telepathy: *I'd like to believe that telepathy exists. I don't know it to be true, but I don't know it not to be true. It may be hogwash, but it's not hurting anybody for me to feel that way. I'd like to believe that a thought itself can work—and only a thought.* As Buck notes, lacking proof of existence, does not prove non-existence. If that were the case, most of astrophysics and a good part of nuclear physics would be discredited by being based on inferential evidence.

Among the group that supports the idea of telepathy is the

Director of the National Center for Therapeutic Riding in Washington, DC, Bob Douglas (p. 173), who states, *People who have communicated with horses, their whole outlook on life is different. I think that they understand life better. I don't knock any of them.*

Personally, I like the idea of telepathy as another mode of connection—human to human, animal to human, animal to animal. Penelope Smith certainly made a good case for it with our menagerie, and I think the possibility of telepathic communication makes life even more intriguing. I'm not looking to prove telepathy one way or another in this book, but I will pass on some observations:

*I believe there's something in the horse/human interchange that is beyond what we can explain physically, notes* Dr. Elizabeth Lawrence (p. 173), Professor of Environmental and Population Health at Tufts University Veterinary School and author of books on the human-horse relationship. *This sense of communication, this sense of knowing...you could use the word, "telepathy," but it would perhaps take away from what you were trying to do because it has a bad connotation. There's an intellectual prejudice against that word, and I think it's important to keep open minds about all of these things.*

Diana Thompson raises a different issue with the term: *I really don't like using the word "telepathy"; to me the term is separating, and it is not a separate thing for me. I call it "tuning in." When I am working with people or a horse, I'm tuning in on every level I can. It's really a full-body sensing, and telepathy is part of that because that's just part of the mind. I'll get mind communications sometimes, and I'll get emotional feelings sometimes. Everybody has that ability. You know when you walk into a room of people there is an atmosphere there; there are moods; everybody picks that up. Or, you are walking down the street, and you suddenly feel, "Uh oh, something's not right here." You look up, and around the corner comes Mr. Bad Guy USA. Your sensing mechanism picked that up before your vision and logic did. We all have the ability. It is just whether we want to bring that out in ourselves and acknowledge it.*

Penelope Smith agrees that the ability is universal, and elaborates: *Anyone can learn to communicate telepathically, but telepathy has been carefully socialized out of in our society. We've been taught to distrust intuitive ability, that it's impossible to receive thoughts and intentions from other beings. The fact is, we do it all the time, yet it's not acknowledged in our culture. From a very young age, kids are taught that it's foolishness; it doesn't exist. So it depends on the layers of socialization that people want to deal with to develop this ability.*

*Some people will read a book, listen to the tapes [on interspecies communication] and it all opens up for them. They go, "Oh! I've been doing this." The ability starts coming to them, and they practice, and away they go. But they still have to practice. This is something that develops over time and you get better and better at it. It is after all, a language—the universal language understood by all species.*

*Some people are not willing to put in the time and energy, and they won't get it. This isn't instant pudding; I can't wave a magic wand and give it to you. This is something that you have to be very sincere about. It is so close to the heart.*

*You have to be willing to face your own barriers. And often people's barriers are extremely emotional. One of the biggest barriers to this is invalidating one's own perceptions and intuitive abilities. When you hear something from the animal, you go, "Oh no, no, that couldn't be;" and cut off the communication. If you would just accept it, even if you don't get it totally correct, or don't understand it right away. If you say yes to it, and ask for more, then it starts to develop. But many people just run around in their own doubts. They'll go, "Oh, no that couldn't be, that's just my projection, blah, blah, blah…" So they don't get anywhere. The animals show you. They are the best teachers. They show you when you've got it right— they're happier, more cooperative. When you get it wrong, when you're misinterpreting, when you are throwing your own stuff at them, they don't like it, and they don't cooperate. But when you get it right, you understand them; you implement what they said; you offer solutions that are acceptable to them, that work with them; they go, "Right, this is great, you got it!" and away you go. It becomes a whole different relationship, a whole different way of being.*

*I remember one cowboy who called me,* Penelope continues. *He had a cutting horse that he knew inside out. Well, he sort of tested me. I told him some things about the horse—what the horse felt and what his life was like. The cowboy said to me, "You know you just told me things in ten minutes that it took me fifteen years to learn about that horse."* It's so simple, it seems impossible.

## Telepathy—The Local Call

So we all have the ability to tune in. Now, with an open mind, consider a few of the experiences reported regarding thought transference: *A student of mine had been having difficulty getting her horse to do flying changes,* Linda Tellington-Jones recounts. *Well, this girl broke her leg, and when I went to visit her she was bemoaning the fact that her recuperation time would set back her training so much. So I suggested, "Why don't you—just for the heck of it—pretend that the horse can see your mental pictures? Each day take ten minutes and mentally go through a shortened form of a lesson that you would like your horse to do. Imagine that she can see it; imagine the horse is feeling you breathe, and do a successful flying change. She ran through the mental lessons daily during her recuperation, and the first time she got on after not riding for weeks, her mare did flying changes! I have so many stories like that it's boring. My experience is that horses pick up our pictures. I have no question in my mind that horses pick up our pictures. I don't just think it; I know it's a fact. If that isn't telepathy, what is it?* Well, some would say perhaps the imaging process had mentally honed the girl's ability so that she gave her horse better cues when they returned to work. With an open mind, it's possible either way—the horse received instruction, or the girl improved her ability. The question remains, can the vivid concentration of imaging be projected to another?

Jane Savoie reports an interesting experience with her horse in Florida: *When my horse was sick, he was on an antibiotic, but the vet still wanted me to work him lightly. Well, when I did work him, I was in a complete and total fog, and I couldn't understand why. I mentioned my fog to the vet, and he said, "Well, you know, you're very intuitive, and this antibiotic tends to space the horse out." He thought I was picking up the vibrations from the animal. He says a lot of people can do that—pick up stuff from the animals.* Is it possible that Jane was so open to communication from her horse that he projected his state of being on to her? Could this be reverse imaging from the horse to the human? If so, might that be the basis for telepathy—the visual and sensory imaging being projected to others—not simply staying within the confines of an individual's mental boundary?

For many, hearing voices out of the blue is a sure sign that you're overdue for a check-up with your shrink. Yet, it could be your horse expressing his appreciation: *After I hurt my back, I almost had to completely relearn how to ride,* recounts Becky Hart (p. 174), world champion endurance rider and trainer. *I had to learn to relax and release, so I started Centered Riding lessons. One day, I was coming down a steep hill with Rio, and he was just walking out terrifically, which he didn't do before I started the Centered Riding. Well, he was doing this great walk, and all of a sudden, I just felt like I heard him say, "I love how you ride me now." It was very interesting. It was just this thought in my head. I don't know where it came from. It didn't feel like it was something I was thinking. It felt like it was put in.* It's interesting to note that the message popped into Becky's head phrased from Rio's perspective, not her own.

*There was a woman who came to one of my clinics,* relates Diana Thompson. *By noon I knew that she was communicating with the animals very directly. She would go up to a horse and pet it, and then the horse would look like, "Whoa, who are you?" They were looking startled at her. Kind of like when you walk up behind a stranger and go, "Excuse me, can you tell me the time?" And that person suddenly whips around when they realize they're being spoken to. The horses were doing that. So I went to her and said, "I know you're doing something, but what are you doing?" "I'm talking to them," she replied. "How do you do that?" I asked. "Well, it's like talking, only with your mind." She explained, "Like talking real loud, but it doesn't come out of your mouth." Her father had been deaf, and she'd developed a non-verbal communication with him. She hears the animals as if they are speaking verbally in her mind.*

## Telepathy—Long Distance

So we've seen some examples up close and personal. But what about connections with animals that are at a distance, or even...on the phone? Obviously being removed from view of the subject discounts body language or physical sensing. *Recently, I was out shopping, having a great time,* says Pat Lawson, *but something—and I can't tell you what—kept telling me, "Go home; it's time to go home. Go home." I'd just started shopping, then got that pull to go home. Well, I didn't balk. I just thought, "Oh, what the heck, I'll go home, and I'll make myself a little lunch." So I drove home. Then, while I was sitting in the kitchen having my lunch, just watching the horses, I saw Star rolling and biting at his sides with colic. Now had I still been out shopping, running from mall to mall, I would not have seen him and been able to help him. God only knows how long it would have taken to put him in a really serious posi-*

*tion, or even kill him.* Most parents can identify with an incident such as this. But is this an example of extra sensory perception or merely coincidence?

At the training stable where I ride, there is a young horse they call Fiddle, because he's constantly fiddling with something... anything...everything. A big, lanky Thoroughbred, he was a bit awkward and unsure of himself in his four-year-old youthfulness. After a year at the stable, our trainer, Macella O'Neill, was concerned about him, for unlike other horses, Fiddle never rolled or even laid down for a good rejuvenating rest—he was always on his feet...fiddling. *I had never ever seen that horse lie down, Macella explains. And I had never seen straw or shavings in his mane or tail. That worried me because I think it's very relaxing for horses to lie down. Now don't laugh, but I used to put him out when it was really hot, and I'd even play with him occasionally, to try and get him to relax and lie down, but he never did. One day, a client was talking to an animal communicator, Jeri Ryan, on the phone about her pony. She asked if I had any questions for Jeri, and I said, "Yes; ask her if Fiddle lies down." Well, she asked Fiddle and said, "No, he doesn't. He's scared that he can't get up." So I said, "Please tell him it's okay; I want him to lie down and relax." So, Jeri talked to him some more, and I went down to put him out. Within an hour, I looked and Fiddle was in the middle of the ring lying down flat as a pancake! He took about a 30-minute nap in the sun. From that day on that horse has been pretty darn comfortable lying down. He sleeps in his stall and everything, now.* Communication or coincidence? It is hard to say definitively one way or the other, but it is very interesting to consider.

Perhaps the most fascinating accounts are the communications picked up over great distances: *When we first started working with Zapatero,* Jane Savoie relates, *my trainer, Robert Dover, sized him up and said, "We have to build this horse's self-esteem. He must feel that there's nothing that he can't do like a champion." Robert knew how important it was for this horse to puff himself up and to think, "I can do that!" So we made sure his training was built on success, and I always gave him lots of praise.*

*Now, I cannot stand the thought that one of my animals may be in pain, and I want to know if there's anything bothering them. So, even though I'm on the East Coast, I occasionally call a psychic in California to check on things. Well, this psychic was talking with Zapatero when he starts to laugh. I asked him what's so funny, and he tells me that he's never heard a horse talk like this before. Every fifth sentence out of Zapatero's mouth was, "I'm a real good horse!" He just thought he was a hot shit. "I do this.... And I'm well prepared.... And I'm a really good horse!" We got his self-esteem built up! He just saw himself as a champion, and that's what we'd been working towards. It was really neat!*

## Communion

When communication flows so naturally and so completely as to be shared in total clarity, that's communion. Subtle, silent conversations that elicit absolute comprehension. Communion is achieved by the few who care enough to know the other so well as to simply exchange and share thoughts. With or without telepathy...it appears telepathic. It is the ultimate connection: *The communication between me and my horse is so intimate,* marvels Anne Kursinski. *What I do, and the level I do it at...it's fragile, and it's finely tuned, yet there's not much verbal communication. It's a very delicate, magical connection, this becoming one. I think horse and rider communication does go deeper with the really great riders than just hands, legs, and voice. There's something more to visualization, too, that you can't really put your finger on. I believe that there is something a little more...psychic.* That's communion.

*One time playing polo, I was doing terribly on every horse I rode,* remarks Rege Ludwig. *It was a bad day for me. Nothing was going right. Then I got on this horse, Mike, that I had been playing for years. All of a sudden something happened, and I started playing well. It was that Mike and I understood one another extremely well. Things that I was not communicating to these other horses or that they were not picking up on from me—Mike was picking up on. The responses were right, and I started playing incredibly better. What a brilliant experience! It was a real high charge, all of a sudden, to get on this horse that understood me, and turned my game around.* That's communion.

*When I first meet a horse I always extend my hand flat so he can see it,* Chris Hawkins describes. *And I try to come up underneath his jaw and give him a soft scratch. Then I very gently lift the head, talk to him, and I lean over and very, very carefully and gently touch my nose close to his nostril and breathe with him very softly. Because that means, I want to be your friend, in "horse language." You've seen horses do it. I have never had a horse turn me down when the breathing said "I want to be your friend."*

*My horses have no words to express themselves, but you haven't lived until you're standing there with your back to them and one of them walks up and puts his head over your shoulder and nuzzles underneath your neck. Hey, if that isn't communication, tell me, what is it?* That's communion.

*I wonder why I always relate my connection with horses to magic?* muses Linda Tellington-Jones. *I think it's because I've always felt I could talk with my horses and knew what they were thinking. That possibly is what has prepared me to be able to relate to the unseen and have a much more spiritual point of view of the world.* That's communion.

*The desire to understand the nature of horses, or the nature of "otherness," is really the main motivation for me with horses,* explains Caroline Thompson. *The desire to comprehend the incomprehensible. It will always remain the incomprehensible, yet there are moments of perfect comprehension. Those few moments of perfect, shared comprehension —communion—are the biggest rush you can possibly have.*

Amen.

## Life Lessons

This is the era of technological intercourse: radio, television, cellular phones, fax, e-mail, the Internet.... Millions of people and billions of dollars are at work making communication more accessible and instantaneous. Communication is perhaps the most important aspect of human life, for it is the basis for all relationship. In this most basic and most complex arena, the horse has many lessons to offer us: *Working with horses has definitely improved my communication skills with people,* declares Jill Hassler. *First, it has made me try to view and pursue things from the other person's point of view.*

*Second, having to break down communication into the simplest basic form for the horse has taught me to speak simply and clearly. As a result, I don't have as many unfinished or bad communications as I used to.*

*Third, with a horse, if you're muddled, the horse continues to be muddled. However, once you're clear with the horse and the horse gets it, the horse forgets that there ever was a problem. That has made me realize that when there is a misunderstanding, it's important to clear it up with the person so that we can go on.*

*So, horses have also taught me to "forgive and forget." Once corrected, I can forgive people and forget miscommunications, Boom, just like that! I absolutely learned that from the horses' example.*

Relying exclusively on our own language doesn't work with

horses; we are forced to tune in to their language in order to communicate: *We've got to be educated enough to read what our horses are saying,* reiterates Richard Shrake (p. 175), trainer, instructor and show judge. *We've got to learn their language. When you don't know what they're saying, it's like living in a foreign country and never learning the language. You have to be sensitive and understanding of others, and you have to listen. When you don't listen to them, or you're not sensitive to them, whether it's a horse, a client...or anyone, you're in trouble.*

Then there are those miraculous equine communications that only the few can hear: *We had an autistic 8-year-old boy in our therapeutic riding program who could not speak independently,* Bob Douglas relates. *If you said, "Let's do that," he would reply, "Let's do that." But he had never initiated an independent word. When I introduced him to his horse, Buster, and was helping him in to the saddle, he said, "No." Now that "no" was probably the most important word he ever said, and probably the most important word I'd ever heard, because it was his first independent communication. From that point on, the dialogue between him and Buster began. The two of them communicated. I am not exactly sure what Buster was saying to him, but he certainly began to relate and to talk to Buster. He'd say, "Good boy, I love you." He was initiating conversation with this horse! Now he's 14 and speaking on his own. What happens with these horses is incredible.* It truly is.

The need to read the character of horses trains us to be sensitive to human nature as well: *I love that expression about the horse— "it has a kind eye,"* says Dr. Elizabeth Lawrence. *When I meet a person and I think, "That person has a kind eye," I'm going back to my horse experience.* And it's usually right on.

In order to understand equine communiqués and feedback, horses force us to look beyond ourselves—into their world to study their ways of communicating. They teach us the immeasurable value of clarity. They teach us that often the most effective communication is achieved with a mere whisper, or in cooperative silence, through "feel". For those horsemen who do converse by feel it's so simple; but for those of us still struggling to gain that simplicity, it's so difficult. Horses teach us that learning takes place through *listening.* They teach us that miscommunications are important to correct, yet hold no import once corrected. They teach us valuable skills and insights to improve both our horse and human communications—through *HorsePower!*

JIMMY FAIRCLOUGH, b. 1958, is president of Fairclough Fuel Co. and a competitive driver who took an individual fourth and the USET Team Gold in the 1991 World Pair Driving Championship in Austria. Driving is a family affair for the Fairclough, with Jimmy teaching his young boys to drive and his wife Robin assisting in competitions. With Robin navigating from behind, Jimmy and the dynamic duo of Speedy (Holsteiner) and Leo (Hanoverian) burn up the track at the 1993 World Pair Championship at Gladstone, New Jersey.

JENNY BUTAH, b. 1945, is a psychotherapist who rode as a youngster until she was 18. Returning to riding after a thirty-year hiatus, Jenny has taken up dressage and trail riding along with Centered Riding training. She is shown on her Thoroughbred, Dusty, during a 1995 clinic working on balance.

LT. CARL CLIPPER, b. 1946, Commander of the Horse Mounted Patrol of the United States Park Police in Washington DC, and New York City, transferred from the motorcycle division of police work to the mounted unit. On duty for many memorable park and presidential occasions in the nation's capital, a stand-out event for Lt. Clipper was commanding the Horse Mounted Patrol at the 1996 Olympics in Atlanta. Lt. Clipper and his vigilant police mount, Midnight Dancer, are pictured during a routine patrol in 1993.

AMY HUBBARD, b. 1980, is a
high school student looking
toward college. One of the
highlights of her riding to date
was qualifying for the US
Pony Club Championship Team
in Show Jumping. Amy and her
handsome chestnut gelding,
B.W. (Bretton Woods) share
a contemplative moment in his
pasture.

DIANA THOMPSON, b. 1956, is a
horse trainer and journalist who
rode ponies at age three and
received her first horse as a
Christmas present when she
was seven. In 1985 she assisted
Linda Tellington-Jones with
TTEAM training the Russian
Olympic team in Moscow.
She is founder and editor-in-chief
of THE WHOLE HORSE JOURNAL, an
innovative publication dedicated
to holistic equine health and
gentle, effective training methods.
Diana is shown with Buckley,
a horse that she has treated and
trained back to physical and
emotional health.

BEV DOOLITTLE, b. 1947, is an internationally renowned watercolorist famous for her unique camouflage technique, in which multiple images are ingeniously woven into the fabric of the main composition. Bev has always been inspired by the strength and beauty of the horse. She is shown with one of her favorite models, an Arab/Quarter Horse paint. Paints are often incorporated into Bev's work, and her trademark piece, "Pintos," is credited with bringing her singular camouflage style to the attention of the art world.

GENIE STEWART-SPEARS, b. 1951, equine journalist and photographer, enjoys endurance riding and has photographed most of the greats in the sport. Genie, with her mare Commander's Lory, are pictured during the 5-Day 285-mile New Mexico Renegade Ride in 1995. The 1994 New Mexico Renegade Ride had been Genie and Lory's first endurance competition together, and they finished 9th with Genie taking first in the lightweight division. Lory is a departure from the more usual Arabian contenders—she is a Saddlebred/Fox Trotter cross.

LAURA BIANCHI, b.1952, joined the San Francisco Police Department Mounted Unit in 1981 as its first female officer. Laura later became the Mounted Unit's trainer and has written articles on police horse training. In 1987-88 she was a member of the championship Grand National Color Guard Team. Laura is pictured with her police mount, Bill, prior to going out on patrol in San Francisco's Golden Gate Park.

PAT LAWSON, b. 1946, is an attorney and founder of Ebony Horsewomen, Inc., a non-profit troupe of African-American riders who support urban youth through drug awareness, criminal justice, health and education programs. The daughter of a jockey, Pat's interest in horses started at an early age and has been a source of strength and growth throughout her life. Pat is pictured giving an inner city child her very first experience in the saddle on her beautiful Palomino, Rising Star.

CHAPTER SIX

# DETECTIVE WORK

## Awareness and Deductive Reasoning

*Horses have taught me to see—to know what I am seeing and what I'm not seeing. —Bev Doolittle*

The sunny afternoon was simply too delicious to waste; so, when our lesson ended, I decided to go for a ride on my Thoroughbred mare, Freddie. After telling my instructor, Kelli, our route, we set out for Napa Valley's Highway 29, where wide grassy shoulders stretch along miles of vineyards, allowing us to stay well away from traffic. The first three quarters of a mile were uneventful, but as we approached Scott Way, a quiet cul-de-sac intersecting the highway, Freddie became agitated and resistant.

When I urged her on, she began crow hopping. "Easy girl, easy, now..." I crooned, as I stroked her neck and collected the reins. Suddenly, she exploded in a violent buck that threw me high above her. Luckily, I came down on the saddle, but no sooner had I landed when she bucked again, then reared onto her back legs, screaming. My mind filled with terrifying thoughts of hitting the ground hard while Freddie ran wild along the highway—or into traffic! I knew I had to stay on; so I flung myself at her neck, hung on, and prayed. Again she reared, this time shearing the metal clip on her tie down, so the leather strap was whipping her head.

I remembered my trainer telling me a horse can't rear and move forward at the same time, so drive them on, and they'll come down. Frantically, I sat up and gripped my legs around her, pushing her ahead, away from the highway. So much for that theory. Freddie went up again and walked on her hind legs like a crazed circus dog. One more buck, and we were off the grass, and onto the hard-top of Scott Way. Miraculously, she stopped bucking and rearing, and merely pranced about, snorting angrily. I walked her up the road, trying to calm her and myself; then I got off to take care of the tie down, which was still swinging wildly from her noseband.

"What was that about?" I asked aloud.... Suddenly the stable seemed a long way off. Less than a mile, but if we had another episode like that, we would never make it back. Still trying to soothe my own shattered nerves, I checked Freddie for bee stings or snake bite—any indication of what might have caused such a violent reaction. I walked around her, stroking, and talking to her until she was quiet again. With all that exertion on top of our jumping lesson, she was quite tired now. I remounted and walked her up and down the street until I was assured that the fury had completely passed.

We walked out Scott Way, then stepped back onto the grass when she began again—a quick rear, then a buck and some jagged crow hops as we progressed back along the highway toward the stable. Finally, she stopped, but continued prancing and snorting until we crossed onto a nearby driveway where she once again calmed down enough to walk.

Back at the stable, I told Kelli about our roadside rodeo, and she said, "That's strange; two other horses have exploded at Scott Way. One actually kicked out so hard he went lame. Luckily no one's been hurt, but there must be something scary there."

On the way home, I stopped and explored the area for anything that might be frightening to all those horses, but came up empty.

A week later, my husband, Kip, and I were riding our seventeen-year-old trail horses: Lucky, a lackadaisical Quarter Horse, nicknamed "Eeyore" because he is so placid; and Haji, a handsome, fairly level-headed Anglo-Arab. As we approached Scott Way, this time from the opposite direction, Haji began to dance. Then he gave a little buck and quickly trotted forward. Meanwhile Lucky kicked out behind and picked up his pace.

"This is too weird!" I said, "What is it about this area?" The horses had moved onto Scott Way and settled down, but Kip and I again searched the area for anything that might be suspect. There was no foul odor, yet we considered the possibility of dead animals, or even evil spirits.

It was as we continued along the highway that we saw them: small neon-orange signs warning against digging without first calling the phone company to locate the underground cable. "Could that be it?" I wondered. It made sense since the horses did not react when they were on the pavement of Scott Way, only on the moist grass that could carry a current. However, I wasn't sure that phone lines, being low voltage, had enough charge to transmit through the ground.

I called the phone company and spoke to a woman who asked, "Are there any overhead wires in the area?"

"Yes." I replied.

She said, "It is possible to set up a flow between the two electrical sources. Is there a wire fence anywhere nearby?"

Again the answer was "yes."

"Don't touch the fence. It may be carrying current; I'll send someone to check it out right away."

Investigators from both the phone and electrical companies came out, and I showed them where the action had taken place—between the buried phone cable and an electrical company transfer box. The wet ground was still visibly torn up with Freddie's deep hoof prints.

The report came back that there was no problem, but from that day forward, the horses never again reacted at Scott Way. (I suspect they fixed the problem yet didn't want to admit anything for fear of liability.) At any rate, the problem went away after that.

After realizing what had caused her violent outbursts, I felt bad for my poor mare, suddenly receiving electrical current through her metal clad hooves and unable to understand. No wonder she wouldn't keep her feet on the ground.

Had this been an isolated incident, I would probably have chalked Freddie's behavior up to willfulness. Yet, once all the pieces of the puzzle were on the table, we were able to put the whole picture together, discovering the real problem and a solution.

Unexpected incidents such as this have shown me that being on a horse is like driving a car with dual controls through a mine field where all but a few of the mines are marked. Most of the time, you are in command of the steering and speed, and, being vigilant, you can avoid the obvious detonations. Occasionally, however, without warning, one of those hidden little surprises goes off, and then your powerful, anxious partner grabs the controls. It's important that a rider be alert for unforeseen blow-ups and be able to retain, or regain, control when his horse spooks.

## Cognitive Alertness

Being around horses is a great training ground for the various levels of mental alertness one must develop to cope with whatever life throws at you. It teaches you that *anything* can happen, and you must be ready to deal with it—in concert with others— often a big, powerful other.

*When I fell off and twisted my knee,* says Tracy Cole, *my father told me, "That's what you get for riding something with a mind of its own. You have to be ready for that." Since he told me that, I've made myself more aware.* Tracy is referring to "cognitive alertness": the recognition that, for your own good, you must be constantly alert. This is a basic equestrian safety point. However, *making* yourself be cognitively alert can cause anxiety and nervousness—both undesirable emotions around horses.

Since being relaxed yourself helps to keep your horse relaxed, one must counteract anxieties caused by the state of cognitive alertness. This takes the experience and confidence that comes with time in the saddle: *A friend and I were riding across a field, talking, with our feet hanging out of the stirrups, just waltzing along easily, when up comes a wild turkey,* recounts Phyllis Eifert. *We both got dumped at once. We were on the ground before we knew it, and off went the horses.... Sometimes when you've ridden a lot, you relax a little bit too much.* Too relaxed!? Being so relaxed that you are not paying any attention to riding, your horse, or your surroundings is not optimal either.

*You need to stay aware of what's going on around you,* cautions Dennis Marine. *But you don't have to be setting up there like you're in freeway rush traffic expecting a wreck. You might program that wreck in there by transmitting your mood to the horse. You need to be relaxed-aware. Don't go to sleep when you're at the wheel.* To achieve a balance between states of nervous red-alert and comatose zoning-out requires that you expand sensing beyond yourself, to your horse, and your entire surroundings. *I teach awareness of one's self through body awareness and allowing* reports Sally Swift (p. 176), developer of Centered

Riding, a combination of visualization and the mechanics and anatomy of movement. *Aware and allow are two important words in Centered Riding. When you get awareness of yourself you also get awareness of other things, but first you must be aware of how your body works and allow your body to function without dominating it all the time. Allow it to function—and the same with your horse. As you become aware of yourself, you then become aware of the horse. The horse can't move properly if you're interfering with him physically—if you're out of balance or rigid—you need to be supple and sensitive to your horse's motion. Once you become aware of your body and your horse's body, then you can allow both to function. When they both function in the optimum way you get wonderful results.* This trains you to get out of your head and into the feeling, sensing mode of listening and being in the moment with yourself, your horse, and your surroundings. Such training allows you to assimilate basic cognitive alertness into the broader "subliminal awareness" of an entire situation.

## Subliminal Awareness

*You definitely have to pay attention,* says Cathy Ziffren. *It's like you're a plug and the horse is a socket—you plug yourself into that horse. You can feel everything that horse is feeling, and the horse can feel the same from you.* By applying the communication skills discussed in the previous chapter, a rider can receive, interpret, and react to messages, feedback, and potential problems before they explode.

*There are two kinds of riders in my book,* observes Richard Shrake. *There's the kind that every day they get on a horse, they've got a problem. They're kind of going from fire to fire trying to stamp it out. Then there's the horseman who rides in such harmony and feel with his horse, that fires never really develop, because that harmony never lets things progress into problems.* That sensitive, aware rider feels a problem when it's a mere spark and snuffs it out before it ignites. That rider has internalized his cognitive alertness to a naturally mellow state of relaxed, subliminal awareness of himself, his horse, and his surroundings.

## Competitive Awareness

Yet another level of mental alertness is "competitive awareness." This has subliminal awareness as its foundation, then adds cognitive alertness in the strategic vigilance of the game, the many players, and the charged surroundings. *To be competitive in endurance riding, you have to be aware of everything else around you,* explains equine journalist and endurance rider, Genie Stewart-Spears. *You have to be aware of all the other players in the game. You have to be realistic about where they are, how they are, and what they're going to do. You have to know what you can do and how much horse you've got underneath you. There's a lot of discipline involved because you have to really know yourself and your horse and stay with reality—not dreams or denial.*

Competitive awareness is mentally challenging and taxing and cannot be sustained indefinitely as subliminal awareness can—especially in the fast-paced action of equestrian competition: *One of the big problems in polo is that we don't look around enough,* claims Rege Ludwig. *When we don't watch what's going on around us, we miss a lot of plays. When you start missing plays, you're going to lose. In polo you have to be so confident in yourself, in your horse, in your abilities to respond properly to all situations, that you can give your attention to the game. You just know that whenever you want something—it's there. All I've got to do is ask, and it's there. When you have that confidence, you won't be focusing on yourself or your horse and miss what is going on around you. Then you can deal with what is going on and respond to it in time to control it.*

Having the secure foundation of subliminal awareness frees a player to add the more focused cognitive alertness to the game. That combination eventually matures and mellows to "competitive awareness," the state in which confident athletes are able to rely on their own and their horse's abilities, thus freeing their attention to respond to in-play opportunities.

## Early Warning Systems

Another important factor of awareness is both the human and equine early warning systems—allowing your own and your horse's instinctive antennae to guide you. Due to a horse's superior sensitivities, a horse can supply vital information through this system: *My big beautiful Quarter Horse mare, Shermanette Tank, and I were doing the Stewart Anderson Ranch ride—where the Black Angus are,* recounts Chris Hawkins. *Coming down this hill, I saw a patch of bright green grass that looked so pretty, I decided we'd ride over and let Shermanette eat some. When we got to the edge of the grass, Shermanette balked and started snorting. Now I should know better than to argue with her, but I said, "Oh, Sherman, what's the matter with you?" And urged her on.*

*Well, she took two steps and sunk down until my feet were on that grass. It was a bog that you just couldn't believe was there! It scared the living hell out of me—I didn't know what was underneath there. Very carefully, I got off, lay on my belly, and just skittered along like a water bug, until I was out. With my weight off her, Shermanette was able to get her feet up higher, and she came out behind me. When I reported it to one of the cowboys on the ranch, he said, "If you'd fallen down far enough, you'd have found a lot of dead cows in there—it's that deep! We intend to put a fence around it, but haven't had time." That taught me to listen and consider my horse's objections in the future....*

Over the years, Lt. Carl Clipper has honed his instincts to find trouble before it finds him. In addition to his own savvy acumen, he relies on the equine early warning system of his police mount: *Being a police officer for over twenty years, it's second nature to try to see a problem before it starts. On the mounted force, you have to be alert not only for yourself, but for your horse as well. You never know what's gonna get them. They can go right down the center of a marching band just fine, and then a plastic bag blows across their face, and off they go! You just have to be ready all the time.*

*Quite often my horse picks up on disturbances much quicker than I do. Horses' hearing is a lot better than ours—they can hear a baby crying, or somebody hurt, that we would miss. Big John will cock his head, then I see that there's an accident or something going on that shouldn't be....*

Years of practice at being alert around horses has turned Macella O'Neill into a human disaster locator: *I have a most unpleasant sixth sense,* exclaims Macella. *Whenever something happens—like when a truck jumped its emergency brake and hit our trailer, or when horses crash and fall, whatever—I'm always the one who sees it. Never have I been physically present and not seen something major occur. Some sense hits me; I look over, and there it is—boom. I always see disasters occurring, unfortunately not early enough to prevent them.*

## Observation

Working with horses trains you to observe. Every time you take a horse out of his stall or paddock, you watch for changes in condition, attitude, action, and general demeanor. As you groom, you inspect his body and run your hands down his legs to detect any soreness, heat, swelling, bumps, or cuts—sort of an equestrian "pre-flight inspection." You want to be assured he's healthy, content, and sound. Observing horses day in and day out develops a mental template of what's right. When the scene doesn't fit that template, you start asking questions: *You become very aware of things that you might not be, normally,* notes Sam Savitt. *In the winter, I know I should have to fill my horse's water bucket again in the evening. If it's still full, I wonder, why isn't he drinking? I know how many loads I should find in his stall. If there aren't that many, I wonder, "Is he blocked?" When he's coming in from the field, I watch to make sure he's walking sound. Sometimes one leg will hang too long, and it will come in a short step, and I'll think, "Geez, I hope he hasn't hurt that leg." You learn through observation and being aware of movement, habits, and sounds....You become tuned in to all their body English. It's another dimension in living, being with animals on a daily basis.*

This essential scrutiny teaches the value of natural cognizance: *I am always watching horses, watching for anything wrong with them,* says René Williams. *I checked every horse at the* [United States Equestrian] *Team, every day. You have to observe all the time, until it's a feeling. That's made me observant in life. I never studied anatomy in school, but I know anatomy. My Lord, I know where every tendon, every bone, every muscle is. I know conformation and soundness and what the perfect horse should look like... I know that. That's why I'm sent out to observe horses people are paying high prices for.* René's keen observation has also paid off in his second career of sculpting. He creates his horses from the inside out: first building a wire skeleton, then applying the wax musculature until he has "living, breathing," thoroughbreds that just happen to be cast in bronze.

*Horses have taught me to see—to know what I am seeing and what I'm not seeing,* states Bev Doolittle—no small claim for a world renowned artist. *There is a subconscious store of information that you get when you actually have contact with horses—the give and take of the flesh and the fur—all those things register. I sense the gait and the gestures, where the horse is looking, its balance.... I want to know what he is seeing, what does he smell.... I start to think beyond myself. Then, when I go to draw horses, I'm drawing from my own feelings—if it feels right, I do it. I call that drawing from the heart.*

A trained eye is obviously an important tool for any artist. It's interesting that all three contributors describing the importance of observation are well-known and highly respected artists. This indicates to me that developing a keen eye and sensitivity to the form and action of horses pays off in many ways: not only for the animal's well-being and to enhance one's own ability with horses, but also as a foundation for fine art, and a more perceptive life.

## Deductive Reasoning

Let's imagine for a moment, that you are just starting a new career. You have finished your schooling, passed all the exams, got your state certificate, and just leased your first office with your name in gold letters on the door under the title: *Private Investigator.* You glance proudly at that sign and smile as you enter that first day to find a number of clients awaiting your arrival. You are struck by your immediate good fortune; they are all good-looking, well-cared-for types with whom you'd be proud to work. They nod a greeting as you say a quick "hello" and walk briskly into your office, instructing your secretary to send in the first client. By the end of that first day, the true challenge of your job is apparent: all your clients are mute! Each has difficulties you could help with, and they want to work with you, but it is up to you to discern their problems, their histories, and the solutions solely from your alert observations, astute interpretations, and perceptive deduction of the silent clues they are able to offer. Now add a second title to your door *Horse Owner; Trainer; Rider; Farrier; Groom;* or *Veterinarian,* and you have an idea of what it takes to work with horses on a daily basis. If such challenging detective work holds no allure for you, you'd best take up golf, instead of horses.

*When I was dealing with my horse, Zodiac's, habit of rearing, I learned that problems and solutions are not always obvious—often there's a hidden issue,* relates Kelly O'Boyle, dressage instructor (p. 200). *It was obvious that Zodiac didn't want to go forward on to the bit, but nobody stopped to think that there might be something other than willful stubbornness causing his reaction. Two trainers told me to put him down because of his dangerous behavior. But I didn't find him aggressive or mean; I found him tense when he was asked to go on the bit. I followed my gut and continued searching for an answer. Nobody, including me, stopped and asked, "Could we have a physical problem?" As it turned out, the major problem was a bad tooth that the bit kept hitting. It seems fair to me that if Zodiac has pain in his mouth every time he goes forward on to the bit, he might not want to do that—he might even fight it by rearing. This has made me more determined to explore lots of avenues when there's a problem: let's check teeth; let's look at feet; let's look at bug bites; let's see what else is going on. In problem solving you need to consider the obvious, but also learn to listen to your intuition, and look for hidden causes.*

Obviously for your safety as well as the horse's, it's important that all tack fit properly and comfortably: *"Oh, he's just being a brat!" I hear that all the time, says Diana Thompson. I went to see a client the other day. I've worked with her horse about four times, and we've got him from a prancing-on-the-forehand fool, to relaxed, walking on loose reins, turning properly, listening, stopping calmly, lots of neat things. She now tells me, "He's been horrible all week! He won't stand still when I get on, and he's running down the driveway again." She was very angry. I said, "Well, that's a switch. We were doing very well. Why don't you get on, and we'll see if we can figure it out. I like this horse; he's honest. Let's look for what's bothering him." So, she gets on, and sure enough, he's an idiot. He's whirling; he's spinning; he's out of control. She can hardly stop him. So I grab him and get her off. So what is different here? She was in a different saddle. "Did you ride in this saddle all week?" I asked.*

*"Yeah."*

*"I'm gonna bet that it's the saddle. I'm going to work with this saddle for a few minutes and try to make this saddle work; then we are going to put the other saddle on and see."*

*As we changed the padding, the horse got better and better. Then I changed back to the client's regular saddle that we'd worked in earlier, and the horse was perfect. He stood totally still at the mounting block, head down, loose rein, didn't tear off when she got on him.*

*What was really nice about this incident was that the woman really saw that her horse was talking to her through his behavior...actually, he was screaming at her. This horse is very sensitive anyway and with a sore back he reacted really fast. He didn't just get cranky—he went nuts! It was a really good lesson for the owner. His behavior was a direct reflection of that saddle bothering him. Any saddle maker in the world would probably say, "That saddle fits him." Well, the horse didn't think so.*

*Over the last ten or twelve years, I've learned to come from total body perspective, listening to the horses, and giving them credit for what they are trying to say.*

Not all problems are solved simply by changing tack: *I had a mare with a very bad kicking habit brought to me, relates Rex Peterson. I studied her, and studied her, and studied her. Finally I called the vet out and said, "I want you to check this mare's eyesight."*

*He said, "Why?"*

*"I don't believe this mare sees well. I'd ride her in the same area every day, and we'd go by objects she'd been by every day—all of a sudden they'd bother her. They wouldn't bother her on the left. But the right eye would drive her crazy."*

*The vet confirmed what I was saying. On the right side, which is where she generally kicked people, the pupil never changed from bright to dark. So his theory was she was probably 80%-90% blind in that eye. She could see movement, but she didn't know what it was. The vet even asked me, "How the hell did you figure this out?"*

*I said, "You're around the mare enough and you're studying her, you'll see it."*

Just as there are different solutions to the same problem, there are often different causes for the same effect. Kicking is again the issue, but in a very different situation: *There was a lady who lived about twenty miles from me who called and said, "My son's little mare suddenly started kicking,"* Rex continues. *A thirteen-year-old mare and she starts kicking—that's kind of odd. But not knowing a whole lot about the mare, I took her, took the kick out of her, and sent her home sixty days later. Now the husband buys a four-year-old horse...supposed to be an awful nice horse. It gets along good for about six months, then all of sudden he starts kicking. That's kind of odd. But not knowing where he'd come from and stuff.... Anyway, I took him, I took it out of him. Within six months, after their other mare foaled, she started kicking. So now, there's something really wrong. I couldn't figure out what it was at first. When the filly was a year old, they called me because she was kicking too. I went out to where they lived. I walked in the yard and I said, "Right there's your problem."*

*"What?"*

*"Those two dogs."*

*"It's not!"*

*"Well, I'm sorry, but I've owned Queensland Blue Heelers. I own one now. They're as good a working cattle dog as I've ever seen, but they are not a backyard dog with other animals. They are a natural herding-instinct animal, and they give you problems." When I combed the filly's tail out, I found a canine tooth in her tail and still the lady did not want to believe me. Yet it was an open and shut case. They got the dogs, and the horses start kicking: How old are the dogs? They're about five. How old is the mare? She's eighteen. Tell me when you brought me that first mare?*

*When she was thirteen. When did you get those dogs? When we moved into this house. When did this mare start kicking? Shortly after we moved into this house.... But to this day, I cannot 110% convince her that her dogs caused the problem. But they did. Those two dogs cost this lady training on four horses, yet to this day, she gets very, very mad when I tell her that. It's so evident; it was written all over the wall. Animals are not born liars. So all you have to do is sit and look at them and read them. Some of them are hard to read, some are easy to read, but they don't lie to you.*

As good as he is at reading horses, occasionally Rex needs to fill in the blanks by researching the animal's history: *Years ago I was brought a little gelding because his owners could not get him into any kind of enclosed area,* Rex says. *They hauled him in an open-top trailer. You could not get him in a barn; you could not get him in a corral with a shelter over it. I studied this horse and worked on him. I couldn't figure out what was wrong with him. One day I started to do research, studying and looking for signs, the whole bit. I found out who owned him before, and I finally found out the whole story of the horse. It was an accident, but it was man-made. This horse was in an old barn as a yearling. A wind storm came up, and collapsed the roof. This horse laid there all night trapped under the roof. So why would he want to go under another roof? I got it out of the horse, but it took some time. I ended up buying that horse and keeping him for three years.*

*Yes, some of them are hard to read. Some of them are talking German, some talking Spanish, you know. But if you study, you can learn Spanish. If you study, you can learn to read them. But you must study. I don't care what the problem is, you must break it down and figure it out.*

Once you're good at reading the animal and observant about its actions and conditions, you can become an impressive equine Sherlock Holmes: *I got a big seven-month-old Paint colt through a sale in Santa Rosa,* continues Rex Peterson. *During the bidding, when the handler raised his hand near the colt's head, the colt knocked him down and was doing a Mexican hat dance on him. He looked like a caged lion in that ring. Everybody jumped out of the ring and just left him in there. They'd had him at $1,800 but they had to start the bidding over again after he exploded. I bid one time on him for $400 and ended up owning him. There was a man sitting in front of me who turned around and said, "Son, what did you buy that crazy colt for?"*

*I said, "Well...I don't think he's crazy...I think he's misunderstood." This guy really thought I'd lost it. I stood up, and I've got a cast on my leg from my hip all the way to my ankle. I went over to the colt's box stall, and he's bouncing off the back wall, more scared of me than I was of him. After awhile he came over to me. You sit and study the colt you could see the whole story written on him. I walked around the colt staying away from his head. I touched the colt where I could and not panic him, and hobbled out of the stall on my crutches. I had a whole group of people watching through the cracks and every place else. I went up to the lady who sold him and asked, "What have you done with this colt?"*

*She said, "Well, we really ain't done much."*

*I asked her, "Well, how many times has he pawed the twitch off his nose?"*

*"What do you mean?"*

*I said, "He's got one ear trimmed, part of a bridle path, part of his whiskers and he's got no hide left on his nose. And when that handler raised his hand towards his nose, he got that guy down in the ring. So I can tell you this, you had a twitch on him, and he learned to paw it off. And if you go near his nose he's gonna paw you right on top of your head."*

*She asked, "Who've you been talkin' to?"*

*I said, "Lady, it's written all over him; I can read him like a book." And to this day, I'll bet she still believes that somebody told me. But if you studied the colt you could see it. You can tell when a horse has pawed a twitch off. This colt is seven months old; there's no reason for him to be mean. And watching the guy lead him down in the ring…this guy put his hand up toward this colt's nose when he come into the ring, and the horse struck him. He's scared to death. Now as I get to talking to this lady I find out more about him.*

*"His momma died when he was about three months old, and we couldn't catch him, so I had the neighbor boys come over and rope him. They had to drag him into the barn; he wouldn't lead."*

*Now why would he lead without training for crying out loud?*

*"Then I kept him in a box stall, but couldn't get near him, so I put a rope around the manger and when he stuck his head in it one day, we choked him down, and put a halter on him."*

*Well now, that's a real good second handling by mankind…then they put a twitch on his nose! If I was him, why would I ever want another man to touch me again? Especially my head. Not on your life!*

*I said to that lady, "If I had done those things to you, would you even let me in the same county with you?"*

*This lady just shook her head and had no idea what I was talking about—and never, ever will—there's the sad part. She made a bad horse from not understanding. I named him Hell on Wheels. If you'd seen him when he went through the sale ring in Santa Rosa, you'd know why. I've got quite a bit of training on him now and did a film with him called THE SILENT TONGUE. He's a stallion, and we breed mares to him, but I've never twitched him another day in his life.*

## Experimentation

In training a horse, it helps to be able to think like one; then experiment with them: *It was amazing to watch Rex Peterson during the making of BLACK BEAUTY—to watch him try to think the way a horse thinks so we could get from the horse what we needed for each scene,* marvels Caroline Thompson. *For example, there is one scene in the film where Black Beauty steals a piece of bread from his master and runs around the field with it to get the guy to play with him. His master chases him, laughing, but finally gives up and flops down. Then Black Beauty comes over and eats the guy's bread, standing over him, while morsels of his bemused master's lunch are falling all over his master.*

*Rex had never given Justin* [the horse playing the part of Black Beauty] *bread before, and since horses love bread, Justin scarfed it right down. Rex would be off camera, hand Justin the bread right before the shot was supposed to go, and Justin would eat it, and we had no shot. Rex thought and thought and finally devised a mock up for rehearsal, so when Black Beauty (Justin) stole the bread, we used a piece of leather that looked like bread. When he ran around with that, he wouldn't eat it. I loved watching Rex figuring out his techniques: he took the leather "bread" and kept handing it to Justin and getting it back from him; handing it to the horse and getting it back, getting the horse used to taking the leather. But when I called "action," on the real scene, Rex handed Justin the actual bread, the horse walked into the shot before he realized he had real bread. Then he started to eat it and half of it crumbled on the actor. It was really charming—it was perfect!*

*Watching Rex put himself in the mind of that horse was a beautiful thing. Rex works a pair of whips like semaphores; signaling the horses with different configurations of his whips. With those remote, visual cues, Rex instructs his horses while staying out of the camera shot. It is fascinating to watch.*

The very same abilities Rex employed to manipulate Justin in that scene—keen observation and intuitive awareness, coupled with deductive reasoning and experimentation—are also the basis for scientific inquiry: *I love studying horses,* exclaims Jane Savoie. *It's a puzzle to find where a horse is locked, blocked, stiff, or weak. Then to figure out specific physical therapy exercises to unblock, unlock, loosen, and strengthen. It's very rewarding. This is an instinct I've developed through observation and experience. You do something and you experiment—that's part of the creativity—it works or it doesn't work. It's like a living laboratory, basically.* Thus, working with horses offers not only a knowledge of equine physiology, but a working application for the creative and logical process of trial and error, as well as controlled experimentation.

## Life Lessons

The mental acuity needed around horses obviously has many applications, not the least of which is driving: *I can still hear Gordon* [Wright] *bawling me out,* muses Sam Savitt. *He'd bellow, "Look, when you're driving, do you watch the hood of the car? No, you don't! Well, don't look at your horse's head while you're riding—watch where you're going!"*

Mary Fenton recognizes additional skills she's gained through riding: *As a practical matter, riding has made me a good driver. As a result of doing a lot of jumping, I've learned about distances, cornering, balance, speed, pace, and an awareness of what's going on around me.*

In addition to driving applications, fine tuning your powers of observation is good business: *You need to know what's going on all the time,* says Tom Moore. *I'm a very observant person; on the farm I can see if a board is broke, or a tree limb is down when other people don't notice.*

Being attentive is also good self-defense: *I'm not by nature a highly observant person,* admits Dr. Robert Miller. *But horses have made me a more perceptive human being. If you're not perceptive around them, sooner or later you'll get hurt.*

Subliminal awareness and an attuned early-warning system are valuable tools of self preservation: *This world has changed,* Lt. Clipper exclaims. *We've lost a lot of trust in people and places. You can't even go into a convenience store without looking in there first to see if it's safe.*

Heightened awareness offers protection against dangers beyond horses. In today's society, where trouble and trauma can strike anyone, anywhere, anytime; being alert, aware, and observant is a vital advantage. The mental habits developed through successful work with horses: cognitive alertness, subliminal and competitive awareness, observation skills, deductive reasoning, and creative experimentation create an astute perception that is an asset in many areas of life—personal and professional. The individual that cultivates these various levels of perception becomes a more active player, attentively taking advantage of the many opportunities life offers through these important cognitive benefits of *HorsePower!*

WILLIAM STEINKRAUS, b. 1925, editor and legendary equestrian, is a six-time Olympian with a 1952 team bronze, team silver medals in '60 and '72, and the first American individual gold medal in equestrian sports in 1968 to his credit. He has served as President, Chairman and Chairman Emeritus of the US Equestrian Team, as Director of the American Horse Shows Association—receiving both its Horseman of the Year and Lifetime Achievement Award—as international judge and also as television commentator for a number of Olympics and World Championships. He has been elected to the Madison Square Garden, National Horse Show, New York Sports and Show Jumping Halls of Fame, served in many executive positions for the Fédération Équestre Internationale and was President of its World Cup Committee and authored several equestrian books. He is married to a noted dressage judge, has three sons, golfs, plays violin and viola, and still enjoys riding—schedule permitting. Here Bill sails over an impressive oxer on Bill Haggard's Bold Minstrel in 1967 at Hickstead, England.

MONTY ROBERTS, b. 1925, is a renowned trainer with world champion western and race horses to his credit, as well as a horse psychologist specializing in equine communication. His best-selling autobiography, THE MAN WHO LISTENS TO HORSES, espouses humane training techniques. In 1997 he was awarded the Equitarian Award for contributing to the welfare of horses and was named Man of the Year by the American Society of Prevention of Cruelty to Animals in 1998. He is pictured with his Quarter Horse, Dually, at home on Flag is Up Farms.

MARTHA JOSEY is a world champion barrel racer, clinician and Vice President of the burgeoning Josey Enterprises who does everything in winning style. Career highlights include being a National Finals Rodeo contestant in four consecutive decades on eight different horses, winning both the American Quarter Horse Association and Women's Professional Rodeo Association World Championships in the same year, capturing an Olympic medal and the National Barrel Horse Association World Champion. Martha is shown at the 1992 Cheyenne Frontier Days Rodeo with Lone Star Oak, a horse that went on to win the National Little Britches Rodeo Finals with its subsequent owner.

Diana Cooper, b. 1946, is a trainer and writer who has authored a book on circus life. She is pictured with her Welsh Corgi, Gaddis at home in Connecticut.

Jane Savoie, b. 1949, is a trainer, writer and motivational speaker who advocates positive thinking and imaging as foundations to success. Jane was selected reserve rider to the United States Dressage Team for the 1992 Olympics in Barcelona, Spain and was dressage coach for the Canadian Olympic Eventing Team at the 1996 Olympics in Atlanta. Jane is shown on her dressage horse, Eastwood, as he returned to competition after recuperating from the loss of his right kidney in 1996.

REGE LUDWIG, b. 1942, is a master polo coach and instructor based in Palm Desert, California, who started riding around the age of ten at a Pennsylvania polo club where his father worked. He loves the challenge of figuring out individual horses, then training each to its potential. One of his career highlights was coaching two different teams in the United States Open Polo Championships and winning both times. Rege is shown on a polo pony preparing to play at El Dorado Polo Club in Indio, California.

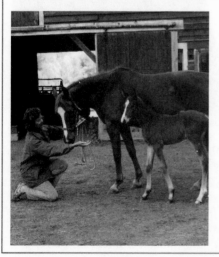

OCTAVIA BROWN b. 1942, is Assistant Professor of Equine Studies at Centenary College, a master therapeutic riding instructor and breeder of sporthorses. She was a founding board member of the North American Riding for the Handicapped Association in 1969, began the first NARHA program in New Jersey, and was the 1981 New Jersey Horseperson of the year. Octavia is shown with her mare, Fire and Smoke, and foal, Jeroboam, in 1991.

JIM BRADY, b. 1940, President Ronald Reagan's Press Secretary, received a debilitating head injury when shot during John Hinckley's attempt to assassinate President Reagan in 1981. Since then Jim and his wife, Sarah, have lobbied for handgun control. In 1993 the Brady Bill, requiring a background check plus a waiting period prior to purchasing a gun, was signed into law. Jim attributes a good part of his remarkable rehabilitation to his equine partners in riding therapy.

# CHAPTER SEVEN

# THE SCHOOL OF SOFT HANDS AND HARD KNOCKS

## The Learning Process

*The world is full of instructors, but not very many teachers.*
   **—Sam Savitt**

*It's so easy to train horses; it's almost impossible to train the owners.*
   **—Glenn Randall**

"Katie, here are your pens and sketch books," her mother said as she laid them on the picnic table overlooking the arena. "You can watch the horses and draw while I help your sister get ready for her lesson."

Katie watched as a tall, slender lady coaxed a powerful Hanoverian over a short course of jumps. After cooling him out, the woman rode to the barn and got on another horse. By the time her sister's lesson was over, Katie had seen that rider put four horses through their paces.

The following Saturday, the scene was repeated. In the arena, Katie saw the same lady riding, while a man called instructions as she guided horse after horse over a jump course. When she was done, the man led that horse away, and a young girl brought a different horse, and held it while the lady pulled herself into the saddle yet again.

This continued for weeks—every time her sister had a lesson, Katie would watch the slender trainer work a variety of horses. One Saturday, shortly after arriving, the woman rode by on her way to the ring; Katie looked at her and asked incredulously, "Are you *still practicing?*"

The trainer smiled down at her and replied, "Sure am! And if I'm lucky, I'll be practicing for the rest of my life!"

Riders are "in training" for life—one never learns to ride definitively—we are always learning to ride. 'The School of Soft Hands and Hard Knocks' has an infinite curriculum in a limitless living laboratory. As with daily existence, each and every ride is a new experience of combined personalities, abilities, energies, equipment, timing, and unfolding events. This ever-changing mix, coupled with the multitude of uses and disciplines in which horses are involved, creates an endless body of knowledge. That perpetual challenge makes the world of horses both frustrating and fascinating.

## Eligibility for 'The School of Soft Hands and Hard Knocks'

One of the most appealing aspects of this particular school is that it is open to anyone willing to apply himself. Granted, the physical act of riding does require a certain amount of balance and coordination. However, given the right horse and circumstances, almost everyone can learn to ride: *In the horse world you don't have to be eight feet tall like a basketball player,* notes Richard Shrake, *You don't have to be able to run a hundred yards in nine point seven seconds...I've given lessons to three-year-olds. I've given lessons to people ninety-six years old. I've taught people who are paraplegic, and I've given lessons to great athletes like Clyde Drexler. You see, riding doesn't rely on strength, athletic ability, or size. What it takes is somebody with feeling, compassion, and finesse; that's why it's an art form.*

Prior to World War II, a young actress from Texas moved to Hollywood with dreams of starring in sophisticated cinema and elaborate musicals. The roles she landed, however, were in rough-and-ready westerns. Riding became an essential job requirement, and she knew she had to learn *pronto* in order to save herself and her career: *Before I started acting, the only thing I ever rode was my uncle's pony, and when I was twelve, I went horseback riding once—and that's all*, claims Dale Evans. *I didn't sit a horse well; I bounced terribly. I knew I had to learn quickly if I was going to do these pictures so I took lessons on lots of different horses. That helped prepare me for the many kinds of horses I had to deal with throughout my career as a Hollywood cowgirl.*

*Buttermilk, the horse I rode in our NBC series, THE ROY ROGERS SHOW, was a little 14.2 [hand] buckskin Quarter Horse, and he surely was a rough ride! He was agile, alert, and feisty like an ornery little boy. And he could spin like a top; I've never seen a quicker rein in my life than this horse. He also had a bad habit when he'd go around a curve. We'd be going at a good clip, and he'd dig his front feet down, bump you up and change leads—it was just terrible.*

*For the Roy Rogers TV series, I used a double in some shots, Alice Van. Alice was an amazing horsewoman; she and her sister were world champion trick riders three years in a row. But even Alice said, "I'll tell you one thing; Buttermilk is the roughest horse I ever rode!"* Glenn Randall had trained Buttermilk as a roping horse and given him to Roy. That little critter even managed to unseat Glenn one time. Eventually I learned Buttermilk's little tricks, got a good seat on him, and loved him.... So even newcomers can learn to ride well enough to be a Queen of the cowgirls!

Nowadays, the barn is also open to the mentally and physically handicapped, thanks to innovative therapeutic riding. Through these programs, people not only learn to ride, they also strengthen themselves physically, mentally, emotionally, and spiritually: *As a therapeutic riding instructor, I'm a specialist,* Octavia Brown explains. *I take people who have very low-level skills and work with them to improve their lives. The best moments I ever have are when my riders with disabilities go off to standard national or international competition and no longer need me because they have made it into the mainstream and can continue with nonspecialist instructors. When I see a rider having great success with very minimal signals, and I know that I've helped train that horse and rider how to do that...those are my joys.*

## Is Talent Required?

No. I can state unequivocally that talent is not a prerequisite to learning and enjoying horseback riding. I have absolutely no natural physical talents in this area—I am not blessed with an exceptional sense of balance, rhythm, or timing. I am, however, blessed with the love of horses and the desire to learn to ride as well as I possibly can. With experience, and time in the saddle, my senses are becoming more acute, sensitive, and subliminal.

*Talent is something that people are born with—a seed planted,* says Michael Plumb. *You can improve and expand on it with hard work, but not everybody is talented. I deal with lots of people who really have to work hard for everything they get. I believe in the work ethic; I believe in the good student who studies, and practices, and takes advantage of all that's available so he or she can learn.*

Even when the seed of talent is planted, it must be tended, nurtured, and supported with the necessary skills in order to flower: *Now I suppose somebody could be dropped out of the sky being very gifted,* muses Richard Shrake. *There are people who have good hand-eye coordination, have a relaxed feeling for animals, and a love, and they're very lucky to have all those things going for them. But you still have to develop the skills. A horse will never get any better than your skill. When your skills as a rider aren't good, it's like sitting down to a hundred-thousand-dollar piano—if you don't know how to play, you can't make music—no matter how gifted you are. The gift is applied to the skills.*

*My dad traded horses. I sometimes hate to tell people that because that's kind of a rogue life, but it was a real advantage for me. When you've got a hundred head of horses in the barn, it's like living in a library. Each one of those horses became a book in my life—I learned my skills by working my way through that living library.*

Obviously any activity is enhanced by inherent talent. But more important than talent in this learning process is motivation, determination, and hard work: *I've had many people ask me,* Richard Shrake continues, *"If you had one rider who was very gifted but not motivated, and another rider who didn't have the talent, yet had the desire, which would you take as a student to the World Show?" I guarantee you, I'd go with the one that wants to go. For me, that's the big thing. You can always work on skill level, refining and sharpening abilities, but if the motivation isn't there, you've got a flashy car with no gas!*

As with gasoline, you need to keep adding incentive to the learning process in order to progress. One such incentive is competing: *Life is a competition,* states Monty Roberts. *When we set goals competitively, we pay greater attention to our lessons. In my opinion, com-*

petition is the most incredible form of motivation for learning available to us on earth.

## Concentration

While desire defines our interests, concentration is needed to focus our faculties on the facts and skills necessary to learn, perform, and progress: *One of the first things that I teach people is how to concentrate and how important that concentration is,* states John Lyons. *To ride a horse correctly takes 100% of our concentration all of the time. When we look up at the clock, when we glance over to the other side of the arena, within a few seconds the horse's performance starts to drop off because he feels us change. Following our lead, his attention starts to drift off. When people tell me, "My horse spooked at the dog…. My horse spooked at the car…." I ask, "So why are you looking at the car? You shouldn't watch what your horse spooked at. When you shift your concentration to look at the dog, or the car, or whatever, then you've just followed your horse, and now the two of you aren't concentrating on what you were doing."*

*Whenever your horse is not doing what you want, concentrate more on what you're teaching, and pretty soon the horse's performance will return to what you're teaching him, and his concentration will follow.*

Working with horses demands an integration of mind and body that almost any parent would be thrilled to have a child pursue: *Riding is really more mental than physical,* notes Adrian Arroyo (p. 200), age 15, who has been riding since she was seven. *I have to think about what I'm doing and figure out how to do it. Think about making my body do it. And thinking what I'm going to do next. Mentally you have to be ready for anything that's going to happen. Riding really helps me think.*

Not only think, but also remember a multitude of instructions. In the ring, kids listen and remember precise directions from their trainer, plus the complex order of jumps for a never-before-ridden-course over a dozen fences. They do this effortlessly at an age when many classroom teachers claim students can't follow instructions for taking a pop quiz.

*One of the things that I've learned from horses that I apply to life in general is how to focus and shut out distractions,* says Jane Savoie. *And not only external distractions, like judges or an audience, or dogs running by. By learning how to focus totally when I'm riding, I've also learned how to get rid of internal distractions. All that chatter from the conscious*

*mind that says things like, "What makes you think you can do this?" or*
*"You're stupid and uncoordinated." or "Everybody's laughing at you."*
*All those things that your logical, analytical, busy little conscious mind*
*tells you that gets in the way of helping you go for your goal. Learning*
*how to focus and shut out internal, as well as external, distractions is an*
*important skill in riding as well as in your life.*

These powers of focused concentration, honed through her
work with horses, have brought Jane Savoie to Olympic heights
in her riding and training careers.

## Teaching Styles

When I first took up riding, I was taking lessons from two trainers with very different teaching styles. One was an "instructional
teacher"—she'd call out instructions as I approached the jump.
These reminders set me up to jump correctly and have a positive
experience. After the jump, she'd analyze what I had done right,
as well as what needed improvement. The second was a "correctional teacher"—she'd watch me jump and tell me what I had to
correct. Well, first off, for correctional discussions, I'd have to remember what I had just done over each jump. I don't retain much
over a fence—I'm just so thrilled to get over still in the saddle.
With correctional instruction, I was always thinking and talking
about what was wrong, which kept me focused on what *not* to do
in jumping.

With instructional teaching, my jumps are much better from
the beginning, for I'm more confident and focused on proper techniques all the time. The verbal reminders became "rhythmic man-
tras" that set me up for jumping well on my own.

I stayed with the correctional teacher for two years because I
thought it would build character to stick it out with her (plus she
had a great school horse who was a real packer, so I got to jump
bigger fences). But I finally realized that concentrating on the nega-
tives wasn't improving my riding, or my life, so I left her. I'm still
with the positive, instructional trainer. Sometimes, when things
click, she tells me I'm a goddess. It's fun; it's constructive, and I
stay focused on the proper way to jump.

There are many teaching styles and riding instructors. Trainers
can make or break a rider—or a horse. I discovered the importance of finding an instructor that gave me a positive experience

from which to learn. That realization has made me more selective with people I choose for any professional service now. I look for the best, then make sure that we work well together for positive results. A nice complement to this is an instructor who is also looking for the best in his students: *In teaching, I always look for the student's strong point*, says René Williams. *Everyone has a strong point: it may be their seat, their legs, their mind, their hands; it may be their balance. Once you find that strong point—that's the secret—keep that strong point and then build on it.*

*I don't think they teach that way nowadays; young riders are being altered to all ride the same way. I look through periodicals and magazines and see the children in particular—they all seem to be taught the same way. When I was a boy, everyone rode as an individual, working off their strong points. Well, that makes sense, doesn't it? Nowadays it's like sending your child to school and finding they're very good in one subject, but then that subject is taken away, and they're made to study only what the rest of the class is studying.* Thus, the insightful teacher identifies a student's strong suit and builds on that individual element of strength, rather than subjugating it to a pat formula of instruction.

Teaching is a tough job to begin with, and riding instructors bear the additional burden of having to be alert to horse, rider, and the action around them. They must be able to read posture, emotions, and situations to avert potential problems and calm fears. They also need to be able to judge and adjust for individual needs: *I have to ride my two horses, Lady and Zodiac, in such unrelated ways that it amazes me constantly*, exclaims Kelly O'Boyle. *My mare takes much more leg at the trot than I ever expect her to, and with Zodiac, I need spurs. I must ask those two animals completely differently for the canter even though it's the same request. They've taught me to be more flexible in my approaches and allow for different personalities, different temperaments, different styles. My teaching has benefited from that flexibility as well. As a teacher, if I can't get an idea across to my student, I have to figure out another way to present it. Part of the fun of riding is figuring out different ways to get the same thing; now I do that with my teaching, I do that with my work as well as with my horses. It's all-encompassing.*

Not all instructors are going to be positive and tell you you're a goddess. Occasionally, unexpected criticism can become the most powerful lesson: *I was taking a riding class from my friend and trainer, Gordon Wright*, explains Sam Savitt. *He asked me to do a course of jumps. I was on sort of a rank horse who tried to run out at every fence, but I kept him moving on, so that he jumped every fence. When I finished I was feeling pretty good about it. Gordon walked over to me and bellowed so everyone in class could hear, "Butcher!"*

*"Butcher?" I exclaimed. "I did it, didn't I? I got him over the course!"*

*He replied, "Sure you did—like a butcher. Now I'd like to see you do it like an artist."*

*And that's when it really first dawned on me, "Like an artist." You know, when you see the best people perform it looks so easy, because they're doing it like an artist. I never forgot that. A great lesson.*

## Teaching and Learning

During the course of this inquiry, I stumbled onto an unexpected controversy: whether or not "teaching" is even possible. Monty Roberts is emphatic on the subject: *There is no such thing as teaching. Period. Teaching implies the imparting of knowledge by pushing it into the brain of a student. I will teach you; he will teach you; they will teach you. There is no such thing. That can't happen. There is only learning. If you're a teacher, you can create an environment in which your student can learn, but you cannot teach. Knowledge has to be pulled into the brain by the student; it can't be pushed in by others. And as soon as we throw away the term "teach" and only deal with the word "learn," then our training techniques change dramatically. You also can't train a horse by teaching him. You can create the learning environment, and the more cleverly you do that, the more quickly he'll learn, but you cannot push the knowledge in.*

Monty's comment prompted me to look up the definition of "teach," which is: "to impart knowledge," with the definition of "impart" listed as "to make known, to disclose." Without getting into a hair-splitting semantic argument in which I think the term "teach" is defensible, I do agree with Monty's basic premise: knowledge cannot be force-fed, for effective learning is a voluntary and selective process. This is why motivation is vital for that process to succeed. A student must have the desire to listen, comprehend, retain, and apply the knowledge made known to him.

Another perspective of teaching and learning is an extension of the principles of imaging, as explained by L.D. Burke: *You can't teach somebody to ride by explaining the whole process; it's just too complicated. You can't explain all the things that come into play, but you can* demonstrate them, then have the student experience them. There's a program called *Cybernetic Learning* where all they do is model the process. They film it, slow it down, put wonderful music with it, and you just watch it, just watch it, just watch it. Your inner guidance gets the picture and knows how to do it. Then you can do it, but you cannot explain it. Perhaps this theory is the basis for such sayings as, "Get the picture?" and "A picture is worth a thousand words."

*That's why kids, really young kids, so young that people think they can't understand an explanation, learn so much faster when the teacher demonstrates,* L.D. continues. *They don't understand what you're talking about, but just demonstrate it, and the kids pick it up right away because they don't have all those words to contend with...and, of course, children are not so caught up in their mind, or ego....* Also, when people are excited about something, they often dream about it, and dreaming is integral to imaging and psychocybernetics.

As mentioned above, when I first started jumping, I memorized a verbal sequence and repeated it in my head before each jump: "Eyes up, heels down, half-seat, exhale, crest release...." As I improved, and my jumping became more refined, there were new commands to add: "Toes out, hip angle, tall shoulders, soft back...." Pretty soon my silent verbal mantra was so long that I couldn't get through it before the obstacle was upon us. It was then I realized the profound value of imaging. A vivid, detailed image of the approach-to-the-jump process contained all those verbal commands—visually—in a fluid mental video that could keep pace with my horse. That picture is definitely worth a thousand words, and doesn't take nearly as long to process.

## Experiential Learning and Apprenticing

When I signed up for riding school at age forty-two, I pictured myself in a class of beginners with a progressive lesson plan of what we'd study each session. I'd imagined that after careful explanation on how to establish the walk, I'd practice on a horse until I'd learned step one—walk; move on to step two—stop; then step three, and so on.... I was not even close. I had one class of signing liability releases and orientation, a class of grooming and tacking up; then it was mount up and join the already spinning carousel of other horses and riders of incredibly varying abilities. As I was attempting to remain calm and keep my horse going—but not "too going"—others were trotting, jumping, cantering, and doing flying changes around me. It was definitely the most chaotic introductory class I'd ever experienced: welcome to Barnum & Bailey Riding Academy! It was then I realized riding is not a linear learning process. It is predominantly experiential—you've just got to do it to learn it.

As with living your life, no one can experience riding for you, then hand you successful coping mechanisms. In order to comprehend and learn to cope, individuals must experience the good, the bad, and the ugly for themselves: *There's a lot of things in riding that you don't feel until you put enough miles in both directions,* notes Dennis Marine. *Then you become more aware of a lot of real subtle things—ways of going that suddenly just feel right when anything less feels wrong.* Here, once again, is a balance point for the mental acumen of riding. Not only do you learn to ride by your wits, but also by the seat of your pants.

Experiential learning is essential for horses as well as riders. Nowadays, expensive sport horses may be foaled, reared, trained, and housed in comparatively confined surroundings: a box stall, a small turn-out area, and an arena. This routine restricts the natural equine experiential learning curve: *A horse who's brought up properly, by which I mean, turned out with other young horses, learns a lot about how to cope, move, defend himself, and how to interact with other horses,* explains Diana Cooper. *He learns manners from his dam, and how to use his body to run, turn, stop, and jump. I live on a hilly farm and I've had horses come here who had never been out in pasture in their lives. I'd turn them out in a hill pasture and they'd start bucking and fall down! I don't want to ride that.*

*This is all part of a horse's education to learn how to keep his mental and physical balance in awkward situations. The whole thing for a riding horse is learning how to balance a load. That's their task. Just as if you had to learn how to dance with a backpack—if you don't know how to dance without the backpack, it's very hard to dance with one. A horse needs to get out and learn how to balance himself—up hill, down hill, how to use his feet.... There are all kinds of experiences that are real important for a horse to have under his belt, yet a lot of horses in this country are never turned out. They know how to do their one thing, and that's all they know how to do. Some of the most valuable and highly trained of all horses, the Lippizaners of the Spanish Riding School, aren't even boxed* [put in a stall] *until they're about five or six*. Everyone, horse and human alike, needs to be exposed to the risks inherent in experiential learning in order to reap the rewards of coping. A risk-free life is not only impossible, it's down-right detrimental.

Many of the breakthroughs I've had through experiential learning have resulted from my instructor taking the time to physically pose me on the horse. "Your heel needs to be down, like this," she'd say, as she flexed my foot beyond any angle I thought possible. "And your leg should be here, under your hip, and your toe out more, like this." That incidental ritual of posing me like an artist's mannequin gave me the opportunity to establish a graphic physical memory.

When I'm actively riding and the instructor calls out, "There, feel that? Now you're in just the right position." What? Where? When? My mind races to identify which instant she was referring to. For in the time it took her to tell me I was going well, my body moved through a myriad of positions, balanced and not, and I was never certain which nanosecond she had in mind. But being posed in stopped-motion gives me insight into what's being sought and creates a physical memory to draw on when things get rolling. It's the difference between being able to study a single frame as opposed to trying to isolate a specific action from running movie footage.

I have since used that physical learning approach to many things in my own life. Now, when I'm teaching others, I take the time to help them establish a physical memory by manipulating their fingers on the reins or moving their hand in the gentle circular motion for currying. This also creates a caring connection between teacher and student.

The experiential learning process within the horse world lends itself to the all-but-obsolete form of teaching known as "apprenticeship." Apprenticeship is an extremely valuable form of education, which should not be lost. But in this day and age of fast food, jet propulsion, and instant everything, the closest thing we have to it is a sadly watered-down facsimile known as "OJT" (on-the-job-training).

The traditions, rituals, practices, and routines of accomplished equestrians are worthy barter for apprenticeships. Often riders will trade their time, enthusiasm, and energy for the opportunity to work, study, and learn from a master. This is an exceptional, comprehensive learning experience that no amount of book-learning, course of riding lessons, or personal practice alone can provide. For a motivated apprentice, learning from a master—his mentor—has an intrinsic magic mixed in with the hard work that cannot be gained through any other method of education.

## Mentors

The horse community is blessed with many individuals worthy of the title "mentor." Glenn Randall was a mentor to Rex Peterson; Gordon Wright was Sam Savitt's riding mentor; and Ray Hunt was a mentor to Buck Brannaman. And so it goes; masters become mentors, apprentices become masters, and the magic is passed on: *Glenn Randall was one in a million, and there will never be another like him,* declares Rex Peterson. *If I live to be five thousand, I could never step into the man's shoes.*

*He was born and raised in western Nebraska, grew up farming with horses, and was with horses all of his life. He was a remount trainer for the Army. He trained some of the greatest horses the movie business has ever seen. He lived with Trigger for twenty years and created the smartest horse in the movies—even housebroke him! To me this man was a legend. Having been raised in ranch country myself, I rode horses for twenty, twenty-one years of my life, but I didn't know anything compared to Glenn. In fall of '76 I moved to California to work with him, and I've been out here ever since. Glenn went to the barn every morning including Saturdays, Sundays, holidays, Christmas, New Year's, whatever....*

*Glenn didn't stand up and say "You're an idiot." Glenn would say, "You know a lot, but there are better ways to do this." Glenn didn't chase horses; he didn't rope horses—Glenn called horses to him. He didn't have horses that kick, that strike, that bite. Now I grew up with ranch horses, and I can't tell you how many times I've been bucked off, kicked, struck, bit, run over. This didn't go with Glenn. He showed me you don't need to put up with that. Horses are big, powerful animals; they have to learn respect—but they cannot be scared of you—and that's a very, very fine line. Anybody can make a horse scared of them. Glenn made a horse respect him and not be scared of him—that's the trick.*

*Glenn passed away a few years ago. It was a very, very hard thing for me because he was like a father to me. I lived in a trailer house right in his yard for fifteen years. I went to work with him every day. There'll never be another like him....* Mentors teach a way of life by example—an inspiring way to learn.

*I wrote an article for* THE CHRONICLE OF THE HORSE *entitled "Gordon Wright, an Unforgettable Teacher,"* relates Sam Savitt. *Gordon was just a natural teacher and became one of the great trainers and coaches in the country; he was just inducted into the Horse Hall of Fame. He didn't have much formal education; only went to third or fourth grade. He was a rodeo rider who decided it was about time he quit rodeo, so he came to New York and bought a stable. He started showing horses, but admitted to falling off once or twice every show. So he started taking instructions from the Army and wound up teaching up in Fort Riley, Kansas, during World War II.*

*I'd been riding most of my life, but not seriously until I met Gordon in 1948 when we worked on a book together,* LEARNING TO RIDE, HUNT, AND SHOW. *We finished the book, but my learning and friendship with Gordon continued; we were friends right up to the end. He's been gone a few years now.*

*At one point I was having a problem jumping, and Gordon told me my timing was off. He said, "Close your eyes as you gallop in, and I'll cluck your horse over the fence so you'll be able to get the feel of it." Well, I had so much confidence in Gordon that when he told me to close my eyes, I did. He clucked, my horse took off, and I was able to feel it correctly. We did that two or three times. I told Gordon, "I wouldn't jump blind for anyone but you." I'll tell you, he was terrific; when I'm down at the barn I can still hear him bawling me out about something....*

Having a mentor is not necessarily an easy path to learning: *Now granted, I've learned a lot from Ray Hunt and Tom Dorrance,* states Buck Brannaman. *But I studied. I sought them out and I worked hard as a student. They didn't hand it to me on a platter—I came and I got it. And that's the only way they'd have it.* And that's the only way it works....

*I've learned that my horse, Magic, is a very good teacher when I listen to him,* claims Mary Mansi. *By paying attention and learning his signals, I've learned to get beyond things I used to do that made him mad. I can see the change in his behavior on certain issues that I've allowed him to teach me. It doesn't bother me to admit that, either. A horse as a mentor? Most definitely. That's what HorsePower! is all about!*

## *Processing, Practice, and Patience*

Being around horses and learning to ride teach the value of process and sequencing. Like a jet pilot, there is a critical list of maintenance items to check and a safety process to follow before each and every ride: Sound legs? Check. Clean coat? Check. Good attitude? Check. Tack okay? Check...all systems go...mount up.

Once aboard, the sequencing of training and learning begins. These exercises work to improve memory, logic, discipline, and organizational skills: *Horses are trained through task analysis: taking a specific task and breaking it down into simple sequential steps,* notes Maxine Freitas (p. 201), counselor and founding director of EquiEd Therapeutic Riding. *In Special Education, we do a lot of task analysis. For instance, putting your foot into the stirrup; that specific task breaks down into 12 different things you have to do in order to lift your foot into that stirrup. Most of us don't need that level of sequencing, but when you are teaching somebody with a disability, you have to break tasks down to their personal function point before they can progress. When a kid becomes frustrated with the process, the parallel with training horses helps him understand this is the way to learn, these are the steps you need to do in order to be able to learn. This common learning process provides a wonderful analogy for these special kids.*

Although the separate steps depend upon individual needs, the process is sequential and must be complete. You cannot skip steps that are the foundation of any learning process. In riding and training the only shortcut is a complete lesson plan: *I spent two winters on a young horse doing lots and lots of ring work,* says equine journalist, Genie Stewart-Spears. *And God, I was so tired of it, and I know the horse was too. But we did it to build the foundation, and the first time I ever went into competition with this horse was so wonderful because he knew what this leg meant, and what this rein meant, what all my body movements meant. We had a fabulous time.*

*I've applied this to my writing as well. I'm working on an article now, and I'm not making great progress, but I'm not upset because I'm laying the foundation: putting down ideas, and moving them around; doing the ring work. And then, once I have the basis for the story, it will click, and then I just roll. This particular story took me days, and those days of preparation were necessary, for now the story just rolls. All that preparation, that ring work, pays off in life as well as in riding. It builds a strong foundation.*

There is no formula for figuring the amount of time it takes to build a strong foundation—it takes as long as necessary and usually longer than desired: *One time a young woman came to Gordon Wright eager to ride and show,* recalls Sam Savitt. *She said to him, "You'll see, I learn very quickly." Then Gordon told her, "With me you'll learn very slowly." And he did teach that way. If he saw a rider who was moving along too rapidly, he'd give him a horse that would set him back, because he didn't want anyone to miss any part of the training.* Hence the adage, "There is no elevator to success, you must take the stairs."

The process of taking each step in turn puts off many seeking an "Instant Learning" course with horses: *Throughout our culture in terms of education, we praise quickness as a sign of intelligence,* claims trainer Diana Cooper. *That's bull. My son's a super rider; he's incredibly intelligent, and he's wildly dyslexic. His route to learning is not through speed. I know a number of dyslexic kids who are top-notch riders, not because they're learning-disabled—a term we don't use because there's nothing wrong with anybody's ability to learn—but because their route to learning is more suitable to the way you work with animals. Through knowing them, I've learned how much we lose when we insist that things be done fast. It's one of the classical premises of good horsemanship that the best results take the longest. If you're going to work with horses, you have to come to terms with that premise. People who don't, fall by the wayside.* Diana's training skills provided her with an approach to education that is beneficial to those who need a more measured method for learning.

Since equine enterprises do not cater to instant gratification, many credit their work with horses with cultivating patience: *Ironically, horses quickly teach us the value of patience,* states Macella O'Neill. *I've learned to be content with progress measured in really small packages, as little gifts. That's one of the reasons I'm a successful horse trainer; I am content with the inchworm path I'm on when no one else can understand why. Often people don't take the time to value the little tiny nuances and details that make for real progress—for excellence. I believe many people would have a greater sense of peace and pleasure if they could appreciate more of those little gifts in life.*

Some of the gifts of learning and progress are discovered through the never-ending process of practice that each and every ride represents: *Out on location when the sun would be coming up, I used to practice to see how steady I could make my head go, by watching my shadow,* recalls Roy Rogers. *You get the rhythm of the gait between your ankles, your knees and your hips. Good riding is all a matter of practice.* Even the King of the Cowboys was constantly working to improve.

*I asked a wonderful old horse trainer in the Dakotas if he had a secret to his great success,* says Jack Huyler. *He said, "Yeah. Wet blankets." Wet saddle blankets—in other words, lots of riding.* So the secret to horsemanship is no secret—it's simply doing it, learning it, living it— one little gift at a time.

## Reward, Reflection, and Internalizing

One of the valuable lessons on learning in the horse world is that intense practice can be counterproductive. Successful training is based on many short practice sessions, rather than repeating one exercise endlessly. Once the lesson has been presented to the horse and repeated a couple of times, he then needs time off to let that learning penetrate. The process is: presentation, performance, reward, reflection, retention, repetition. Unlike people, who may become obsessively repetitious when bent on perfecting personal skills, there are no compulsive equine workaholics. The equine need for recess is an effective balance point in the learning process: *Horses can get stale from having you constantly educating or working them daily,* remarks William Steinkraus. *They, like people, benefit from a chance to go out in God's green pasture on a loose rein.*

Release, relaxation, and rest are valued rewards to a horse. Thus, when the horse has done a good job, it's best to quit the lesson and reward him with rest so the positive performance penetrates: *One of the things that I love about good circus work is whenever a horse gets one tiny little thing right, the horse gets put away,* remarks Diana Cooper. *Say they're teaching a horse how to rear on command; they'll ask and ask, and then the horse leaves the ground an inch with both feet. With that minute progress the trainer says, "Bravo! Bravo!" pats him all over, gives him a handful of grain, and he goes back to his stall. When the horse makes an effort in the right direction, reward it, and end the lesson. Then the horse comes out of his stall knowing more the next time.*

As essential as this particular aspect of equine education is, it frustrates me; for when my horse and I finally do something really well, my instructor calls out, "That's great! Stop with that." But I'm sitting there thinking, "Wait a minute! We did it right? Let's do it again! Let me do it until I cement that feeling."

"Nope. That was perfect—lesson's over."

The frustration is that I need the repetition while my horse needs the reward: *That is why I applaud those great unsung equine heroes—school horses*, adds Diana Cooper. *A horse that will tolerate that kind of repetition is solid gold because that's what people need. It's not what most horses appreciate, but some horses are really tolerant about that, and they're the ones you've got to have. The packers. The old schoolmasters. If you find one, I always tell people, it doesn't matter what it costs— buy that horse.*

The process of learning is a combination of imparted knowledge and shared experience, with the most powerful lessons being those of internal realization. No one can give another internal realization. Whether human or equine, that knowledge and ability must come from within oneself: *My mare, Lory, is such a willful animal that I was often scared of how she'd react to new experiences*, reports Genie Stewart-Spears. *We were in a clinic where we did a lot of cavaletti work. Lory would rush through it and knock everything over. She'd do fine until she got right to the cavaletti, and then it was like, "Oh my God! What am I supposed to do?" So I would try to direct her. But I was so nervous about her reaction that I'd take a tighter rein, a tighter grip with my legs and thighs, and that control just brought her bad reactions about. The instructor kept telling me, "Back off and let her figure it out." When I could talk myself into releasing and letting her figure it out rather than tensing myself, we would go over the cavaletti smoothly. I realized I have to relax, trust her, help direct her energy, and let her think it through. When she figured it out for herself, she gained self confidence and did fine.*

With internal realization, suddenly all the lights go on. Eureka! Lory finally realized rushing the cavaletti wasn't working and ultimately paced herself for success. That independent, internalized knowledge creates a much more fulfilling confidence than having to rely on another for direction. There are times when the teacher must relinquish control in order for the student to progress. Teachers can't push in learning—it must be taken in by the student.

## Diverse Challenges

The horse world offers such diversity of disciplines, activities, sports, professions, experiences, and studies that one need never fall into a rut: *If you're a horse trainer, you must always be learning*, says

Ron Harding. *Your mind is never idle—you could have two or three lifetimes and never learn all of it. That's one of the major attractions. Training horses keeps me going because the challenges always get better and better. Sometimes I may get tired of one thing and think, "I'm gonna quit horses." But I never do. I just find a new game to play on them. I train saddle horses; I teach them to rein; I'm training a three-year-old of my wife's now we call Danny Jo. The other day I told my wife, "Danny Jo would make a good buggy horse; I might get a set of harness and make a buggy horse." I've never trained one, but I know I can; so I might go off in a different direction before too long just for the experience and the challenge of it.*

Helen Crabtree has been riding, training, and showing for more than seventy-five years. Recently, she was forced to quit riding due to encroaching blindness: *Blindness is not an easy thing for an athletic person like me to adjust to,* says Helen. *I thought when blindness forced me to give up riding, that would be the end. But what I didn't count on is that I've trained my mind to enjoy all aspects of riding and training, so that I can live in my mind, and I'm still learning every day. I'm smarter now than when I was actually riding, because I'm immersed in the challenge of understanding the "why" of it. The "why" is so much more than the "what." They're both important, but the why leads you to think of the horse first, and that's a mental game that is so challenging it never quits. If you just ride the tack, you'll be a very poor rider; you must think from the horse's viewpoint. A good rider can correct mistakes; a great rider anticipates and avoids them—that's the thinking rider.*

Rather than curtailing her horse activities, as she believed blindness would, Helen found it has simply redirected her thinking about riding. Her schedule, now freed up from the time-consuming routine of physical riding and training, can focus on more cerebral exercises, such as restructuring the riding program at Kentucky's Midway College and writing another book on her equestrian experiences. Even in blindness, she is still living and learning from horses.

## Mastery

An expert rider is not necessarily a horseman, and a horseman is not necessarily an expert rider. Though each has mastered an art within the horse world, these are two distinct titles: *"A rider keeps a leg on both sides and his mind in the middle,"* quotes Buck

Brannaman. *Anybody can do that. But real horsemen have got heart, desire, and concern, plus a genuine feeling of oneness with the horse.*

Ron Harding elaborates: *Anybody who desires to be with horses is a horse person. But a true horseman is a person who is fully involved— they're sold out. They are not comfortable functioning without horses, and they are not comfortable short of learning everything they possibly can about horses. When I read, it must be educational, and it must be about horses. I don't care if it's pedigrees, training, or genetics…I want to learn everything I can. I've trained horses for forty-one years and thought I was getting pretty good—I was pretty cocky—but five or six years ago I found out I hadn't even scratched the surface. The more I learn, the more I know I don't know. When you get past the point of thinking you've got all the answers, then you're beginning to get somewhere—maybe—I say maybe.*

The horseman is the true master of the horse world. This is a title that carries a great deal of hard-earned respect: *There are lots of riders, but not very many horsemen,* states Jack Huyler. *Riding is a science, while horsemanship is an art. Horsemanship is a never-ending study: the experience of knowing a lot of horses. There's input from each of them into you, input which you use with your dealings with the next horse. Nobody ever learns all there is to know about horses, any more than anyone learns all there is to know about people. Horsemen are willing to show you what works for them; when horsemen get together, everyone learns. As my dad said, "A horseman improves every horse he rides."*

## Limitless Learning

*Horses are capable of more than most of us know how to ask of them,* declares Dennis Marine. *There's always so much farther to go. You need to take that in the right frame of mind; otherwise you could end up real frustrated.*

After a long successful career as a champion bronc rider, Larry Mahan also realized his education was just beginning: *When I quit riding bucking horses in the rodeo game, I really felt I knew it all,* says Larry. *But then I got involved in the sport of cutting horses and found out just how sensitive horses really are. That opened my eyes up to riding and changed my whole life. That was the beginning of my getting into horses seriously; I jumped in with both feet. One goal was to enjoy the competition, but the main goal was just to become a better horseman. That's still my goal.*

Larry works toward that goal every day, for he realizes there is no quick and easy condensed course in horsemanship; it's an ever unfolding body of knowledge, not merely a set of physical skills to be mastered: *Learning to ride is not just riding the tack; it's learning what motivates a horse,* Helen Crabtree elaborates. *That mental challenge of working with horses has always been what I enjoy the most because I've approached horses, not through their skin, but through their mind. In order to do that, you have to understand yourself as well. That's the root of all good horse training.*

*The last horse I broke was a two-year-old colt named Santana's Best Man,* adds Helen. *Since my eyesight was failing so fast, I was pretty sure he would be the last horse I'd be able to train personally. He was a beautiful little horse—soft big eye, keen ears, not quite enough motion to be a stakes horse, but a vessel you could pour everything into. So I thought, let's just take all I know about control and teach this horse. I concentrated on the voice aids; I never let him move without a vocal command, plus body language, particularly leg aids and responsive hands.*

*Now when I reverse a horse in the ring, I automatically throw the bight (loop) of the reins to the outside. I know they say, "The bight's to hang to the right," but I think it looks neater kept to the outside. So when I reverse, I always flip the reins over the horse's neck as I turn the horse. One day I just flipped the reins over and Santana turned around and I realized, "My heavens, we are teaching these animals all the time whether we're aware of it or not, and we have to be accountable for what we do!" Experiences like that have made me more aware of all my actions with horses—and people. Sometimes we casually do or say things that we're not anticipating a reaction from, and suddenly there it is surprising us. Just because we didn't expect a reaction doesn't mean we're not accountable for causing the reaction. That's what happened with this last horse. I've been riding and training horses all my life, and this is the first time a horse was cued by the flip of my reins—I hadn't expected him to turn around, yet I'd actually trained him to that signal unknowingly.*

*So you see, every horse is different just as every person is; plus we all vary from day to day. We can't always predict how every one is going to react to what we do or say—yet we're ultimately accountable for the action causing the reaction. My work with horses has taught me to be more aware and sensitive and keep an open mind. I learned from the first horse I ever rode seventy-five years ago, and I learned from this last one I just trained and all the thousands in between. Santana was the last horse I trained and showed, and it was so rewarding. I stopped with a tremendously inter-esting horse.*

## Coaching

*It takes a lifetime to learn how to live a lifetime,* states Buck Brannaman. *In order for me to get out of my life what I want, I have to be a student first and a teacher second. There's never a point where I'd be able to say, "Okay. I'm done; I got it all now." Because the only competi-tion, really, is with yourself.*

Being a lifetime student calls for a lifetime of coaching. No one ever outgrows their need for a coach. The better the rider, the stiffer the competition, the more a coach is needed: *No matter what level you're at, you should always have a coach,* claims Laura Bianchi. *Coaches should have coaches. When you're critiquing someone, you teach yourself as well; you recognize what you need to work on by watching others' riding. It works both ways so everyone gains from it.*

Again, some of the best coaches have four legs: *I learned an important lesson from my horse, Jeep, when I was looking at movies taken at the state championship barrel race we'd won,* recounts Jack Huyler. *In that race, as we were heading to the finish line, I was batting Jeep with a rolled up program I had in my hand. Every time I did that, Jeep's ears flicked back to me, and he'd check a little speed. I thought, "What's he trying to tell me?" Well, that's when I realized that batting didn't speed him up; it slowed him down! From then on, when I wanted my horse to go wide open to the finish, I'd just chirp with my mouth and urge him on audibly. That showed me the importance of studying the horse and the situation to learn.... There's always more to know....* Studying the race from a different perspective gave Jack new insight—from his horse!

## Lessons Learned

If you're not listening, learning, and improving, you're dormant, declining, or dead: *Lots of people tell me, "You're always thinking; you're always training,"* says Martha Josey. *Well, I love it, so I'm constantly thinking of how I can improve my riding and improve the horse I'm on; through the years, I have really changed my techniques. The things that you do in barrel racing are the same things that you do in life when you really want to succeed: you're motivated; you're organized; you're a good image; you're setting goals, and you're always looking for ways to do it better.*

When we are open to listening and learning, each horse and every ride teaches us every day, for 'The School of Soft Hands and Hard Knocks' never ends. Anyone with desire can enroll in this school and be exposed to many worthwhile lessons through the process of being with horses and learning to ride. This school accepts all applicants, yet no one ever graduates. Since the course of study is infinite, students are perpetually earning credits of insight and know-how toward their lifelong degree in *HorsePower!*

IRVING PETTIT, b. 1907, is a retired mortician whose avocation was harness racing. He bred, trained, raised and raced Standardbreds for forty years until retiring from racing at the age of 80. Irving is shown here being greeted by Dr. Pettit, a Standardbred colt named in honor of Irving's brother, a dentist.

VICKI HEARNE is a philosopher, poet, and award-winning author and renowned trainer of horses and dogs for almost thirty years. Her books, ADAM'S TASK, BANDIT, and ANIMAL HAPPINESS offer unique perspectives on animals, pets and humans. Vicki is pictured with Bandit.

DOUG LIETZKE, b. 1944, psychologist, is a National Top Ten Competitive Rider in endurance riding who specializes in equestrian sports psychology through his many articles, tapes and seminars. He is a winner of the solo divisions (riding one hundred miles in one day without any support crew) for the Old Dominion and Race of Champions endurance rides. Doug and his Arabian gelding, Atizer, are seen riding in the Black Hills of South Dakota during the 1993 Race of Champions, in which they placed 6th overall (out of more than 100 riders) and won the solo division.

BOB DOUGLAS, b. 1933, Executive Director of the National Center for Therapeutic Riding, recently relocated from Washington D.C. to Burtonsville, Maryland. As a research biologist at the National Institutes of Health, Bob helped develop a vital screening process for rubella in women. Multiple sclerosis cut short his research career in his late thirties, and he turned to horses for personal therapy. In 1972 he started a new career that has brought therapeutic riding to hundreds—including Presidential Press Secretary, Jim Brady. Bob is shown here aboard his handsome show horse, Magistrate.

DR. ELIZABETH LAWRENCE, b. 1929, Professor of Environmental and Population Health at Tufts University School of Veterinary Medicine, is both a veterinarian and an anthropologist. This combined vocation, coupled with her deep affection for horses, has inspired Dr. Lawrence to research, write, teach, lecture, and author three books on the subject of the human–horse relationship. Dr. Lawrence, shown with her beautiful Morgan mare, Easter Bonnet, loved riding "Bonney" through the woods near her home in Massachusetts.

BECKY HART, b. 1954, trains endurance horses and is a Centered Riding Instructor in San Jose, California. A three-time world champion, Becky has won both the Tevis Cup and the Race of Champions— twice, been North American Champion, the 1990 American Horse Shows Association (AHSA)/Hertz Equestrian of the year, CHRONICLE OF THE HORSE Rider of the Year in 1990, has been elected to the American Endurance Ride Conference (AERC) Hall of Fame in 1992, and was United States Equestrian Team (USET) Master Rider in 1994. Becky is pictured with her champion Arab gelding, R.O. Grand Sultan, aka "Rio," after taking first place at the 1991 Race of Champions.

RICHARD SHRAKE, b. 1944, is a professional trainer, instructor and judge whose resistance-free training methods have produced national and world championship horses and riders. Richard is pictured with a beautiful Quarter Horse ready to show.

SALLY SWIFT, b. 1912, master riding instructor, developed the innovative and highly effective Centered Riding techniques that combine clear visualization techniques with the knowledge of anatomy and kinesiology she acquired from her lifelong education to counteract the physical effects of scoliosis. Centered Riding makes the rider aware of his body's actions in relation to those of his horse, thus promoting more relaxed and integrated interactions. Sally is shown giving instruction in 1983.

# CHAPTER EIGHT

# *RIDING HIGH*

## *Self Confidence and Self Image*

*If ya' done it, it ain't braggin'* —**Old Texas Saying**

The loudspeakers trumpeted "God save our gracious Queen..." as Princess Michael of Kent stood up in the Royal Box in the Grand Hall at London's Olympia. The 1980 Olympia International Show Jumping Championship was featuring a special exhibition: six riders from the United States introducing the American Saddlebred to the British public.

At the in-gate, the youngest member of the delegation awaited her cue to enter. When the crowd settled to a rustling murmur, the American announcer introduced the pair: "We are proud to present, from the great state of Texas, Miss Camille Whitfield, on her champion Saddlebred mare, Elation!"

Camille (p. 201) was surprised and touched to hear the vast hall fill with "The Yellow Rose of Texas" as she directed Elation into the arena. Impeccably turned out—Camille in the traditional fitted riding suit and top hat, and Elation with gleaming tack and flashing hooves—they were show-stopping gorgeous. Glowing with excitement, the pair sparked the crowds as they strutted around the arena. Before their first circuit was complete, the stands exploded in cadenced applause, delighted by the two American beauties.

That spontaneous eruption created a combustible atmosphere; energy surged between the charged crowd and the spectacular pair. Elation responded to each pulse of the crowd's exhilaration by pumping out more voltage with increased animation—that mare actually swelled in size before their eyes! The horse-savvy audience loved the elegance and energy of the American Saddlebred.

In that electrified performance, the four minutes allotted for their royal ride evaporated like water on a hotplate. When Camille heard, "Your time is up," she smiled radiantly at the steward and refused to leave—Elation, Camille and the crowd were having too much fun to quit now. The crowd rose to their feet, cheering, as Camille and her glorious Saddlebred gave an impromptu command performance.

This was not the first time Camille had created an unorthodox stir at a prestigious show. The tradition of horse shows is long and deep, and to many, deadly serious, but Camille Whitfield had always shown for fun first, standings second. The fact that she and her mounts won so consistently was a result of that attitude, not in spite of it. Camille's parents had never pressured her to win—only to do her best and have a good time.

When Camille was thirteen, she was participating in the Pin Oaks Horse Show in Houston, Texas—a competitive and venerable event on the national show circuit. Camille's horse, Eli, had just been sold, so this was to be their last competition together: the Equitation Stakes. With their current standing, Camille knew she and Eli were not in contention for a big win. Nonetheless, Camille was determined that she and Eli would have a memorable final round.

As they waited at the in-gate, Camille's trainer noticed his normally animated young charge was unnaturally quiet—even dour, but he attributed that to this being a bittersweet final ride. Camille didn't even give her usual smile as he wished her luck and sent them into the ring.

It wasn't until they were headed down the straightaway in front of the box seats that Camille smiled. When she did, there was an audible gasp of shock, then a rising crescendo of giggles and laughter as Camille continued around the arena with her wide, totally toothless grin of blacked-out teeth: a childish prank, but not one to be taken lightly at a show of Pin Oaks' caliber. Camille's mother couldn't believe her eyes, "At the time I didn't think it was very funny, but in hindsight, it was hilarious."

But Camille made a lot of friends with that heretical act. A renowned Saddlebred trainer's wife brought their daughters over and said, "I just have to introduce my girls to someone who would have the nerve to go in there and do that, at this show!"

Although to some, such actions may seem egotistical or insolent—flying in the face of tradition with a silly prank at so serious a competition, and defying the steward at the Olympia Horse Show—Camille was actually a youngster with the poise and presence of a seasoned trooper and just a "bit o' the devil" in her—a talented competitor who did her best and won precisely *because* she loved to play with her horses.

It was no accident that the horse that brought Camille Whitfield to the height of her showing career was named "Elation," for when Camille showed, she was happy, confident, and exuded elation. Their winning attitude was appreciated by the Saddlebred community, and in 1980, HORSE WORLD magazine's readers voted Elation Amateur Three-Gaited Horse of the Year. Prior to their trip to London that same year, an editor of NATIONAL HORSEMAN magazine commented, "May the thrill of this Royal Exhibition repay Camille and Elation for all the thrills they've given audiences over the years." As Camille remembers, "That tribute means more to me than winning a slew of world championships because it acknowledges what Elation was—a real crowd favorite."

## Self-Confidence

One of the toughest periods of transition in life is the teen years: a time of replacing the insecurities of youth with the confident maturity of an adult; a time of developing skills needed for self-expression, personal support, and independence; a time of connecting with peers and life partners while individuating from parents. The assurance that comes with riding and handling horses offers a solid cornerstone from which to begin building inner strength: *When you're young and you master a horse, you get leadership qualities that stay with you over the years,* remarks rancher and horseman, Allan Jamison (p. 202). *You can learn a lot from these horses and get more confidence in yourself.*

As we've seen, Camille Whitfield Vincent gained enough confidence through her riding to test traditions, both in the ring and in training: *My trainer, Charles Smith, found Elation when she was only three,* relates Camille. *At the time I thought, "I can't ride a three-year-old," because normally trainers rode the young horses through their fourth year, and then put the amateurs on. But Elation was just so well-man-nered and had such a great temperament that I tried her one time, and we bought her. I was showing her in Ladies Amateur Classes as a four-year-old. I was told we set records for the youngest rider on the youngest horse, but I don't know how true that was.* Taking on a new, young, exuberant Saddlebred mare and being the youngest in the show class might intimidate some, but Camille's years of show experience and winning attitude bolstered her confidence so that she took it on and won with it.

Being proficient with horses allows for measurable success at a time when a teen may not be feeling so secure in other areas: *Riding gives me such a great feeling,* says seventeen-year-old Tina Schuler (p. 203). *I concentrate when I'm riding, and when things go well, I think, "Wow, I can do this! I can't do math, but I can ride!"*

Almost every schooling barn has groups of young people who become acquainted through their shared interest in equestrian sport. Since the act of riding is still an individual pursuit, personal dependency within these peer groups tends to be less than in many other teen activities.

*Entering adolescence…that's such a tremendously difficult time for young adults,* notes Octavia Brown. *But having an honest, simple, nonjudgmental "stable relationship" is reassuring. That stable relationship remains secure—a horse is not fickle—he doesn't get on the phone and wreck your life five times a week. My God, this in-group/out-group that I'm seeing with my teenage daughter and her friends…they are all so mercurial. I'm sure these are typical teen behaviors, and because my daughter has that stable relationship in her background, she's got her feet on the ground.*

Young equestrians learn early on to make choices for themselves and their horses, so it is easier for them to disregard peer pressures or criticism: *Some of my friends at school think that my riding is stupid; they don't think it's a sport,* notes fourteen-year-old Amy Hubbard. *They're like, "Oh, yeah, all you have to do is you get on a horse, and you sit there and go 'Whoa, or come on horse.'" And I say, "Do you want to take my horse and jump three-foot jumps and have perfect position? Go do it." I don't let it bother me because I know what it takes.*

Learning what it takes, and then being able to perform, builds a rider's confidence, and there are times when we must do the same for our equine partners: *When my horse, Jenny, started jumping, she was really gutsy and would do anything,* reports Adrian Arroyo, *but then she crashed a jump. After that, every time the jumps got higher than three feet, she got really scared and wouldn't do it. Even with my trainer she'd stop—she just wouldn't do it. Eventually, we worked her up, and now she's comfortable jumping 4' or 4'6". It took a long time, but now she'll do it. I feel real good about bringing her back because I wasn't sure I could do it, but I did.* By working to rebuild her horse's confidence, Adrian had a successful training experience that built up her own confidence at the same time.

Gaining confidence is often a two-way street: rider to horse or, as in this case, horse to rider: *My daughter, Jill, has ridden and shown all her life,* explains Richard Shrake. *While she was at college, majoring in broadcasting, she wrote me a letter and said, "I'm flunking speech."*

*I called her, and said, "Hold it. You're in broadcasting, you can't be flunking speech!"*

*She said, "Well, I get really nervous when I'm in front of people on stage."*

*I said, "Jill, you've ridden in a hundred horse shows, some of the biggest in the country—the Quarter Horse Congress, the Cow Palace, and Del Mar—how can you be nervous in front of people?" Then I told her, "The next time you give a speech, just pretend you've taken along ol' Brownie and tied him up right next to the podium and you're in a showmanship class." And darned if she didn't mentally image that, went in there, and A'd the course! But it took that—it took that horse being with her....*

Still, the most compelling trials are those between you, your horse, and Providence: *The biggest thing that I look forward to in my life are multi-day rides because they bring me down to the bare essentials of life: food, water, rest (when I can get it) and meshing with my horse to find out what he and I can do,* states endurance rider Genie Stewart-Spears. *There's nothing else out there; it's a matter of survival and a rejuvenating of the soul. You find out that you can do a whole lot more than you imagined—that you're a lot stronger than you thought you were. It builds self-esteem. To me the accomplishment with the horses is a personal thing. Nobody else may ever see it or understand it, but you know, and that's what's important.*

Since self-confidence and self-esteem are personal qualities that develop from the inside out, the individual is the first to feel their effects. Yet once acquired, these qualities are visible to others through the peace, strength, and assurance that naturally emanate from a confident person with a comfortable definition of self.

## Poise

Although self-confidence and self-esteem develop from the inside out, poise and attitude can be created from the outside in, as Holly Peterson Mondavi explains: *The way we use our bodies is so important—it's "motion creates emotion." If you want to feel confident, sit up, put your shoulders back, and sit in a confident way; if you want to feel tired, then slouch down, or if you want to break out of depression, sit up and smile—put a great big silly grin on your face, and you can't feel depressed—just the way you look cracks yourself up. Pretty soon you're laughing and thinking, "Well, it's not as bad as I thought. I'm still breathing, and there are some good things about today." Being around horses has made me think a lot more about how I use my body and create my own attitude.*

I was able to experience this process recently myself. The evening I returned home from four days of Centered Riding instruction with Mary Fenton, in Watsonville, California, there was a message from my sister, Rachel, saying that our mother's progressively failing health had suddenly turned critical. I immediately made reservations on the first morning flight to Boston. Rachel called at 1:15 a.m. to report that Mom had quietly died in her sleep.

In planning the funeral service, Rachel asked who wanted to speak, and I said that I did. Secretly, however, I wondered if I could actually get through the ordeal of standing before family and friends who knew and loved Mom and deliver my personal remarks without falling apart.

I wrote out my thoughts and practiced a few times. I managed to get through most of it, but was unable to recite the poem I had written without breaking down with images of Mom in mind. Doubts were overshadowing my confidence as to whether I could pull this off at a graveside ceremony.

The day of the funeral was truly spectacular—a perfect New England spring day, with more than one hundred attending to honor Mom. When it was my turn to address the crowd, I had already been brought to tears by my uncle's heartfelt tribute and was fighting to regain my composure.

As I approached the podium, I thought back to what Mary Fenton and I had been working on with the Centered Riding techniques. I silently chanted, "Relax..., breathe..., center..., and grow." I stood at the podium, softened my eyes, deepened my breathing, centered myself, and delivered my remarks and the poem composed, poised, and confident.

This is just one more illustration of what I have found so valuable in my short time in the riding community—*riding* lessons being *living* lessons. I have Sally Swift and Mary Fenton to thank for giving me the tools of centering in riding—and in life.

## Assertiveness

In order to handle horses well, one needs to be assertive, rather than aggressive. Developing that quality affects many areas of life and generally strengthens character. Helen Crabtree broke a lot of social rules to become the first professional female trainer of American Saddlebreds back in the thirties. Helen is every inch a lady, yet her unorthodox career path both demanded and provided the strength of character for which she is renowned: *I'm a very strong person now because of riding. I am. That strength has come from constantly learning how to control a situation, to control myself, to evaluate what is important, what is not important, how I affect other animals and other people, which is so much of riding and life.*

## Independence

Working with horses and honing equestrian skills give many of us a boost in confidence. And for those with physical challenges in life, horses have special gifts to offer: *I got a phone call from a lady in Oregon who has a ranch in the Cascades where they do therapeutic riding,* recounts Dr. Robert Miller. *She said she was very interested in imprint-training and wanted to come and talk to me about it. So we set up an appointment. Then she told me, "I'll be coming with my mother and sister. I can't drive myself because I have a rare form of multiple sclerosis. I've had it since childhood, and it's grown progressively worse. My family's interest in the horse program developed because it has helped me so much."*

*This woman was in her twenties. Her head is normal sized, but her body is undeveloped and doll-sized. Her mother or sister pick her up and carry her in their arms like you would a little child. She has partial use of one arm—just fingers. She's unable to hold her head up straight, so her mother or sister had to prop it up for her. They set her on the couch in our living room, and we talked. She's extremely intelligent, is a public speaker, and an incredible person.*

*"I have a specially constructed saddle and a gentle, well-trained horse whom I can control with the one hand I have use of." she explained.*

*"So what do you do with this horse?" I asked.*

*She said, "I ride the Cascade mountain trails alone."*

*"Alone?" I asked.*

*"Yes, I cross streams, and I go all over the wilderness by myself."*

*"Why do you do this? The risk is so great of something going wrong—a bear...the horse falling on the trail...and you're tied to the horse!"*

*She said, "It's worth the risk. I have been totally dependent on other people all my life: I can't dress myself; I can't even feed myself. How can I explain what it means to me to be able to ride those trails—to hear a waterfall thundering around the bend and be able to ride and view that by myself without anybody's assistance? How can I explain that? Without my horse I could not experience this. It's worth every bit of the risk."*

*I said, "There is a compromise—don't ride alone. Ride your mountain trails on this horse, but have somebody with you."*

*She said, "Yes. But then I'm dependent again...."*

*I'll never forget that woman. That's an extreme example of what horses do for people who are disabled....*

For those of us who can throw a leg over our horse and head out for a ride, this sounds like a tremendous risk for the pleasure of experiencing the trail on your own. Yet that simple pleasure is worth a life's gamble to this woman who has been restricted and dependent all her life. Her horse, her courage, and her determination afford her the only means for that level of independence and the ancillary gift of being *able.*

## Self-Esteem and Self-Reliance

Having been born with multiple sclerosis, that young woman has had to deal with personal limitations and dependence every day of her life. For James Brady, physical limitations and the resulting dependence were thrust upon him by a wild bullet from

John Hinckley's gun. Jim has had to reorder his entire life from the dizzying height of doing for himself and others as Ronald Reagan's Presidential Press Secretary to being dependent upon family, friends, therapists, and caregivers. The sudden changes in lifestyle and self-esteem are difficult to imagine, but Jim has adjusted with courage, humor, love, and help from hippotherapy [riding therapy]: *If I was being a wuss during my riding therapy, Bob Douglas would say to me, "You think you're feeling anxious now? I'll make you feel anxious..."* Jim recounts. *Then he would say, "Trot!" Well, that was another one of my horse Bernie's vocabulary words, so suddenly I'm bashing up and down on that tiny slippery English saddle. That can put the fear of the Lord into you. We'd go around with Bob chanting, "Trot, trot, trot, trot, trot, trot...," until I finally say, "Bob shut up! Enough with the trot already!"*

*But I learned to rebalance from those exercises, and that is one of the greatest results of hippotherapy—a renewed sense of balance and rebuilding my self-esteem. That has taken me a long way down the road of recovery. Everyone should go out and get on a horse—it can do wonders for you—it's made me feel a lot better about myself.*

Bob Douglas, Director of the National Center for Therapeutic Riding, understands Jim's predicament intimately. Bob suffers from multiple sclerosis and receives daily riding therapy at the center he founded in Washington, D.C. His therapy is extremely painful, yet Bob never misses a day because he knows the benefits are well worth the pain: *What I get back from riding—the two most important things—are self-esteem and self-confidence,* says Bob. *I have to reinforce myself everyday that this is where I want to be. It would be much easier for me to stay in bed in the morning and not come to work. It would be less painful, but by doing that I would not be happy about it. At some point I have to be happy about what I'm doing, and being at home—even though the pain is less—that is not part of my happiness.* Life is not necessarily about "easy." It's about learning and doing and struggling and improving. The fact that Bob and Jim struggle and have pain riding, yet do it religiously, is an impressive endorsement for the physical, emotional, and spiritual gifts they receive from riding.

## *Self-Image*

The maxim, "There's something about the outside of a horse that's good for the inside of a man," reflects the feeling of pride and power horses transfer to people. Just being on a horse can give a person a feeling of supremacy and privilege: *Mounted societies were noted for being more aggressive, fierce, and imperious because the horse gave them that kind of power,* reports Dr. Elizabeth Lawrence. *With each conquest over sedentary foot people, warriors on horseback became more bold and proud, more daring and defiant. After the Plains Indians mastered horses, they became known as "Lords of the Plains," whereas before they had been considered a little inferior. Throughout history, horses have been symbols of victory and superiority. Being on a horse increases self-worth—there's a status elevation on an individual as well as a cultural level. This is indicated in the expression, "Get off your high horse" when someone has too much pride…. Horses elevate the human self-image.*

Tracy Cole found that riding allows her a sense of equality since locomotion difficulties, due to her cerebral palsy, are evident when she walks but not when she rides: *Riding makes me feel like I'm an equal,* says Tracy. *If I'm on a horse and you came up to me never having seen me walk, you wouldn't know that there is a problem. My position may be a little off, but not everybody has perfect riding position.*

*One of my friends at work asked why I don't like it when people try and help me up if I fall down. I explained to her, "When people—especially guys—help me, they will literally pick me up and put me down on my feet, then let go and I'll fall over again because I don't have a chance to regain my balance. Whereas, if I get up on my own, I have a chance to equalize my balance to where I am and what I'm doing, and I can usually stay on my feet. Now that she understands, this friend tries to help me by not helping me. One day I tripped getting in the elevator at work, wound up at this guy's feet and my friend runs over yelling, "Don't help her up! Don't help her up!" You should have seen the look on this guy's face when she did that. I had to explain to him as we went up in the elevator. Actually, the more I get up on my own, the better I am at doing it. Sometimes I fall down now, and I'm up before anyone even realizes that I was down.* The sense of equality Tracy feels when on a horse helps Tracy develop independence and a stronger self-image.

Lt. Carl Clipper experienced the enhancement of horses when he went from the police motorcycle unit to the mounted unit: *In this line of police work, it's a proud feeling to be on a horse. You stand out a little bit special amongst the other police officers. It's a mixture of pride in your horse, being a horse-mounted officer, and the duties that you perform.*

*I was on Harley Davidson motorcycles for nineteen years, and it's a world of difference. When you're on that motorcycle, your job is enforcement more than friendly type of work. The horse-mounted unit is about a 100% turn-around: everybody's happy to see you; they want to pet the horse; they want to talk to you. On the motor, they just want to keep away from you unless they really need help; but on the horse, they go out of their way just to talk to you. The horse-mounted unit is a much softer, humanistic field of work. Officers who like to work with people, and public relations, gravitate toward the horse unit. The hard chargers, the ones who want to be out there enforcing the laws every minute of the day, will stay out on the motors, go into the drug units, or investigation.*

*I think being a horse-mounted officer builds the ego—it certainly helps the females because it puts a little beef under them. When a small person has to go into a group of people that are towering over them, they may feel a little intimidated. But you put them on a horse, they lose that intimidation and gain both public respect and self-respect. Now they also have to be able to control that—they can't get too big an ego—there has to be a balance. In police work, that's the main name of the game—balance.*

During my interview with Lt. Clipper, I noted a telling difference in terminology when he described going from riding a Harley Davidson to a horse. He said he went from being a "motorcycle cop," to a "mounted police officer." "Police officer" connotes a higher regard than "cop," reflecting the underlying respect humans hold for horsemen.

Almost everyone who gets on the back of a willing horse feels exceptional, and that feeling can be the catalyst for a whole new sense of self: *There's a young lady who joined our program when she was about twelve and had just lost her father,* says Octavia Brown. *She has a mild cerebral palsy and learning disabilities. She was shy, rather a loner, not really popular, and not much of a worker at school. Her mother reported that the riding immediately made her feel like she was special—a feeling she was definitely not getting from her school situation or any of her peers. Her mother saw the boost riding gave her and realized that her daughter was suddenly achieving, where before she'd refused to try and nobody could push her. On the horse, it was easy to push her—I'm taking you off the lead line whether you like it or not. Feeling able and special through her riding, she came to learn, to want to participate, and to overcome fears. She then used riding to increase her school work, by doing extra credit projects about the horses, because she wanted to. Her teachers were very impressed. She substituted the horse for learning a lot of life lessons she wasn't learning in other social settings.* As a result of feeling special through her riding, this young girl developed a new self-image, which caused a shift in attitude. This in turn inspired her to discover new aptitudes, to participate in activities, and to expand her abilities.

People tend to live up to expectations. When the expectation is limited by a handicap, we adjust accordingly. But when your self-image disavows that limited expectation, you may excel well beyond it: *Two years ago, I was in Denmark and ran across Lis Hartel, a Danish rider who contracted polio at a very young age,* relates Bob Douglas. *Lis is not totally paralyzed; she uses two canes to walk, yet she won the Olympic Silver Medal for Dressage in 1952 and 1956. I was talking to her about being handicapped, and she said indignantly, "I'm not handicapped!" That's a nice feeling to have. That's the feeling I have when I'm on a horse—I'm not handicapped. It is a nice feeling to get there, yet so many people are not able to achieve that. I'm convinced that no matter where you are in life, what you feel about yourself is very important.* In spite of having to be helped on and off her horse due to paralysis from her knees down, Lis does not consider herself handicapped and proved her point by becoming an Olympic champion two competitions running (Events & Athletes 120). That's a wonderful example of how self-image can make or break one's attitude toward life. It starts with feeling special and able enough to want to participate, then you choose your level of participation, and *go for it.*

## Pride and Self-Satisfaction

There are a number of human personality traits that can be easily confused: pride and vanity, self-esteem and conceit, ego and arrogance. The confusion results since differentiating between these traits is a matter of degree and subjective judgment: too much pride can be read as conceit; too much self-esteem may come off as vanity; too much ego becomes arrogance.

Another distinguishing factor in these traits is the genuineness of the individual in question. Deserved pride is not conceit; sincere self-esteem is not vanity; and authentic ego is not arrogance. The attributes of pride, self-esteem, and ego are beneficial when they are balanced, genuine reflections of an individual. However, when allowed to fall out of balance into excess, these positive attributes can transmute into negative characterisitcs.

As mentioned before, horses can be wonderful mirrors for human emotions, since they read people easily and honestly. Thus, dealing with horses can help people learn to stay in balance, since emotional excess is not advantageous: *You can't have a whole lot of ego around a horse,* states Holly Peterson Mondavi. *You need a clear idea of what it is that you want to accomplish, but blind ego doesn't get you anywhere. Ego isn't always negative; ego is essential. One facet of ego is pride, and I see horses as extremely proud creatures, which is wonderful. It's very important to take pride in yourself, or to be proud of who you're with, and have pride in what you can do. It's critical not to hurt that pride because it's fragile, and ego is very fragile as well.*

A sound self-image is a vital foundation block for generating an active, accomplished life from which personal pride is a natural outgrowth: *I believe you nourish your soul with your accomplishments,* says Helen Crabtree. *It isn't necessarily "ego," which can imply that you think you're better than somebody else; it's the personal satisfaction gained when doing your best is reward enough.*

As life's achievements generate gratifying results, self-esteem can develop to the enviable point of self-satisfaction: *I am seeing a nice man now, and when we were talking recently, I went into this little schpiel of mine that as a woman, I've never felt not equal,* claims Mary Deringer Phelps. *I've just felt that I was me—completely satisfied: I had my children; I had my horses; I had my career. I was just waiting for him to say, "Gosh, you've got a good grip on life..." But you know what he says? "You've been smelling too much horse manure!" Like a lot of people, he saw the inner strength and self-definition that I've gained through my career with horses and my family as conceit stemming from being horse crazy. But it's not conceit at all; it's just that I'm totally self-satisfied. I'm just so comfortable with myself.*

Many very talented people fail to recognize their gift or are pulled by other priorities and never follow their passion path. Much of Mary's personal satisfaction and power comes from the fact that she recognized her gift with horses early on and committed her life and lifestyle to it. That's not conceit, that's contentment.

## Character Tests

We are constantly being tested in life. Some tests we sign up for through competition, and some are simply thrown in our path. At times we surprise ourselves by completing a test we thought we'd never finish: *The need horses fill for me is pushing me beyond what I thought I could do,* says Becky Hart. *When I think I cannot go farther, I'm so tired and sore that I am going to have to pull from the ride; but I can't because we're out in the middle of nowhere. I have to go on, yet I always seem to be able to find a little bit more in me. When you think you are at the bottom, it's not fun at the time, but it really feels good afterward. It certainly explores physical boundaries in many ways.* It also tests character boundaries, and succeeding not only feels good, but strengthens character as well.

Occasionally, when we know we're going to be tested, we may require some support: *I'm extremely shy and I don't think I could ever have gotten up in front of an audience, as I've been having to do all my life, were it not for show jumping,* claims Vicki Hearne. *The way I managed to get myself in the ring was by telling myself, "It's not you who has to do the jumping; it's the horse." So you're okay....*

*I was very lucky in having Peppie, [Peppermint Twist], because he was a very tough horse. He was an outlaw horse of the county; people were afraid to ride him. He was housed in a two-dollar-a-month corral down near the dump when I found him. It was not very safe at first riding him on the flat—he'd walk around on his hind legs like a poodle or throw himself on the ground. He was as agile as a snake—you couldn't leave him in a stall that had double doors, because if the top or the bottom was open, he would get out. And nothing would stop Peppie if there was a fence in front of him; so I was able to learn from a very bold and clever jumper. Obviously what I learned was to jump—to take risks, to take leaps.... So, whenever I speak in front of an audience now, I have an imaginary horse who gets me over the obstacles.*

Sometimes life's perverse little "pop quizzes" are thrust upon us, and we're suddenly forced to cope with embarrassing character-building incidents: *Big John and I were at a busy intersection, waiting to cross,* recalls Lt. Carl Clipper. *Big John was a little hot that day for some reason; I don't know what was spooking him up. Well, I leaned out to the right to push the crossing button when something spooked Big John, and he jumped left. I did a complete flip out of the saddle and ended up standing there—still touching the button and holding the reins! It was like we'd practiced. I ended up standing there with the traffic stopped—I should have taken a bow.*

*Then there was the time I was taking a training class out on the trail after I'd got a new saddle and stirrup leathers,* Lt. Clipper continues.

*We'd gone maybe a quarter of a mile and came to some long jumps on the trail. I was bringing up the rear, and when we went over the jump, one of the leathers snapped like somebody took a knife to it, and it took me right off that side. So, all the trainees made it across, but here's the Lieutenant sitting in the dirt. I just take it in stride.... It was a good lesson, not only for me, but for them too—that it can happen to anybody.*

And then there are those special times when we surpass all expectations: *I met an older lady from Maine at one of the horse shows. She was almost crippled in one hip from a horse accident many years before,* relates Helen Crabtree. *She had a mare, "Stonecrest Aber," who was little, and kind of...well...she could be better. Elona said she wanted to come and train with us in Kentucky, so I took her. When I vanned in with that underweight, rather ordinary, little chestnut mare, Redd and Charlie nearly dropped dead. But I said, "I want you to meet the lady who owns this mare."*

*The mare improved nicely with proper care, nutrition, and training, and we took Elona and her little mare to the World's Championships at Louisville. She went in the Amateur Ladies Three-Gaited Class and came out absolutely crying her eyes out— she had taken sixth or seventh place. She had gotten a ribbon—at Louisville—when she'd never dreamed that she would ever be able to compete at that level. She was so excited! Now here's a lady from Auburn, Maine, who never thought she'd be able to ride well at all...so, while winning isn't everything, it is great. But with her, that was a personal triumph—just to be privileged to be in the World's Championships and to get a ribbon was beyond any of her expectations. So it was an exciting accomplishment. I'll never forget that woman; I could draw a picture of her right now.*

These life tests, from the embarrassing pop quizzes to life-threatening exams, are as prevalent in the world of horses as they are in life in general. It is the cumulative results of these tests that determine self-esteem, self-confidence, and strength of character.

## Competitive Ego

The need certain individuals have to test their own limits—to see how far they can go in a given sport, talent, or activity—is ambition. As that ambition sets them apart from others, it may be considered an ego factor as well: *We are all ego-driven people,* states Bob Henry. *Without ego, I don't think much would happen. But you'd better have a pretty good grip on your ego if you're going to get serious about being competitive on a horse's back because a horse can humble you in a heartbeat. The course is going beautifully; I'm feeling the rush—everything's going great—suddenly my horse stops, and I take the jump without him and land on my less than attractive ego...it can be a very humbling experience. But I love it—I've never felt humiliated—you have to be able to take the ups and the downs. That's where the joy is. Without the downs, how would you measure the ups?*

In equestrian sport, ambition and ego are vital parts of the competitive mix: *Ego is very important,* says Jimmy Fairclough. *You want a competitive person to have an ego. You want them to be forward and bold and a little brazen, because they're going out there to beat everybody. And the reason you want to beat everybody is your ego—whether people own up to it or not.*

Even within a team sport, individuals are challenged by personal ambitions: *Polo is a dangerous sport. Polo is an exciting sport. Polo is a demanding sport,* states Rege Ludwig. *Polo is a sport of interrelations between humans, and between humans and horses. Therefore, it is a multifaceted, multi-interrelated game of communicating on many different levels with many different elements at the same time. When you are capable of handling all that complexity, some players feel justified in having an ego. You almost have to have an ego to play polo. Otherwise you don't have the inner fire or drive to really be competitive at the upper end of polo.*

When ego and ambition turn toward arrogance, the competitive edge can start to dull: *More and more I'm finding that there's no place for a false ego in our sport,* says Michael Plumb. *I just finished an event this weekend where I had four horses to ride and a bunch of students to worry about. There were three separate divisions, and I had one horse in each division. The jump courses were all together in one arena, and I went right along on my advanced horse and jumped the intermediate combination, and got eliminated because I jumped the wrong course. That was just another reminder that when you go to events, you have to walk the courses; you have to pay attention to what you're doing, and you've got to have your priorities straight. There's so much to think about that I can't imagine having an ego. I'm reminded of it all the time, but that put me right down and made me think about it.* Yet another balance point—you need the ego, ambition, and confidence to be successfully competitive, and you also need to be graciously accepting of yourself and life's predicaments.

## Humility and Horse Laughs

*There's a beautiful saying I read in a book. "The rider throws his heart over the fence, and the horse jumps in pursuit," recalls Mary Deringer Phelps. And to me, that's always been the way to ride. I had a wonderful jumper, Blood, Sweat and Tears, whose barn name was Tom. Tom could humble ya' in a second because he would not tolerate any form of showing off. He was business. Strictly business. With Tom it was always, "You want to win the class? We'll go to class. You want to show off? Go over there and pick somebody else. I don't have time for that." And he could dump me like that! So, one time when he did throw me off because I was showing off, a friend said, "Well, Mary threw her heart over the fence, Tom galloped up to it and went Phhhllltttt."*

*I learned from Tom that you don't need to show off. If you're talented, you don't need to say, "Hey, look at me; I'm terrific!" People are going to look at you anyway. And they like you a lot better when you're not showboatin'. Tom definitely taught me that, but it took me a long time to learn it.* Tom taught Mary to keep her focus on what's important—the job at hand. When you do that and do that well, others notice.

One of the hardest yet most important lessons humans can gain from horses is humility. Humility helps to keep our egos in balance. False pride, embarrassment, mistakes, looking foolish are all a part of human nature. The lessons in humility that we encounter daily as a result of those very human foibles and fears are often easier to bear when buffered by a sense of humor. Horses are constantly offering humans lessons in humility—not-so-subtle reminders that in the horse world, as in life, humans are not necessarily in control.

*Not too long ago, I was out on the trail with a group of my riders, recounts Octavia Brown. I was on my unpredictable mare, Fire and Smoke. We were trotting up a hill, and as I was rising to the trot, Smoke saw something and jumped out from underneath me. I just had time to think, "I'm either going to fall on my ass, or I'm going to do something about this," so I flung my arms around her neck, vaulted off and ended up facing her. She was so startled, she stood completely still. All my riders were roaring with laughter saying, "Ha, Ha, You fell off!" and I'm saying, "No, no, I jumped! I did a 'flying dismount'.... Yeah, that's it! That's my story, and I'm sticking to it!" Just when you think all's under control, horses can suck the wind right out of your sails.* Quick thinking and a quick wit such as Octavia's often spell the difference between an amusing anecdote and an indignant explosion.

*A sense of humor is so tremendously important, declares Helen Crabtree. If you can see the funny side of your mistakes and say, "We all make mistakes, but I'll never do that again," and then be able to laugh at yourself…. The ability to not take yourself too seriously plus a good laugh…that's seen me through a lot in my life, and it's seeing me through a lot now. That's really the saving grace.*

*In showing you don't have to win a competition to have fun because the competition itself is fun. You are going to lose more often than you win, I can tell you that. I've lost a lot, and most of the time I think it was negligence on my part. I could have done better. But I don't dwell on that, and I don't wallow in self-pity—I learn from it, improve from it, and go on. If you don't learn from your mistakes, you're never going to learn. You truly learn more in losing than you do in winning.*

*I was privileged to work with a real champion named Warlock, Helen continues. As a four-year-old he was World Champion Junior walk-trot horse. He was probably the best three-gaited horse in the country when he lost an eye in a barn accident. After that, he made an incredible comeback as a wonderful equitation horse.*

*Several years ago we had Warlock at the American Royal Riding Finals in Kansas City. One of our owners had bought Warlock for her daughter who was sweet as can be, but just not a brain. Now I never believed in coaching my riders. I'd just slap them on the knee, say, "Have fun, and show me what you know," and then shut up. But I knew this young girl needed help, so I'd gotten a place behind her in the line-up for the workout in the finals medal class. I told her, "Now Susie, it's been a long hard week, and they've worked these horses to pieces. You have three numbers on your back, and when you hear the first two that are like yours, reach back and just tap Warlock with the whip." Now Warlock had never been hit in his life, but I thought, "We've just got to pull out all the stops here." So, Susie's all cocked and primed, they call out her first two numbers, and when she reached back and tapped that horse, he popped his artificial eye out!*

*Well, I was aghast. I leapt into the ring, trying to be unobtrusive and retrieve the eyeball. But the show announcer saw me and yelled into the microphone, "Wait a minute! Helen Crabtree wants to say something." Well, I thought I was going to die. I thought, "Oh, no. He thinks I'm out there trying to tell them how to run their show." That's what it looked like—I really thought I was going to die.*

*Warlock and Susie continued on without his eye. Luckily, the ring master saw it, picked it up, held it behind his back, nonchalantly backed up and passed it off to me. Everybody knew what he was doing. But we had to get it out of there—you know, a four-thousand-dollar eye out in the ring with horses stepping on it wasn't all that great.*

*Another strange thing about that situation…Susie and Warlock had to do a figure-eight. Warlock went out and centered himself, but when Susie gave him the aid, that horse broke out with the loudest whinny you have ever heard. It was very strange—the only vocal horse I'd ever heard in the ring. After that night, whenever he went up to do a figure-eight, he'd always whinny. Very unusual. The last time he showed, he won the World Championship, and he was seventeen years old then.*

Show rings are a literal breeding ground for lessons in humility as well as ability: *When that wonderful Selle Français mare, Quibel, came to us for training,* Macella O'Neill explains, *she was shipped into the Santa Cruz Horse Show the first night of the show. Even as a new ride we just clicked. I loved her to death and felt spectacular on her—she was such a magnificent horse! She jumped so beautifully, she was so well schooled, she had such a great temperament, I was so proud to have her. I felt I was finally worthy of a horse of this caliber—like learning how to handle a Ferrari and then actually getting one—all that exciting.*

*Well, I couldn't wait until Sunday for our first Grand Prix. We entered the arena in an elegant frame, circled smartly, moved into a fabulous sitting trot to cross the diagonal, and I am in Heaven! I could sense the crowd's admiration, and I felt proud, beautiful…perfect. I'm thinking, "This is nirvana."*

*When we arrived at center-ring, as quick as a snake, this magnificent mare reaches out and grabs a huge potted fern and trots the rest of the diagonal with this enormous foliage, complete with terracotta pot, swinging from her mouth. My visions immediately switched from celestial to bestial as my elegant bubble was burst by the crowd's laughter. "Well, there you go…," I thought, "A horse is a horse is a horse, and she's eating the goddam plant…and I can't get her to drop it." I had to stop and pry it out of her mouth—she was like a junkyard dog with a bone. I tell you, horses can pull you back down to earth quicker than gravity! That was just another equine humility check for me.*

It's really hard to stay on those egotistically "high horses" we occasionally put ourselves on when we have down-to-earth horses to throw us off: *If you ride a lot, you're going to have falls,* declares Sam Savitt. *Around here we always ask, "Did you buy property?" Wherever you land, that's your property. Over the years I've become a major property owner. We also have walls named after people who have fallen at them. There's even a Gordon Wright wall.*

*Gordon was doing an article for* SPORTS ILLUSTRATED *entitled, "Forty Years Without a Fall," since it was Gordon's fortieth hunt season and he'd never come off during a hunt. So we were all out hunting, going along nicely, when Gordon's horse went over this stone wall, stumbled, went partially down, and Gordon came off. As he got up, slapping the dirt off him, somebody yelled, "Hey, Gordon, 'Thirty-nine Years Without a Fall?'"*

*You have to have a sense of humor with all of this. Actually it improves your sense of humor because you learn to shrug it off and not dwell on it. Things like that happen all the time, and you laugh about them at the time and afterward.*

*I was riding with my brother one day, and he was behind me. We were going down and ducking through trees and all. I turned around to say something to him, but he wasn't on the horse. He had been scraped off. He was all right. But these things happen all the time. And you know?...that little uncertainty, that little fear, that little risk is enticing. If it was too easy, too safe, it wouldn't be as exciting as it is. You learn about yourself and how big the risks are that you're willing to take. The spontaneity is the adventure.*

Embarrassment, shame, pride, errors, and stupidity are all part of the human condition. Learning to deal with them, improve from them, and balance them out with humor and humility are lessons well learned through *HorsePower!*

## Balanced Ego

Horses do have a way of humbling people in a nanosecond, and that humility helps keep the human ego in balance: *The sooner you can get your ego figured out and tucked away, the better off you are,* states Dennis Marine. *No matter what you're doing, a big ego is not a benefit; it gets in the way. You're bound to ask too much when you're worrying about your ego. You're gonna go out there and conquer whatever in the next forty-five minutes.... That's what you've got in your head that you're gonna go do. The sooner you can get your ego checked and put away, the better off you'll be.*

The human ego is the only power on earth with the imagination, hubris, and delusion to seek perfection. Since absolute perfection is not part of human existence, attempting to achieve it is futile, so we must redefine the quest: *What I've learned with the horses is that it's wonderful to strive for excellence every day—you should do that; you should take such pride in your work that you'd be happy to sign your name to whatever you do,* claims Jane Savoie. *I feel that that's important. And I've also realized that perfection is not attainable. I can strive for excellence and have high goals, but I'm never going to reach perfection, and if I accept that in the horses, I have to learn to accept that in other areas of my life and learn how to be kinder to myself and not so demanding. It's taught me to be more tolerant of myself—and of other people, but mostly of myself. I think perfectionists are harder on themselves than anybody else. So it's allowed me to not have to be perfect. I don't expect my horses to be perfect, and I'm comfortable with striving for excellence and not reaching perfection knowing I'll never get there.* To quote L.D. Burke, *"When you realize you ain't perfect, life eases up."*

*One of the points I try to make in my motivational lectures is that it's great to be the queen of positive attitude, but everyone says, "Well, everything's going so great for you,"* Jane continues. *But it's when things are NOT going so great that you need positive imaging more than ever. And what I find with the horses—and I'm going through a period like that now with Eastwood—is that it's all a game; I call it "Chutes and Ladders." That's basically what it is—you climb up there and in a heartbeat you're down again…you have to learn to go with the flow. You learn to enjoy the highs and not to be destroyed by the lows. And you learn, after you've had a low, to pick yourself right back up and start climbing that ladder again.*

Horses, like life, help keep us in check where the search for perfection is concerned: *There are only two emotions that belong on that saddle when we climb on: one is a sense of humor and the other is patience,* states John Lyons. *All the other emotions, anxieties, frustration…just need to be left in the tack room and not put in that saddle when you get on a horse. Sometimes the ego factor can get out of whack and be a major problem with people and horses. When they say, "Well, I taught him this lesson, he should do it." Well, that's not necessarily the case. A horse is never ever going to be perfect—not even for fifteen minutes is he going to be perfect. And we have to give him room to be imperfect so that we don't ruin the very relationship that we're trying to build. Ask somebody who's been married for fifty years, "Is your husband or wife perfect?" And they say, "No." Then ask, "What if you started asking him to be perfect? What would happen?" "Well, it would ruin the relationship to put that much pressure on them." That's exactly the same thing that happens with horses. A demanding ego doesn't belong on top a horse, just like it doesn't belong in life.… Most people I have found that are exceptional riders and trainers are not people with big egos.*

The arrogant self-importance of egotism may not be desirable in the horse industry, but a healthy balanced ego is a real plus. A person secure in his own abilities and gratified by his life's work realizes that coveted ego balance: *The less of an ego you have, the better off you are,* states Buck Brannaman. *And if you happen to have a big one that you have to live with, it should be your life goal to try and keep it under control. Yet everybody has one…* Yes, we all have an ego. The trick is learning its critical mass, for like a fragile balloon, the pleasing result is lost if it's over-inflated or under-inflated.

*If you're a successful trainer, you don't need an ego,* concurs Curtis Steel. *A person shouldn't let accomplishments go to their head, because about the time you really think you're doing something great is when the bottom falls out.*

*Cowboys don't run big egos,* claims L.D. Burke. *And they don't run big egos because, hey, if you've never been thrown, you never rode. Tomorrow you might be thrown again; I mean, that's very humbling. I don't care how good you are; every day you stand a chance of getting thrown into the bush. Every day.*

## Ego Separation

Another aspect of ego we must consider in order to relate to horses is its state of separation. The term "ego" refers to an individual's ability "to distinguish itself from other selves." This definition presents ego as having a singular focus. In working with a horse, you are always dealing with another being outside yourself. While you must be able to distinguish that otherness, you must also subjugate your individual ego to the alliance of partnership: *To me ego is a place of separation from total self, and that brings us to a state of separation from the horse,* explains Linda Tellington-Jones. *There are some very, very successful egos who have certainly done well in horse circles. They are out there, but to me they're not inspirational. I think there's a way of going beyond ego, beyond the individual, beyond that state of separation by learning to become one with the horse and realizing the high that comes from that. Of communicating with another being—that's where the spiritual side comes in. Being with horses has the potential for being inspirational in our lives...ego doesn't have a place in that inspiration.*

## Life Lessons

Given the fact that humans are ego-driven, lessons from a horse can serve as a valuable ego governor. People who are weakly meek, or arrogantly egotistical, are normally not very successful with horses since horses are most comfortable with people who reside in the calm, confident middle grounds of ego. Having such an equine sounding board can help us recognize, strengthen, and maintain that equilibrium. Horses are wonderful vehicles for developing self-esteem, poise, self-confidence, independence, assertiveness, pride, humor and strength of character in kids, teens, and adults. Horses can lift us up to seek perfection, or dump us in the dust of humility, thereby testing who we are, what we can do, and what we're made of. As L.D. Burke advises: *"Ride tall, He's always watching."* Be proud of yourself and your gift—whatever it is—you are an instrument of God. When you're feeling good about who you are and gratified by what you're doing, you don't need to climb on your high horse to ride tall; all you need is *HorsePower!*

KELLY O'BOYLE, b. 1963, trainer and president of Carpe Diem Enterprises, purchased her Thoroughbred mare, Independent Lady at a racing facility for $1. At the time Lady weighed only 650 lbs and could barely walk since she'd been confined to a stall for two years, without exercise. Kelly brought her back to health and trained her in the sport they both enjoy—dressage. Lady, at her healthy weight of 1100 lbs, relaxes with Kelly in the Georgia shade next to their show sponsor's Hummer.

ADRIAN ARROYO, b. 1978, is a student living in the wine country of Northern California. She has been riding since she was seven and enjoys jumping, competing, caring for horses and helping and training other riders. Adrian is shown at the 1995 Santa Rosa Horse Show on her Thoroughbred mare, Hurricane Shirley.

CAMILLE WHITFIELD VINCENT, b. 1959, after retiring from the show ring settled in California, where she is happily busy caring for a growing family and taking her Saddlebred gelding, Steve, on leisurely trail rides. Camille and her 1979 Ladies Three-Gaited World Champion mare, Elation, are shown at the Olympia International Horse Show in London, 1980.

MAXINE FREITAS, b. 1953, is a counselor and founding director of EquiEd Therapeutic Riding. Maxine was an active rider and horse owner through high school, then re-established her connection with horses later in life while recuperating from breast cancer. She is shown after a schooling class at the West Coast Championships Paso Fino Horse Show in Monterey with her Paso Fino filly, Pistolera.

ALLAN JAMISON, b. 1925, grew up in the steep beauty of northern California's Coastal Mountains. Living with the risks and rewards of mountain ranching Allan became an accomplished horseman, pragmatic administrator and a highly respected rancher. Horses and humans all work hard on a ranch. In this shot—taken during a particularly long and hard cold snap—Allan is on Charlie, a palomino Quarter Horse, preparing to pack vital feed to cattle that are inaccessible by truck.

TINA SCHULER, b. 1976, was 18 and looking forward to college when interviewed for LIVING WITH HORSEPOWER! Riding since she was seven years old, Tina has found riding lifts her spirits and helps her rebalance from a busy school schedule. Tina is pictured with Heron, her riding partner when she was attending college in Maine.

BOBBY CHRISTIAN, b. 1917, has trained, worked and enjoyed farm horses since he was a child. In retirement, Bobby devotes his energies to his hobbies: restoring carriages, training hackney ponies, and teaching neighborhood children values such as responsibility and honesty through horsemanship. The July Fourth parade wouldn't be complete without Bobby driving a carriage with his Hackney, Cocoa, in harness.

CHARLOTTE DICKE, b. 1972, is a publishing assistant who began riding at five years of age and rode English until the spirited Peruvian Pasos won her heart at age sixteen. At nineteen, Charlotte began showing Peruvians and has won a number of championships and national titles. She is pictured on her Peruvian Paso mare, H-S Marinera during a mares gait class at the 1992 National Championships in Reno, Nevada.

# CHAPTER NINE

# PAYBACKS

## Concern and Compassion

*If you learn anything from horses, the very first thing is the give
and take of love.* —*Ron Harding*

Shadows were overtaking the late afternoon sun as the dusty
truck and trailer pulled into the ranger's station at Oregon's Ochoco
National Forest. Chris Hawkins and her husband, Hawk, climbed
out of the cab and shook hands with their friend, forest ranger Joe
Giron. Joe studied the horse in the trailer and commented, "Lookin'
real good, Chris." The jet-black stallion eyed him through the slats
of the trailer, then whinnied loudly. "Seems he knows where he
is, too," Joe added.

"I'm sure he does," Chris replied. "Seven years running free in
these mountains...memories of his harem...he knows where he is,
for sure."

The Hawkinses were returning just a year after helping round
up the first of the wild mustangs to be legally adopted out of
Ochoco. Chris had worked alongside Velma Johnston, ("Wild
Horse Annie") and Joan Blue to win government protection for
America's dwindling herds of feral horses. Her reward was the Wild
Horse and Burro Protection Act of 1971 and then adopting Tajhe
Manache,★ her fabulous wild stallion.

Tomorrow Chris was to receive official title to "Taj" from the

---

★Tajhe Manache, (Ta'he Man ee' che): Comanche for Man with Big Balls, "A Stud"

Secretary of Agriculture of the United States in a ceremony pub-licizing the newly instituted adoption program. The Secretary of the Interior, plus the governors of Oregon and Washington state, were also present to support and endorse this new era of wild horse protection.

"Put your horse in the main corral, Chris, then join us down at the cabin," Joe said. "We'll see you down there."

Chris unloaded Taj and led him into the same corral she had taken him from just twelve months earlier. As she dumped his evening flake into the manger and checked his water supply, she talked to him softly, as a loving mother gives running commen-tary to a tag-along child. When she was finally satisfied that all was right with Taj, and he seemed settled, Chris drove the mile and a quarter to the cabin to join friends and dignitaries who had gathered to honor her, her horse, and the new adoption program.

The next morning Chris awoke before dawn from sheer ex-citement. She quickly dressed and drove to the corral to feed and groom Taj until he glistened. His picture was to be in all the major papers, and she wanted him looking his spectacular best. Chris smiled as she thought of the bold white blaze on his face, which made his ebony glow all the more dramatic.

As the truck swung into the parking area, the headlights scanned the corral. Suddenly Chris's breath left her. The corral was empty. Leaping from the cab, Chris searched all the other pens calling his name. Her cries echoed in the stillness, but no reply came from her beloved stallion. She ran frantically around the compound searching, calling, but finally realized Taj had jumped the fence and returned to the wild. Taj was gone!

"My God, he's left me! How could he?" She felt betrayed and despondent, like a jilted bride—and yet, a part of her understood. "Taj, I know you love me, but if you love your freedom more, I can understand."

With the first rays of the celebration day lighting the sky, Chris climbed numbly into the truck and headed back down to the ranger's cabin. As she drove, Chris realized there was much about Taj that reminded her of what had happened to her people, the Comanche. A wild stallion is not meant to be fenced in; a wild stallion is not meant to be broken; a wild stallion is not meant to be controlled by the United States government. A wild stallion is meant to run free.

The irony hit her hard. Chris had allied and worked with the government so that wild horses would be captured, contained, controlled, and consigned to well-meaning adopters. She knew that government protection on reserves was the only way America's wild horses could escape extermination at the hands of profiteers. But wasn't that nearly the same argument the government had used a hundred years earlier when rounding up Native Americans and confining them to reservations?

At the cabin, Chris stumbled into the tiny bathroom, placed a soaking, cold washcloth on her tear-streaked face, collapsed onto the side of the tub, and wept desperately for Taj, her people, and her own confusion.

After listening to her own ragged sobbing until she was mute, Chris suddenly detected a different sound. She held her breath to listen—a chuckling nicker—she pushed up the pebbled bathroom window and there was Taj! She called his name and ran out to the yard where Taj was waiting for her. Chris saw from the depression in the soft grass that he had spent the night under her bedroom window. Taj had indeed jumped out of the corral, tracked the mile and a quarter down to the cabin and found her bedroom window to sleep under! That night Taj made his own choice; he was no longer a wild stallion. It was then that Chris Hawkins understood that she didn't need a government decree to give her title to Taj—he had given himself to her.

The subject of paybacks—incidents of care, love, or protection that people receive from horses—brings us once again into the shady area of anthropomorphism. Are there situations in which horses actually protect or reward their human charges, or are these simply acts of horses taking care of themselves to the incidental benefit of the rider?

Since horses are by nature wary, sensitive animals with a vigilant eye toward self-preservation and herd safety, caretaking others in the form of parental protection, adoptive foal tending, and herd sentries are vital components of equine society. The question remains, however, do horses transfer those roles to human companions? And if so, do such acts indicate conscious compassion or mindless acts of instinct that humans interpret as heroically other-oriented? (As we know from human experience, the term "hero-ism" is usually assigned to an act of instinct by an appreciative witness or beneficiary—rarely is it the conscious intent of the protagonist.)

This chapter cites situations in which the usually aloof nature of horses melts into something closer to a conscious, connected caring for their human companions. As with Chris Hawkins and Taj, these horsemen and women are convinced that their particular relationships or incidents transcended the gulf of indifference and entered the realm of caring, compassion, and even love. Whether real or imagined, most firmly believe that their horses communicated concern.

## Giving

The scenario of the unridable, crazy horse that suddenly gives himself up to a young rider is the stuff of legend and movies. When such a relationship occurs in real life, it is remarkable: *My daughter had a horse that was a beast,* exclaims Phyllis Eifert. *Everybody around here hated him—just couldn't ride him—they said he was wild, he was awful....Well, we bought him—cheap—took him home, and my daughter showed him well—winning champion or reserve in every show. He loved her, and he did what she wanted him to do. She was a soft rider, and she knew the horse; she had compassion for him, and he had compassion for her—she was the only one he'd behave for. In the end, we ended up having to give him away because no one else could ride him.*

While restricting the gifts of riding and winning solely to a single rider may be unusual, horses frequently single out people they like and those they don't: *In the movie,* BLACK BEAUTY, *there is a pony that plays the part of Merrylegs,* Caroline Thompson reports. *In one scene, Merrylegs runs down a row of stalls and opens all the doors, as horses will do. To film this, the latches on the stall doors had been set up so that the pony could pull the latch clean out, drop it on the ground, and go to the next one, pull that latch and drop it...all the way along. Behind each of those doors a groom was crouching so that after the pony moved on, the now unlatched door would be pushed ajar as if a horse were about to come out of the stall. Well, this pony absolutely detested one of the grooms, (and I didn't like the guy much either). When the pony got to the door behind which that groom was hiding, I watched him hesitate a second, then he pulled out the handle. But instead of dropping the handle on the ground as he had been trained, and had been doing all along, he threw this handle over the door hitting the groom on the head—practically knocking him out. The look in that pony's eye was sheer mischief and merriment!*

A young horse that suddenly lives up to Olympic expectations rewards his rider with gifts of courage, confidence, and accomplishment: *One horse I rode that bailed me out of a lot of trouble— bailed us both out of a lot of trouble—was Better and Better in the Three Day Event at the 1976 Montreal Games,* remarks Michael Plumb. *He was a seven-year-old horse that was not slated to compete, but he was a horse that I had faith in. I had the choice of riding an older, experienced horse, Good Mixture, who I rode to second in the World Championships in '74. I chose the younger horse, I think, just because of his sheer determination, heart, and courage. He jumped around that cross-country course and finished and really didn't have any business doing it. He was green, he was young, and he did it all from heart. It was a gut feeling on my part of which horse to ride, and I happened to be right.*

There are few gifts exchanged between horse and rider more valuable than trust: *When Zapatero and I were at the dressage finals in Orlando, Florida, the temperature suddenly dropped to about fifty-five degrees and it was really windy,* recounts Jane Savoie. *Behind the bleachers were the flags of all the countries. It was a very electric atmosphere as we rode into the arena. The cold wind was whip, whip, whipping the flags, the halyards were pinging against the poles, and Zapatero stopped—he was terrified! I could feel his heart pound through the saddle. I patted him on the neck and said, "You're okay. You'll be okay." Then I literally felt him take a deep breath and accept, "Okay, if you say I'm okay, I guess I'm okay," and off he went. That was such a wonderful moment. That this legitimately scared horse—not knowing what to make of all this— went on for me because I asked and he trusted. He trusted that I would not put him in a situation where he would be threatened, and that's what it's all about.*

Occasionally, that gift of trust transcends expectation and blossoms into total faith. At a clinic in the spring of 1996, John Lyons administered a medicinal injection to his Appaloosa stallion, Bright Zip, to combat a minor respiratory ailment. He had used the same antibiotic on Zip before without incident, but this time, the animal suddenly collapsed and stopped breathing—a victim of anaphylactic shock. John was horrified, believing he'd killed his talented and willing partner of so many years, of so many triumphs. Everyone at the clinic prayed as a veterinarian from the audience worked to save Zip. Miraculously, their prayers were answered and Zip came around. Within a couple of weeks Zip was back doing clinics with John, showcasing his talents of bridleless jumping and cutting—impressing audiences with his fluid response to John's imperceptible cues. It wasn't until days later that John noticed Zip seemed a bit disoriented. Upon examination, it was discovered that at the time of the drug reaction, Zip had been blinded by a stroke. It was only then that John realized the true miracle of their partnership. Zip had been cutting and jumping, not only without a bridle, but without sight (Morel 45). What a gift of trust, faith, and heart! What an incredible horse, and what a special alliance.

## Being Careful

The discussion about whether horses knowingly take care of humans, or are merely looking out for themselves, begins with the observation that any horse could cause major harm to a human handler at any time: *Horses show concern for us all the time,* notes Macella O'Neill. *A gentle horse is the rule rather than the exception. Gandhi laid everybody down in front of the British cavalry because it's known that horses won't step on people. So when a horse does something that is purposefully malicious, that's remarkable; and it makes you realize how careful they are in their everyday lives. There's a gray horse at our barn, Dweezel, that broke his owner's arm—twice—when he was just swinging his head. Now every horse could do that all the time, they're that strong. And if you've ever watched a horse tear a trailer apart, you'd realize that there's nothing that can hold a horse if it doesn't want to be held. They are incredibly strong. So every normal, passive move they take exhibits compassion and caring. That's just part of their nature.*

While the argument can be made that a placid temperament does not indicate conscious concern, another equestrian considers every successful ride indicative of equine generosity and care: *I think anytime that they are kind and nice enough to let us stay on them all the way home, they've saved your life,* states Mary Deringer Phelps.

Yet another rider raises the following question: *I've been in situations where I ended up on the ground and almost all of the horses involved have stopped within a short distance and waited,* notes Doug Lietzke. *They could have run off, but they didn't. And why not? They knew the way back to the barn. Was there some concern? I think so. Yes, I think there is some concern for horse and rider.*

Since injuries can make them easy prey, horses diligently avoid falls: *Some horses take care of riders who aren't that competent,* René Williams states. *That's what I call an insurance horse. My dad always bought the best hunting ponies he could for children to learn on. He bought one pony for the daughter of his wealthy employer, who rode sidesaddle. One day in the hunting field, the pony ducked around a groundhog hole and the little girl went off. Upon hearing of the mishap, the father came to the stable demanding, "You've got to get rid of that pony!" Dad had to explain how much insurance that pony was worth—for avoiding the hole and averting a more serious accident.*

In protecting themselves horses do offer a degree of protection to a rider: *A good fox-hunting horse, a good event horse, has to get you out of trouble over and over and over... but I don't think it's out of compassion,* says Diana Cooper. *I had a snappy, fourteen-one hand pony who taught a lot of pony clubbers how to ride, several of whom went on to become Olympic riders. She's quite famous in this part of the woods. Her name was Miss Muffet, which was a terrible misnomer because it was a cute and cuddly name for a NOT cute and cuddly pony. She was a real hot ticket, one of those bitchy little mares who did not like to cuddle, crossed her teeth impatiently with children, and even ran away with them when she was quite young. Muffie was winning at training level back when training level in eventing was quite a lot more substantial than it is now. In all those years of teaching kids, nobody was ever injured on her even though she was really fast and headstrong, because Muffie looked out for Muffie. She said, "You hold on and do the right thing and we're going to have a good time." She inspired kids to throw their hearts over fences because she'd always be there with them on the other side. The only times she ever stopped was when the child brought her into a fence the wrong way. Muffie was not going to get herself in trouble. If I'm looking to be taken care of, I want a horse who's going to take care of himself. I want him to be clever and quick and balanced. I don't want him to worry about me. I want him to worry about his job. He'll do his job, I'll do my job, and we'll get there together.*

As Diana indicates, riders should constantly strive for the best balance and position possible, for even the most athletic of horses can compensate only so much to avoid harm: *In teaching riding and jumping, I've seen what some of these horses do for people,* Anne Kursinski observes. *Very often when I'm teaching, I'll say, "If I were that horse I would stop and throw you into the jump." This horse is being very nice, you know, he's really taking good care of you. Or, when a rider, who I know can do better, isn't being too conscious, not helping the horse with a jump by putting it to a bad spot until they're almost crashing, occasionally I'll say, "Why don't you get off and I'll push you into this jump a couple of times so you'll know how it feels." Horses really do help people out by helping themselves out. Again, a lot of people think it's owed to them— he's supposed to take care of me—not thank you, thank you for taking care of me.*

There are times when a rider is convinced that their horse helps them out: *I was jumping for the first time in my life on a little pony named High Time,* says Tracy Cole. *I lost my balance over the jump and High Time, feeling the shift, stopped cold on the far side. Now most horses would keep right on going, but High Time stopped and let somebody help me get back in position. He was definitely concerned about what was going on, rather than just charging off and leaving me biting the dust. He died at thirty-five, and I think he's giving lessons in heaven today, he was a real teacher. The horse I ride now, Freckles, is another good teacher because she takes care of any rider who gets up on her. Freckles actually corrects my posting diagonal when it's wrong—I can literally feel her shoving me to the correct diagonal. I never worry about her when I'm on the trail— she's so happy out there, nothing seems to frighten her. (Of course, I say this now and the next time we go out on the trail something totally off the wall will happen.) I've got a lot of trust in her because she's earned the trust.* And Tracy realizes that her *trust* is still not a *guarantee.*

When a horse's actions consistently change under specific circumstances, the resulting pattern can indicate cognizant behavior: *I had a mare, Brandy, who would startle whenever anything was different,* explains Octavia Brown. *The trash can gets moved to a new place and she's saying, "My God, what's that?" When we'd be on the trail, she would shy and jump at every little thing. But as soon as someone with any kind of special needs got near her, you could see a total personality change. She would simply stand quietly for hours if necessary. One time we even put a wheelchair on a picnic table, put her beside it, mounted the person from the picnic table, and that flighty horse never moved a muscle. Part of it was that at those times I was not focused on her; I was focused on some other task. It seemed that her attention went with mine. If my attention was not on her, she'd relax and let happen what happened. But as soon as I was focused totally on her, then my whole body was giving her a different message and she was ready for anything at a much higher pitch. When I was on the job, and she was on the job, all thoughts of playing or responding that way went away; she didn't do it.*

Octavia continues with another example: *When that same horse, Brandy, was only four, she was lying down in the field and I looked up to see my two-year-old son, Duncan, toddling out to her. Now at this point, that young horse was really unpredictable, I had not used her for therapeutic riding at all. Duncan went over to her, sat down and curled up in the middle of her legs. I went out—heart pounding—but walking slowly so as not to alarm, with my hand out saying, "Nice Brandy, stay...." I had never been able to walk up to her and have her stay on the ground; but if she scrambled up with Duncan tangled in her legs, it would be a disaster. As I'm walking, I'm quietly coaxing my son, "Come to Mommy darling; get up, move away." Brandy watched me coming, but waited for Duncan to get up and stagger over to me. When he was well clear, she got up and trotted away. I don't know what caused this flighty filly to just stay there, but I believe horses have an innate sense of the helplessness of other animals.*

Since maintaining balance can be a matter of life or death to a horse, the horse attempts to control it as best he can. When a rider is placed on his back who has no knowledge of cues or balance points, very often the animal will take the initiative to balance: *I know Zodiac babysits beginner riders,* says Kelly O'Boyle. *I've put people on him who can't ride, and he's very careful with them. You can see his stance change. He kind of opens up his legs and balances underneath them as opposed to having them balance on him. Put an advanced rider on him, and he'll give them the ride of their life, too. He will question them and make them ask correctly. Watching those differences—horses are definitely sensitive to who's on them.*

It's obviously important, especially in therapeutic riding, to have horses that will balance up a rider. Some horses are good at this while others are not: *Most of my horses will move under a rider who is unbalanced, but some horses get impatient with that and don't like it,* reports Octavia Brown. *By and large, they want to, because they don't want to be unbalanced, so it's a physical need for this to be a working relationship. If you're going to be on my back, let's balance this out. But you can see some horses do it better than others.*

With an untrained or disabled rider giving no discernible cues to a horse, the horse may take over the balance and action. When a rider is on board giving conflicting or harsh cues, the horse may become confused, agitated, or resistent. This could explain the equine personality changes evident with riders of varying skills: *As we advance, we tend to push our horse, then that horse has to think harder,* notes Bob Douglas. *He has to think more about his balance and foot placement. He has to think whether you are asking him to do this, or are you asking him to do that? A rider can unwittingly ask his horse different things at the same time, then the horse decides which to respond to. If he picks the one you didn't know you were asking, that's when you can get in trouble. I think horses are extremely intelligent and want to please, and I think it is very easy for man to confuse them.*

## Caretaking

Perhaps the most striking examples of equine caretaking are those where the horse has a clear opportunity *not* to perform well, yet does: *One year my wife judged the dressage event of the Special Olympics in Minneapolis,* relates William Steinkraus. *When the dressage ring was set up, the installer failed to put a functional gate at "A" that could be shut after the riders were in the ring, so the ring was left open. These contestants, some of whom didn't even recognize their own name, were doing this dressage test on quite a variety of horses. All those horses knew they could go out of the ring anytime they felt like it. Only one of them even thought about it. He got about half way out and then came back in. You could see that these horses were making a real effort. I had the distinct feeling that if something happened the horse would make it right. They understood the problems of the riders and were not taking advantage of them. I remember thinking at the time of all those cowboy stories of horses coming back and rescuing their riders.... Most horses want to be good horses and are truly very generous.*

In the frenetic excitement of a harness race, a Standardbred's good behavior saved her driver from greater harm: *One time I got dumped out of the sulky in a race,* Irving Pettit reports. *I fell off the cart, kept a hold of the lines with one hand, and tried to protect myself with the other, and broke my arm. Now that horse stopped and stood there, she didn't try to run away which most of them will do in a race. A lot of horses would drag you on, but she stopped right away and stayed. There are not too many race horses that mild-mannered; they're inclined to want to run with the others.* Mild-mannered, well-trained, or concerned? The specific motive may not be important, for the fact that she stopped and held her ground against the field of horses gave Irving the protection of the larger sulky-with-horse hazard for the others to avoid, creating an oasis of protected space.

*I do think that horses can have a genuine concern for the rider,* states Jill Hassler. *I fox hunted as a kid, and one time jumping a wire fence, the horse got caught in the wire and we went down. The horse flipped and rolled on top of me. To this day I carry the mental snapshot of that horse on top of me. My elbows were on the ground, I was holding my hands up and the whole horse was on my hands, but I did not break a bone! That horse had to deliberately make an effort when he was rolling over not to crush me. There are times that you do get hurt by a horse, but definitely, that horse tried hard to avoid hurting me. That's my feeling.*

I'd had my mare, Freddie, for almost a year when we popped a jump, I was unseated, and came down on her neck. Freddie leapt sideways, and I was off. I landed flat on my back, and the wind was knocked out of me, so I couldn't get up. At first, Freddie ran around the ring, but when my instructor caught her, the horse dragged the instructor over to me. When Freddie reached me, she sniffed and nickered around me, nudging me to get up like she would a newborn foal, showing genuine concern. Kelli said she'd never seen anything like it before, but thought her reaction was a result of Freddie having had foals. She wanted me to get up to prove that I was okay. It was a very maternal reaction.

A legendary, elder horseman told me of a special training session he once gave: *A gal I know had a stroke when she was twenty years old and lost the use of her right side so she had to be boosted onto her horse. Well, she thought maybe if somebody could get her horse to kneel she could get on by herself. I told her the horse would lie down for her to get on. If her horse lies down on his right side, since it's her right side that is paralyzed, she could put her left leg over and get on. She hadn't thought of that; she hardly believed it. Her horse was fairly easy to get started, only took about twenty minutes to get him to lay down that first time; then the gal and her trainer got him trained over time. It worked real well for her.*

*About two years ago, she was getting ready to go on a trail ride with some other riders. Now this gal likes to visit, and while she was visiting with someone, the others were taking off. I was back a little ways just watching what was going on. While she's visiting, her horse was watching the other horses leave, and he's kind of moving around waiting for her— she had her back to him. It wasn't too long 'til that horse laid down right behind her. Then he moved a little and bumped her leg to get her attention. So she finished her conversation and got on.*

*Another thing about that horse—if other horses came too close, he would move off—he drew a line there to let them know. It was like a mother mare taking care of a foal, he took possession of her. It was so obvious that he understood—and that gal had been advised to get rid of that horse.... Now not all, but a lot of horses, like this one, seem to understand that younger children or handicapped people are at the mercy of a situation.*

Since horses are concerned with and do protect one another—the stallion and sentries safeguard the herd and mares protect foals—the concept of caretaking and protection is a part of their nature. It seems clear that some horses apply that same concept to the humans in their life: *One time my wife and I were doctoring cattle on our ranch, relates* John Lyons. *I had broken my lower leg, and had a cast on it from my knee down. When you're a rancher, it's hard to take time off—you even have to work on Christmas Day—you need to go out and feed those cows no matter what. So I was roping the calves and then my wife would get off her horse and go over and doctor the calf—give it pills, or shots, or whatever it needed. Susie was riding a black Morgan/Quarter cross mare, Misty. We're in a hundred-acre pasture, and if I was standing at north and the calf was at south, then a little bit farther south was the momma cow, probably another forty yards away. Misty was standing at northeast and she's ground-tied. The cow starts coming in closer and closer to my wife, wanting to protect her calf, acting like she's going to come stomp my wife into the ground. Now the mare is off by herself—a good thirty feet from me, a good forty-five feet from my wife, and sixty or seventy feet from this cow—she walks over on her own and cuts that cow off. Then everywhere that cow goes, Misty kept that cow away from my wife while she was doctoring that calf. That's a horse with cow sense and people sense. Horses are super.*

An action that goes against the very nature of the animal is a dramatic example of protection: *Several years ago there were fires in Griffith Park on the other side of the park from where I ride, recalls* Caroline Thompson. *My horse Chester and I were up on the top of one of the trails when suddenly a helicopter came around the corner, taking water to the fire. It was traveling at about the same level that we were. Chester took one look at this strange thing coming around the corner, and he reared up and charged it. Horses are usually flight animals, not fighters, and I've seen Chester spooked by the silliest things, but this day he was feeling protective. He is such a character; I think he would have been happy as a cavalry horse.*

There are times that a mounted officer has no doubt that his horse understands and practices the concept of protection: *One Fourth of July in Washington, D.C., there was a fight going on at the Washington Monument grounds,* reports Lt. Carl Clipper. *As I was breaking that up, a person came running up and said a gang was coming through armed with a sawed off shotgun, robbing people. I was on a seventeen-hand horse, Midnight Dancer. When we got there, the gang took off running, so we chased them. There were nine of them; we pursued for about a quarter of a mile, and caught all of them. When we came up on the one with the gun, he was turning toward us, and Midnight Dancer ran right over him. That same night, there were other fights and that horse kept putting himself right in between me and trouble. He protects me all the time. Then you'll get some dummy that's trying to mess with your horse and then you protect him.*

## Connection

Such a belief in mutual caring sets the foundation for various ways of connecting that bind relationships: *For years I didn't believe that horses could love you back,* Ron Harding admits. *But my wife, Beth, said, "Those horses love you, Ron." I said, "Nah, they don't love me. They just want me out there feeding them." But then I started watching, and some of them do love me. They do have that feeling. I've got a little filly I'm training called DanDee, because she is a dandy and she's out of the Quincy Dan bloodline. Now, all of my horses, when I throw their hay out, they go to it; they want their feed. But I'll throw DanDee's hay into her tub and she won't go to it until I pet her. She wants to talk to me before she does anything. This filly has some kind of an affinity to me. She wants to see me. When they're drawn to you, you're kind of drawn to them a little bit. If you learn anything from horses, the very first thing is the give and take of love. You love me; I love you. Sometimes it takes a lot of loving before they love you back, but once you gain their trust... Love, that's the first lesson.*

Connection tunes us in to one another: *I've gone out to work with my horse when I had not been feeling well, and Star was particularly more sensitive to me because he knew I was not feeling well,* says Pat Lawson. *He chilled out and decided he would be easy that day because I was not feeling well. There have also been times when I wasn't in my best form and Star made allowances for it. His skill rose where mine fell to try and complete the goal.*

Connection is enjoying just being with one another: *My horse had a great personality,* claims Amy Hubbard. *He'd just roam around free—no pasture, nothing. He'd always come back. He never ran off. He'd come up to the back door looking for carrots. It was like we understood each other and had communication.*

Physical connection encourages caretaking: *Brian, a learning-disabled kid in our summer therapeutic program, was a tough-guy leaning toward gang associations,* Maxine Freitas relates. *The first day of class, he was wearing real long, baggy gang-banger pants with his defiant "I'm not gonna change my clothes" attitude. Since he didn't like his pants dragging in the dust and dung, he went around all day hiking up his pant legs. When we taught the class how to approach a horse, Brian saunters up to the horse and goes, "Hey, dude." This kid needed an attitude adjustment, so we asked him to start grooming the horse. He went at it with a vengeance until I told him their skin is very sensitive, so you have to go gently. With that, he turned his hand to the back side and started stroking the horse. Another teacher was watching and at that moment, with that small physical connection, it was like a veil was lifted. Brian softened in front of our eyes. The rest of the time there was no attitude. Touching that horse touched his heart and softened his being.*

*In order to continue in the program, the kids have to fill out forms; Brian was the first one to return his forms the next day. By the end of the four-week session, he was side-walking for kids who were less able, and he was in heaven. He found that he had something of value to offer others. This is a four-week program—not a lot of time—but in that time Brian went through an incredible change. I deal with kids all day long as a school counselor, and I have never been able to effect that kind of change in my office. Never. Most therapeutic riding programs do not have time for the kids to do the grooming. But I think that tactile connection, for many of the kids who are not touched at home, is the most important part. They have a big animal that they can make pretty, see the results of their efforts, and in that process, they are touching this warm, living creature who is not judging them.*

Empathic connection can help heal: *When I worked at the local hospital, one of my patients, Gary, had been a rodeo rider,* Maxine Freitas continues. *He was also a roofer who'd fallen forty feet, suffered major brain trauma, and is now in a wheelchair. He had owned horses, but when he was hospitalized, he'd had to sell them. He asked if he could watch me ride. So I had his physical therapist bring him over to the house. I was a little concerned when I brought my Paso Fino mare out because she is bonkers most of the time and she'd never been around a wheelchair, but it didn't bother her at all. Gary has a hard time speaking, so I brought her over close to him. She walked right up and put her head on his chest. I couldn't believe it! Then Gary took the brush from me and just started brushing her. Horses are pretty powerful medicine.*

Silent connection can foster compassion: *When I'm in a time of need, I go to a horse,* states Jill Hassler. *Horses have genuine compassion; they take us as we are and don't put any expectations on us. If you want to laugh or cry, it's okay, they're there. Horses don't try to inject anything into your venting whereas people tend to feel they can't just be there. This has taught me a lesson about just being there for other people instead of feeling like gee whiz, if I'm here, I should be contributing. But just being there...now I can just be there for someone—in total silence. If asked, I will respond; but I rarely inject what I think I should be saying anymore. This ability is a direct outgrowth of my being with horses and their silent compassion. I think true compassion means that you're available to give a person the support they want, not what you think they need. That's been a good lesson for me.*

Profound connection inspires strength: *I made a lot of money in the movie industry, did very well for about five years, and put it all back into very expensive horses,* remarks Rex Peterson. *Then I went through a divorce. I came home one day, and it was all gone. I only had one horse left, my big paint horse, Hell on Wheels. He pulled me through a time in my life that I didn't know from one day to the next if I was going to be here, or what I was going to do. Not everybody has a horse like that. That's why I say I've been very fortunate. I guess that's why I spent so much money saving his life. I really believe if it hadn't been for him I wouldn't be here today. He honest to God saved my life on several occasions where I was ready to give up. We sat and had a lot of long talks and a lot of tears flowed. Because of that, I fought as hard as he the day he almost died. I sat right there in the operating room all night with him while they saved his life.*

*The vet said, "This horse means a lot to you...."*

*"Yeah, he does." I don't think anybody knows what this horse means to me, not my wife, nobody, knows what this horse means to me. He's an outstanding horse, but I've ridden other horses that are better than him in*

*a lot of things. He's well worth the money I spent on the vet bill on him, that's for sure, maybe not to anybody but me. He's the one horse I had left, and I still have him today. When I lose him, it's going to be very hard on me, I realize that. He is a great counselor; I think that's one thing that all horses are. Horses can counsel the most inexperienced rider to the greatest rider. . . . Why? I have no idea.*

## Paying Back

The give and take of the equestrian relationship is constant and uneven. There is no ledger in which one records debts owed for services rendered. Each gives what they can and takes as they need: *I bought Chester off the trail for $300; I just liked the look on his face,* notes Caroline Thompson. *He turned out to be an incredible athlete who really loves working and playing. He's an amazing animal just in terms of character, and he has such a sense of fun. He's been like one of the best buddies I've ever had. I had to retire him, which breaks my heart, but I did that for him. I remember a [Hollywood] producer asked me how long I thought the horse would live and how much it was going to cost me. I don't care; this is not about money.* Indeed it's not about money—it's about paybacks.

Since paybacks are gifts given and received without expectation, they may arrive in surprising circumstances: *Jeannie Scoggins was a girl who rode with me for years, and when she was eleven years old, her horse died in the middle of a horse show,* says Richard Shrake. *Well, we found a new horse for her, called The Highwayman. This horse had never been shown; he was just being broke. We were preparing him for his first show, the Pacific International. Jeannie was staying with us the week before the show, because this was going to be her horse's first outing. Just before the show, I got a call from Jeannie's mom; she said, "Richard, Dave died. He just went to the hospital and three hours ago we lost him."*

*I was in total shock. Number one, it was the hardest thing I've ever done in my life, to tell this little girl her dad had died. That was tough. Jeannie asked, "Would you please take The Highwayman on to the show?" And I said, "Sure." Then she grabbed my hand and said, "Richard, would you win this one for Dad on The Highwayman?"*

*Well, I was stuck—now, how do you go win a class on a horse that's never been shown, in a ring where they've got rodeo events on one end and this is a major AHSA* [American Horse Shows Association] *A-rated show? How do you just go win it? Well, we showed the horse. The very first time he was in the ring he won the open, came back and won the championship—the first three classes he had ever shown. Now, I'll tell you, that was an eerie feeling because this horse had no right to do that well that quick and beat that competition, but he did. He won the whole thing. That horse came through.*

Paybacks don't always come directly from the horses themselves: *I've been retired over twenty years, yet I have never been idle,* notes recreational Hackney Pony driver, Bobby Christian (p. 203). *My interest is children, and I go through the horses to get to the children. With these ponies and the children they attract, I'm expanding my life and theirs. I'm very sensitive to raising children right. I think that's our duty in life: to lead them. I teach them about duty. I never let them leave the barn until everything is in place—the brushes, the combs, the bridles—everything. A parent told me the other day, "Little Lynn comes home and teaches her sister, 'Now you must put that back.'" So you see, I feel that I'm doing some good. Another parent told me they would like me to be their child's godfather in case something happened to both of them. Those are the things—the invisible rewards—that are important to me.* Bobby's ponies give him the opportunity for connecting with children and their families in a meaningful and mutually beneficial way.

In her attempt to gratefully pay back the horses in her life, Anna Sewell touched off an international movement for humane treatment of animals: *Anna Sewell was a lifelong cripple who got around in a pony cart,* relates Caroline Thompson. *When she was in her forties or fifties, she was given eighteen months to live, so she decided to write a thank you to the animals who'd looked after her her whole life. It took her six years to write the book,* BLACK BEAUTY. *It's the only book she ever wrote; it's beautifully written and makes the point that a horse is a sentient creature, a creature with feeling, as alive as humans are.*

*Clearly, a hundred years ago, being a horse was probably not the greatest thing in the world, for people were inclined to treat horses as machines. They needed them to be their machines. Until the 1830's carriages were heavy and had to be drawn by big draft horses. Through the middle part of the nineteenth century, technology improved and lightened carriages, bringing finer-boned animals into harness. As aesthetics became increasingly important, wealthy owners jacked their horse's head up in bearing reins to achieve the proud look they considered so appealing. This high head position was extremely hard on horses in harness, especially when pulling uphill. Anna Sewell wrote about this abuse in* BLACK BEAUTY *and as a result a law was passed limiting the use of bearing reins. Because of her book, watering troughs for the cab horses were installed throughout London and homes were established for retired horses. BLACK BEAUTY had a phenomenal impact. Sadly, Anna Sewell died shortly after its publication and did not live to see the impact her book had on humane treatment of animals all over the world.* Not only was Anna Sewell's book a wonderful payback to her equine companions, BLACK BEAUTY became a catalyst for the creation of humane ideals and humane societies around the globe.

Jane Savoie wrote her book, THAT WINNING FEELING!, to share the skills she employed to enhance her riding career. The paybacks from her audience have been widespread and heartfelt: *The most rewarding thing about my book is the people that are touched by it,* says Jane. *I had a letter from a lady going through chemotherapy, who used techniques from my book to help her. I've had people starting off in business call to say that my book helped them. Three days ago I had a message on my machine from a lady who said, "You don't know me. I'm just somebody from Pennsylvania, but I want you to know that I bought your book a while ago, and I've read it many times, and I've got your videotapes, and I can't tell you the difference it's made, not only in my riding, but in my life." Then she started crying on the phone, and said, "I just wanted to thank you from the bottom of my heart..." and she hung up. I can't tell you what that means to me.*

Books are not the only way to acknowledge an equine payback: *I want to read this letter,* said Bob Douglas. *It is a very short letter, but it's a very, very important letter received by one of our riding instructors, dated February 4, 1994: "Dear Joan, Thank you very much for teaching me how to ride Buster. Buster is a good horse. Buster was very good. Tell Buster I am now getting out of Special Ed."*

Buster is a very good horse, indeed: we met Buster earlier when he inspired the young autistic boy to speak in Chapter Six. *Buster is an interesting horse; he has only one eye due to an accident, so he's also disabled,* notes Bob. *He's had to regroup, but he still jumps, and seems extremely happy.* It appears Buster gives a great deal to his therapeutic riding charges.

## Life Lessons

Obviously every incident between horse and human is open to interpretation, so it is impossible to know conclusively whether a horse is acting out of self interest or caring for another. And does motive really matter? Since the human experience is a product of personal belief systems, if people believe that their animals acted out of concern, protection, or love, isn't that perceived payback valuable in and of itself? Whether the above examples are fact or fantasy, intention or interpretation, they remain meaningful lessons of caring, concern, compassion, connection, protection, and courage—through *HorsePower!*

# CHAPTER TEN

# SAYING GOODBYE

## Empathy, Letting Go, Death

*If heaven don't have horses, I ain't goin.'*
*— © L. D. Burke III, Santa Fe*

*God gave us the gift of tears... —Dale Evans*

The somber parade made its way down Pennsylvania Avenue to the slow measured pace of military drums. The only being out of step in the long procession was a lone black horse. Unable to vent his energy or control his anxiety, the nimble creature danced nervous jigs around his handler. His athletic vitality was in sharp contrast to the mute, stunned throngs gathered along the route.

The horse was saddled and bridled, but carried no rider, only a pair of empty dress boots turned backwards in the stirrups. A mournful symbol of loss—the riderless horse, tacked up, yet unmounted. This was but another soul-touching confirmation that America had lost her beloved president. A man who, in spite of chronic back pain, was so full of "vim and vigor" himself that he had ignited the flame of national pride, infusing Washington, D.C., with the dynamic spirit of Camelot. He created the Peace Corps and inspired citizens to ask what they could do for their country. John F. Kennedy was assassinated during the honeymoon of his term, and the entire country mourned along with his elegant widow and their impossibly young children.

The mental snapshots that have remained with me from that day of national mourning are many, but aside from little John-John saluting his father's flag-draped coffin, the image that is burned into the memory book of my mind is that beautiful, confused black horse—all tacked up and riderless.

## Moving On

Loss is perhaps the most difficult life lesson to accept or comprehend. Often a young rider's beloved first horse or pony becomes the object of his initial lesson in loss: either through progression to a better horse, the sale or retirement of the animal, or its death.

The loss of any loving relationship is hard to bear, but when it came time to sell my first equine love, Freddie, I did not foresee the emotional toll that it would exact. We had been together almost four years—years of mutual learning in which Freddie was transformed from a sullen beast to a willing jumper, while I went from equitation on the flat to courses over fences. For the last two years, however, I was becoming increasingly apprehensive, while Freddie became stronger and more imperious. I'm still not sure whether my budding fears were a reaction to Freddie's growing dominance, or the cause of it. At any rate, we were no longer a great team: we couldn't even complete a short course of jumps without the mounting tensions in both horse and rider leading to an ugly scene. Like long-term sweethearts who fail within marriage, we were still warmly affectionate on the ground, yet desperately incompatible under saddle. Both of us needed a change.

Even placing Freddie's name on the sales list was difficult, for I had never sold a friend before—and that's what we were—best friends who got along well in all areas except work. I expected a local rider would fall in love with my beautiful chestnut mare as I had, and I'd be able to visit and keep up with her progress. Then I got the call.

My trainer, Macella, said, "My friend, Lynn Lloyd, is here and adores Freddie. She's a terrific horsewoman. She's ridden horses across the United States—literally—ridden from coast to coast. I've known her a long time and Freddie couldn't find a better home."

I was thrilled by such a glowing endorsement, for my first priority was a good situation for Freddie. "Okay," I said, after a moment's consideration, "Let's do it."

"Fine," said Macella. "Lynn lives in Nevada and wants to take her home today. Do you want to come over and say goodbye to Freddie?"

That's when it hit me: "Say goodbye to Freddie..." suddenly it echoed hollow and final.

I grabbed some carrots and raced to the barn trying to control my tears. "Say goodbye to Freddie." I really hadn't expected those words to have such an impact.

I met Macella and her friend at the barn. By then, all I could do was apologize for my bawling. Lynn was kind and understanding. I went into Freddie's stall, gave her hugs and carrots and left after signing the necessary papers—still crying hysterically. As I drove out of the yard, I pulled off the road to watch as they led Freddie to the trailer. Freddie calmly walked up the ramp, and out of my life.

I cried for three days straight, and pined for weeks. The depth of my despair shocked me. It wasn't as if Freddie had died—she was going to a good home—yet I simply could not dispel my sadness. Ultimately I realized that these were more than tears of loss; they were also tears of regret, remorse, and failure. Regret at *having* to sell Freddie, remorse that I lacked the abilities to have made our partnership work, and the feeling I'd failed both Freddie and myself.

A month later, a large envelope with a Reno, Nevada, return address arrived. Inside a letter from Lynn described how she loved Freddie and what fun they were having hunting (Lynn is Master of Foxhounds for the Red Rock Hunt). This was obviously a heavenly match, for Freddie had always come alive on trail rides, whereas arena work seemed to bore her to distraction.

Enclosed with the letter was a fantastic photograph of Freddie with Lynn in her scarlet jacket returning from a hunt leading a pack of hounds. They looked absolutely regal, and Freddie was literally *smiling*. I was so happy for her...I cried.

I thought a large part of my reaction, or over-reaction, was due to the fact that this was my first horse, my first sale, my first failed partnership, my first equine loss. I soon learned, however, that amateurs are not the only ones who have a hard time saying goodbye to their teammates: *This last year with Starman was very difficult,* declares Anne Kursinski. *He was still relatively sound—he wasn't limping, he was still galloping and jumping—but I know what it takes to go around the Olympic games, and so did he. I didn't think he could really be an international show jumper anymore. I knew in my heart that it was time to let go. We kept him around about a year, and he got a little better. I competed him in Palm Beach, Florida, but then we retired him to California to breed. That was very hard, but a very good lesson because it's about honesty and what's best for the horse. It's also about being thankful and appreciative for all he'd done for us, then moving on to something new and positive. The day I retired Starman in Palm Beach we had a ceremony. Then Eros, who was coming along, was second and third in probably the biggest grand prix of his life. With that, Starman's retirement took on a more spiritual end—with each ending, there is a new beginning—Starman was going out, Eros was coming in....*

Neither my loss nor Anne's was terminal; we both knew our horses were going to good situations, yet there was still a palpable sadness at the closing of particularly memorable chapters of our lives.

*Three months ago I retired a horse that had been on the beat with the same officer, in the same barn, for eighteen years,* reports Lt. Carl Clipper. *We took him to a ninety-two acre grass farm for his retirement life. As we drove away, that horse came trotting down the fence line following after our trailer. Within the first month the officer was down three times to visit him....* Even the best of retirements can be a difficult adjustment.

*When we came home from the Tokyo Olympics,* [eventing champion] *Grasshopper was seventeen or eighteen years of age,* notes René Williams. *We kept him a year, then it was decided to ship him to his owner's place out in California and retire him. I argued that it would be so much better to keep him here* [in New Jersey] *and give him to some boy or girl in the neighborhood so he or she could hunt him and keep him happy. No, that wouldn't do, it was decided, he had to go into retirement. Within six months, he was dead. They say he got colic, but I think he pined away; I think he died of a broken heart. I guess when you're associated with animals as much as I've been, they get pretty human to you—most of them.*

## Sudden Death

Sudden death is the most sinister of losses: it ambushes, shocks, and stuns, supplanting security with cruel reminders of how tenuous life truly is. On May 27, 1995, my husband Kip's birthday, we'd decided to take a short trail ride before turning our attention to dinner preparations. We enjoyed a peaceful ride up the mountain to a neighboring vineyard, down through the redwood groves, then along a narrow path still scarred from the driving March rains with deep crevices in the rusty clay soil.

Suddenly Haji stumbled off the trail into one of the clefts and went down on all fours. I managed to stay on as he quickly scrambled up, but when we took stock, Kip said, "He's not putting weight on his left hind leg; you'd better get off." I jumped down and examined Haji's leg: the gaskin felt warm, but thankfully, there didn't seem to be any broken bones. I loosened the girth, and we began a solicitous walk back to the barn.

After stripping off the tack, I offered Haji his post-ride carrot; he wouldn't take it. In the six years we'd had him, Haji had never refused a carrot.... I phoned our vet. He was not on call that weekend, and his replacement was on an emergency; the woman at the exchange promised he'd call as soon as possible.

I groomed Haji, and put him in his stall to minimize movement, then went to shower. Checking on him forty minutes later, he seemed listless. I called the vet's exchange again; still no doctor available. I rubbed his neck and told him to buck up; it was only a sore leg and we'd get him some good medicine and a nice massage as soon as the vet took a look at him. I went in to fix dinner. Our guests arrived and I excused myself to check on Haji once again.

This time—just an hour and a half after our return to the barn—Haji looked horrible: he could barely stand. I called the exchange again and insisted they find someone to help. I phoned my trainer and left a message on her machine; I called our friends with horses and left messages on their machines. Haji was obviously in serious trouble—but WHY? I phoned the veterinary exchange again and asked if our vet's wife was available. "Yes, but she's a small animal vet," said the woman. "She knows horses—put me through!" I demanded.

As it turned out, our vet, though not on call, was home. As I explained what happened, I watched Haji go down, then try to struggle to his feet. The vet said, "Try to keep him calm and lying down, but stay away from his hooves. I'm on my way." I went to where Haji now lay flat out. Kneeling beside him, I stroked his ivory neck, then lifted his head onto my lap. His eyes were wild. He tried to get up, but I held his head and he didn't have the strength to fight the leverage. I quietly caressed and talked, telling him the vet would soon be here and he'd be all right. After all, it was just a little fall, nothing broke, he'd be fine.

Shortly his breath started rattling and his eyes lost their focus. I screamed for Kip to come. Haji's legs were doing the loping death dance, only we didn't recognize it as such. As his breathing became weaker, Kip and our guest began what they imagined equine CPR to be: rhythmically pressing on Haji's chest to force out the bad air, let in the good...they were still working when the vet arrived, but Haji's eyes had clouded....

Dead! How could that stumble kill him? He didn't even break a bone—what happened? I was confused and inconsolable. Why had he *died?* The vet took out a syringe and plunged the needle into Haji's abdomen. "There it is," he said indicating the syringe, now full of blood.... "Abdominal aneurism. He bled to death internally. That may have been what caused the fall, or in the scramble to get up, the aneurism tore. It's not common, but it happens."

So that was it. In less than three hours, our beautiful, funny, personable Haji had expired due to a burst blood vessel.

As with the adage, "Time flies when you're having fun," time spent with the few very special horses in our lives always seems too short: *When I was just a squirt, Dad had a little mare he called "Belle,"* Dennis Marine recounts. *You talk about one that was willing and good-minded! One morning he went to get her out of the pasture.... Well, she'd got kicked, and it just about took her leg off, so Dad had to shoot her. That was the first...(his voice breaks). It still affects me...you see, it's never the ones...there are some horses that are just plain dinks...but it's never those; it always seems to be the outstanding ones.*

*I don't know if I'd say that death hardens you, but it makes you look at things pretty practically. That just goes with farm or ranch life and growing up. Nothing lasts forever.... Never say "never" and never say "always" 'cause it will make a liar outta ya.' You can't help but get a little attached to the really good ones in your life, but keep in mind nothing's permanent...There are lots of good horses, but the outstanding ones...it always seems to go by so fast with them. The less they are, the longer they seem to go—dinks seem to last forever.*

Horses constantly present us with unanticipated twists in life and death: *One horse I rode, Buddy, was a fourteen-year-old sweetheart; I had a real good relationship with him,* remarks Tracy Cole. *He was western-trained and very comfortable—this horse could go from a jog to a lope, and you'd never know he'd changed gaits. He had a stone bruise, so I hadn't been riding him recently, though I was definitely expecting to start back where we left off when he recovered. But the next thing I heard he was dead! Somehow he'd got out and was struck by a car. That was the first one that really put me over the edge: "What do you mean he got hit by a car? He can't be dead!" That was the worst....*

At times even the best of intentions and care may prove fatal: *My wife, Judy, and I have lost several good horses, but the hardest death we've had was my wife's favorite mare that we'd raised from birth,* notes Curtis Steel. *She'd just had a colt, and I gave her a shot of penicillin; Judy was to give her the second shot the next day. When she did, the horse had a reaction and fell over dead. Why it didn't happen when I gave her the first shot—it might have reacted somewhere else, but it didn't react to her heart... We raised her colt from a doggie, and we've still got it here.*

*That same spring, another mare had a colt,* adds Curtis. *Judy had checked it and everything was all right. Judy went back down an hour later and the colt was outside the pen with its neck broken. It had got out under the pen, panicked, tried to get back in, and broke its neck. So Judy had two real horrible experiences that year and it took her a while to get over it. That one mare that died from the penicillin reaction she was awful crazy about.... My wife has a hard time because she's really close to her animals.... But you know, you got to own 'em to lose 'em and if you own enough of them, you're gonna lose some—it's gonna happen.*

As mighty as modern medicine is, even the most competent professionals are reminded daily of the limitations of human endeavors: *When I was twelve I rode a champion barrel-racing mare named Lillie's Star,* says Dr. Patty Latham. *In the spring of that year she foaled, but because she had competed so heavily she did not produce a lot of milk, and the foal was not real vigorous. I spent every afternoon after school and every weekend with that foal. She would lay down and take her naps with her head in my lap. Unfortunately, when the foal was about four months old, my dad's job required that we move back to California. I thought I was going to die. Then the rancher gave me the foal. I named her Lillie Too, and that horse went everywhere with me. My poor parents dragged that horse around with them from Missouri to California, to Texas, to*

*Colorado, and back to California. She went to vet school with me. She taught all my kids how to ride. When she was about twenty-three she was injured in a trailer accident: part of the window in the front door of the trailer snapped, blew open, and when Lillie jumped back, her foot went through the trailer wall severing most of the tendons. We tried surgery and corrective casting for about two months, but we could not get her comfortable, so we ended up putting her down. As vets, we have to deal with death on a pretty regular basis, understand it, and accept it.*

*My philosophy is that quality of life is the most important factor that we have, so death is almost a gift if there is no quality of life. I don't want to die in a hospital. If I cannot be out with the animals, if I didn't have any music...if I were just a vegetable, I would definitely not want to be alive. My kids believe in that also. Having grown up with us, they have seen a lot of severe traumas. None of them react at all to blood, and they've all been in the office when I've had to put an animal down. They've watched autopsies and have become scientifically interested. But I have not seen any reduction in compassion because of that...they still cry with us.*

While sudden death highlights our own mortality, it can also lead us to build the emotional reserves needed to persist in the face of devastating loss: *To tell you the truth, sometimes it's harder for me to accept one of my horses dying than it is to accept a person,* admits Jimmy Fairclough. *I guess that's because of the one-on-one relationship and the training time I have with the horses. I train seven days a week with them, except in November and December when they get six weeks of R&R. The rest of the year, especially in the height of the season, I work some of them two to three hours a day. I become very dedicated to them, so when I lose one, it's hard to accept.*

*Right before the World Championships I had a tremendous, young, together group of horses—we had won the gold medal in Austria—but then Avedon died of colic. Then another really good back-up horse was turned out in the field, rolled, twisted up, kicked, and broke its hind leg. We tried to save him, but we couldn't, and I had to put him down. Then the last selection trial before the pair championships in '93, another horse herniated his stomach wall. We didn't know it until the small intestine slipped through the hole and he died. I had to replace him in the championships with a horse I had only driven in one small, mini-competition. What all that's taught me is to get up the next day and deal with what I've lost, then try to rebuild to go on. You have to go on in life, there's no doubt about it. But it's hard to accept. None of it's easy.*

And some circumstances are more brutal than others: *My father was always a tough guy: he was a horseman who timber-raced, foxhunted, showed, and evented,* Michael Plumb reports. *I guess he taught me to be strong, and I think I am. But I feel sad for horses when they're hurt—when they have a broken leg, or neck, or a broken back—they're entirely helpless, and it's pitiful. It's tragic. I suppose people are helpless in those situations, too, but I feel more sorry for horses because we've put them in harm's way for our sport. And when they give it 100% and fall or have an accident, then you feel responsible. If they have a heart attack and die trying for you, doing their best for you, it gets hard to be tough like my father taught me to be.*

*In 1964, I went to the Olympics in Tokyo. I had a very good horse, Markham, who had been raised by my family and was the first horse I rode internationally. I rode him in my first Olympics, in Rome in 1960, when I was eighteen and neither one of us knew anything. Tokyo was to be our second Olympics. Horses don't get to successive Olympic Games very often. For Markham to come back and be competitive four years later was quite an accomplishment.*

*Markham had had a bad road trip, so we were concerned about him in the horse trailer. Back in those days we didn't have a lot of knowledge about how to deal with horses that didn't ship well. For some reason we thought he'd be all right on the plane to Tokyo. After we took off from New York, he threw a tantrum and broke his restraints. One of the links of the chains shattered a window and the plane started losing altitude. Markham was going crazy wild! When that happens in a plane with a group of other horses, they go wild too, so we had to put him down. We made an emergency landing in Chicago, unloaded him, and went on from there. That was the most tragic and awful thing that ever happened to me—I was still a kid then and I had a hard time with that one. I went on to Tokyo, and a famous horse, Bold Minstrel, was shipped for me to ride in the games. In the end, we won the team silver medal, so the Olympic ending of the story was a nice one. But losing Markham that way was an awful thing to have happen. First for him to lose his confidence—that was the sad part. He was a very confident horse, yet a couple of bad rides in the trailer just shook him incredibly. Then having to put him down and leave him unceremoniously in Chicago.... The tragedy of losing a good friend...that loss is still with me.*

While it's difficult to measure the impact of each loss in one's life, experiencing death and grief through the passing of animals we love serves to prepare us for the inevitable loss of those closest to us: *One of life's biggest lessons is dealing with the shock of unexpected loss; I went through all that with a horse before going through it with a human,* says Anne Kursinski. *My mother was an alcoholic, though nobody ever called her that until finally I did. When I was in Europe for the 1990 World Championship trials, my family was doing some work to help her with the alcoholism. Everybody thought she was fine, but her poor body just said, "I can't do this anymore." It was her liver...and I guess it was her time to go...but it was so sudden! I had just spoken to her a few days earlier. My God, I had no idea she was going to die! When I heard, it was a nightmare trying to get on a plane, flying from Europe, and coming home still not believing that she was dead and gone. Afterwards, returning to the world championships and trying to ride and pay attention with all those pressures and all the grief—that was very, very difficult. Mother was probably my biggest fan. I reflect on what she would have felt or said even though she wasn't with me physically. Spiritually I know she was cheering me on when I did make the world championship team. It's comforting to believe that. Yeah, she was definitely my biggest fan. She was great.*

## Terminal Illness

To be diagnosed with a terminal illness is devastating, yet it contains a measure of kindness in that it gives one time to prepare. For some there is great comfort in that, while for others it merely increases their level of stress. Since animals hold no concept of time or expected life spans, a terminal illness is simply their life's condition until death ultimately occurs. They do not agonize over their demise, they do not regret deeds left undone or hopes unfulfilled; they merely live the best they can until they die. Deep sadness, depression, anger, and bitterness over a death sentence are products of the human condition, not nature in general.

*I'm an animal person—I love animals,* declares James Brady. *If I'd had a choice, I'd have been St. Francis because he's got the best saint beat going—being pals with all the animals. I rode one horse, Bernie, at the Center* [National Center for Therapeutic Riding] *for three years. Bernie took care of me. He knew to cool it when we were going up a hill because of who was on his back. Bernie was not just a steed, not just a mount—Bernie was a pal. Well, Bernie got terminal cancer and had to go live at the equine veterinary hospital. I would go out to visit Bernie and take him carrots…I'd think Bernie was probably wondering, "What am I doing out here with all these pal horses? Why am I getting this treatment? And now Jim comes out and has a whole bag of carrots. Is there something wrong with me? Am I going to die?"* I left that up to the vet—to talk to Bernie about his medical condition. Well, Bernie did have to be put down. I cried for months. He's been gone for about a year, and I still grieve over him. This has made me realize "shit happens." That's something my son would say, and he's right—it does.

Though Bernie probably didn't agonize over his terminal diagnosis, Jim certainly did. I find it striking that even with his devastating history, it took dealing with Bernie's terminal illness for Jim to realize that "shit happens." It does. Yet the animals' simple acceptance of their situations remind us of a simpler truth: life happens, then death happens. Humans who cannot accept that ultimate simplicity may end up increasing "the shit" by not accepting or dealing positively with the situation.

## *Fight for Life*

Fighting for one we love, only to lose, is an arduous lesson at any age. Though the ending is incontrovertible, it is still hard to accept: *When we lived in Arkansas, my dad allowed me to have two cows so I could sell their calves,* relates Ron Harding. *That money was mine, and it was the only pay I ever got. We had a little paint horse, Thunder, that we bred to a nasty old mustang bucking horse named Outlaw. We knew Outlaw was ruined forever as a riding horse; we'd bought her just to raise colts. Before Outlaw foaled, I decided I wanted her, and traded one of my calves for her. Dad and I both thought we had a great deal. Outlaw foaled and had the prettiest little pinto filly foal you've ever seen—to me it was—I was probably fifteen at the time…. I'd go see her everyday. We had a big pasture: like six hundred acres of river bottom, lots of trees and brush…I'd go out and look them up. One day I went out, and nowhere is my baby; this was about a week after it was born. So I start searching and searching and I found it in this big old ditch—probably thirty feet down. It was steep and there were logs across the front end of it so the mare couldn't get down to where the filly was. So here this baby couldn't get out and had gone without milk. I got her out and that little foal followed me back to the house. When we got there, Outlaw wouldn't take it back, so I got cow's milk for the foal. Of course it hadn't had anything in so long, it went to colicking that night. Now, you've got to understand the oldtime farm people: "If it's gonna die, it's gonna die; if it's gonna live, it's gonna live..." and you don't spend any money on them. Nobody helped me with this baby. There I was...about one o'clock in the morning and my baby was dying. It's eyes glazed over and she went into the loping movement that they do and I cried and cried—it still upsets me.*

*But I learned to accept death through that. This is the way things are and it doesn't matter how badly you want it differently, it's going to happen the way it's going to happen and you just have to accept it.*

When something we love turns up hurt or damaged, we naturally fight for it until we exhaust every power and hope available: *When I was thirty or so, I had to put a twenty-year-old stud, Benlowe, down because he'd broken his leg in a fence,* John Lyons recounts. *That was really hard. I kept him alive for almost two weeks trying to come up with a way to bone plate that leg. Since I had been in the orthopedic implant business I tried to think of everything I could to save that horse. But when it finally came down to it, there was nothing, so I had to put him down. That was really hard and I cried a lot. Losing a horse that you really love is tough. It makes you recognize we're all temporary; relationships are temporary, and we're to really enjoy them while we have them, not just take them for granted.* Were it not for loss, we might never appreciate what we had—and what we still have.

Unfortunately, most horses do not make good patients because their survival nature demands a whole, healthy quality of life. The equine mindset of constant readiness to flee at first alert is not conducive to the patient compliance required by immobilized recuperation of a broken leg, for instance. When that quality of a free and healthy life is no longer available to them, death may very well be preferable to the stress caused by restricted vulnerability. As Mary Fenton observes: *Horses have taught me that it's okay to die. They accept death as a natural thing—not a save-your-life-at-all-costs. Death is simply part of the cycle; when it's their time, it's okay....*

Regardless of the hierarchy of relationships, it is easier to accept the finish of a life fully lived than one terminated prematurely: *Brandy was my big love, and in a sense, her death was worse for me than my father's death,* Octavia Brown admits. *My father died at eighty-two; he'd had a lot of strokes, was hospitalized, and was ready to go. We'd been through it all with him and were sad, but it was inevitable and you could tell it was something that he needed at that time. But Brandy was just seventeen when she got an intestinal condition that made her waste away for eighteen months. We couldn't diagnose it and we couldn't cure it—we still don't know what it was. She had endless diarrhea and just dwindled down to the point where we had to have her put down.*

*The feeling of helplessness was tremendous because not knowing the cause, there was nothing we could do, and yet we held on to the hope that an answer would turn up. One problem was that we didn't have endless amounts of money to spend trying to find the cause and the cure. We did what we could do, but the family was not in a position to shell out thousands of dollars, and we had no insurance for something like this. The vet knew that, and, in fact, we got lots of care for free, but we couldn't really go all out as we might have if we'd had more resources. So that was part of the problem and the frustration. A group of us went through it together— I wasn't the only one who loved her so much. Several therapeutic riding people, one in particular, Sandy, a paraplegic rider, said Brandy had really been her lifeline back to sanity after spinal chord injury. Sandy went through all this with me. She's in her wheel chair and we took Brandy down to New Bolton* [University of Pennsylvania Veterinary School] *and had her put down.*

*I found out that when you are so totally involved with an animal it leaves a huge hole in your life. Her death still has the power to reduce me to tears because of the horse she was. In 1989, she was named Therapeutic Animal of the Year by the Delta Society in Washington State. They explore the human-animal bond and have annual awards for therapy dogs and horses. That was the year Brandy died, so we accepted it for her.*

*So you're up against all these hard, real things with horses. What this experience with Brandy showed me was that I needed to reach out to other people. You need to lean on others for support and you need to talk, and you need to mourn; it's really difficult to just put it behind you.*

Octavia's admission that Brandy's death hit harder than her father's may sound shockingly out of balance to many, yet I had the exact reaction when Haji died so suddenly—just a month after I'd lost my eighty-seven-year-old mother. It certainly wasn't that I loved Haji more than Mom; it was that Mother had graciously prepared us for her passing. Hers was a complete life that reached its natural end: her mind, body, and spirit were literally used up like a candle burned to the very last of the wick and wax. Her light extinguished; she was ready to leave this world. Haji's death, on the other hand, was an unexpected blow that felt unfair, premature, and incomplete. When he died so suddenly it was as if he'd been stolen from us. Perhaps that's the difference: I'd had time to emotionally release my ties to Mother, while I felt robbed when Haji expired in my arms. Irrational as it may sound to say the loss of a horse hit harder than that of a parent, I can understand Octavia's admission.

## Euthanasia

One of the hardest decisions in life is when to release a beloved animal from its earthly struggle. Love and hope fuel the search for a cure, while limited knowledge, finances, and mortal resources factor in to the final decision. The experience of euthanasia colors our view of death, and we may come to appreciate a quick, painless exit: *The worst thing in the world is to let an animal starve, suffer, be crippled, or hurt,* declares Valerie Kanavy. *I had my old horse put down. I had her in the apple orchard, eating an apple out on a sunny day and the guy stood there and put a bullet behind her ear and she never knew what hit her. I don't have any problem with that at all. What I wouldn't feel good about is these old starving rack of bones that can hardly chew their food—now don't tell me they're enjoying life! Horses don't know there's a tomorrow. We are all going to—if God wills—outlive our animals. Their life expectancy is not what ours is. That's sad. But we have to accept the joy that they give, and then we have to give them the relief they deserve.*

Doug Lietzke concurs, *I just read an article in which the medical editor of* EQUUS MAGAZINE *Matthew Mackay Smith, said, "There are worse things in a horse's life than dying."*

Living under the control of ruthless, callous people is often worse than death: *I watched a horse almost beat himself to death from* [struggling in] *pain,* Rex Peterson recounts. *It was a sad, sad deal. They would not let us put that horse down because he was insured for a large amount of money. It was a terrible, terrible, sad thing to do to a horse. The guy said to me, "What do you care? It's just a horse. We've got twice as much insurance on him as we could get for him—who cares? We'll collect the insurance." I said, "Partner, as far as I'm concerned that horse has more right to live than you do. Now get away from me." I never spoke to that man since and never will again.*

Thankfully, such criminally cruel individuals are still the exception rather than the rule. Many more owners have compassion and love for their horses to guide their actions: *We had to put my first horse, Cede Reed, to sleep here at the ranch when he was twenty-five,* relates Martha Josey. *He couldn't get up and down anymore, and I didn't want him to suffer. He was such a personal horse to us, we'd won so much...we still miss him.... I thought, "I'll never have another horse like this..." but I did in time...I've got a really good horse right now; it's not a replacement for Cede Reed, but it's another great partner.*

There are times when even Mother Nature makes mistakes, and if the defect causes suffering and can't be corrected, euthanasia is the only humane option: *The horse I had to put down had the most beautiful big black eyes,* remembers Charlotte Dicke (p. 204), who trains and shows Peruvian Pasos. *He was an adorable black and white pinto Miniature, only five months old. He was born a twin, and there wasn't enough room in the womb for both babies, so his front legs had not developed properly: they were curved and kept getting worse and worse as he grew. The vet examined him and said that the chances of any treatment being successful were highly unlikely. I had to take him to a euthanizing room; it just stunk. I couldn't stay with him; I just couldn't face it. I felt like I wanted to throw up all day. It was really hard, the whole feeling of loss. I'd never had that before, and it really was terrible. I just kept crying and crying and crying. He was so sweet and so nice. He had a great personality. I've had dreams of his big black eyes. It was really hard to deal with. But things like that, if somebody dies or something, it makes you stronger and you have to deal with it.*

As upsetting as having to have an animal be put down may be, actually having to do the deed yourself has got to be the most difficult of compassionate acts: *I'll never forget the first horse I had to put down,* says Jack Huyler. *In the old days in Jackson Hole,* [Wyoming] *we didn't have veterinarians. When I was about fifteen, my father said "This is the time for you to learn that fact of life" and I had to take this old mare off and shoot her. I made sure she didn't feel anything, but WOW! I made our oldest son do the same thing and I'm not sure yet— and he isn't either—whether it was right or wrong. You learn that death comes to all of us.... Now, of course, we have the veterinarians do it with a shot, but I never just turn the animal over to them—I'm there patting that horse. When my time comes, I hope I'll have somebody there who loves me and is patting me, you know....*

Anyone whose life involves animals may find himself in a situation where compassion demands immediate action: *I've lost several horses in my lifetime that I thought very highly of,* recalls Rex

Peterson. *It's never easy. Glenn Randall used to say, "Son, if you can't stand to lose one, don't be around them, because you're going to outlive them five or six times over." I've had to put two down myself because of the situation we were in at the time. It's one of the hardest things I've ever done. I put one down—it's been fifteen years ago now—he was a trick horse, a horse I had a lot of training in. He fell down and broke his leg. It was on a Sunday afternoon, and I couldn't get a vet. One of them said he could be there in an hour and half. I wasn't going to stand there and watch this horse any longer: he was in tremendous pain, tremendous shock, and was hurting himself worse, so I put him down myself with a gun. It was the kindest thing I could do for him because he was fighting so severely. To me there's a time to ask, are we doing the horse any good? Euthanasia…a lot of times that's the best thing you can do for them. It is never, never easy. But I knew it was the kindest thing I could do.*

## *Coming to Grips with Grief*

Grief is a Gordian knot woven from unfinished conversations, deeds left undone, broken dreams, fear of mortality, confusion, anger, abandonment, loss…and unanswerable questions. *When I was little my mare died, and I remember just not getting it,* recalls Anne Kursinski. *Why did she have to get sick? Why did she have to die? I just couldn't understand WHY?* The "why" of death can become an instrument of torture for the human mind. Aside from objective pathological explanations, the answer is clearly metaphysical: it was her time…. Until such time as one can accept such a simplicity, healing will be impeded by that frustrating, inexplicable *Why?*

Grief over the loss of a loved one, two-legged or four-legged, needs attending: *Shortly after Buddy* [the therapy school horse] *was hit by the car and killed, we had to put our dog to sleep; he was really old,* Tracy Cole explains. *I had a riding lesson that night, and when I told Octavia what had happened, she said, "Come over here and groom this horse. It's the best way to get it out." And that's what I did. I groomed that horse and cried and groomed…I wasn't fine right away, but I felt better than I had all day. I was connecting with something warm and fuzzy that loved me.* Obviously one being cannot *replace* another, but the simple act of re-connection reaffirms the possibility of future relations.

*I have such passionate feelings for horses that when one dies it's terrible,* says Carol Grant. *I had one horse, Babe, from the time I was about seven until she was twenty years, so I was a teenager when she died. That hurt. I'd love to say that I learned to understand death more, but I just learned that it hurt.... One lesson I did learn from it is to be more compassionate with others when they lose a loved one.*

That gift of compassion is not restricted to human loss, as Sam Savitt explains: *A while back, we had a cat named Jamie who adored our old black mare, Pat. Jamie moved into the barn and became a barn cat to be with Pat. He was always around that horse. Once when we went away, I took Pat off to board temporarily, and asked the neighbor to feed Jamie. They never saw him, but the cat food would disappear. When we brought the horse back, suddenly this dirty cat appeared over the stone wall—came running over. Jamie had just let himself go to hell—he was filthy. But that night when I went down to bed-check our horses, Jamie was sitting on the door of the stall clean as a whistle—he'd cleaned himself for Pat.*

*When Pat died, I buried her on the grounds with a bulldozer. That night, I went out about midnight to see if the cat was okay. The cat was sitting right by the mound of earth. I could have reached out and picked him up, but I felt this was his thing and I should keep out of it...but it bothered me.... You know, the next morning that cat disappeared. I went all over looking for him, but he never came back. I have often felt that all he really wanted was that horse, and this time he knew that Pat was not coming back. You see, before, when she was boarded, he had hopes, I guess. But this time, when he was there and saw it all, he knew that was it.... I was so touched by that cat and his devotion to that old mare, that I included their story in my book,* THE DINGLE RIDGE FOX AND OTHER STORIES.

*Occasionally I'm invited to elementary schools to meet with the children and discuss my art and writings,* Sam continues. *One class wanted me to read some of my stories so I started reading about Jamie and Pat aloud to them. Well, I never finished. When I got towards the end, I just broke up. I was embarrassed and angry with myself, and said to the teacher afterwards, "I'm sorry about that, I thought I could do it." She said, "That was just the right thing because a lot of youngsters don't think adults have those kind of feelings. What happened was real, and they respond to that. So don't feel that you've done the wrong thing." You know, I've tried to read that story to other classes and the same damn thing happened...so I don't read it anymore.*

Although Sam was upset by his tears, they are a natural expression of grief that should not be denied. Disavowing the grieving process can cause distress, either mental or physical, and crying is a fundamental element of that process: *You know, God gave us the gift of tears,* notes Dale Evans. *Tears are a gift, because if you can cry, eventually—if you're calm about it—He will show you.... There will be glimpses of "why?" But you must weep with faith—not without hope— with faith, and then He gives the sunshine back to you.*

As Dale Evans has proven with her books after each of three of her children's deaths, writing about the loss of a loved one can be therapeutic. It honors them, allows the author the luxury of dwelling in their memory, which helps to work through the loss and the grief, and offers solace to others in similar circumstances.

*We had a little palomino Shetland pony named Yankee Doodle,* relates Phyllis Eifert. *He was like one of my family—like one of my children. He'd been with us for twenty-six years. We'd got him when he was nine years old, and he was thirty-five when he died. Actually, I had to have him put to sleep because he could no longer chew. His death was a traumatic experience not only because I had to arrange it, but because I also felt that his death somehow represented the death of my children's childhood. Even though I was fifty at the time, and my children were grown and gone, I felt that that pony was a last vestige, a living connection to their childhood. Putting that pony down was hard to deal with. I picked a nice sunny day, arranged for a back hoe, and the veterinarian. When it was over, I told the vet, "There's one thing I want... I want to keep his tail." I'm sure the vet thought I was insane, but I got it. Afterwards I went upstairs, pulled the shades, got drunk holding on to his beautiful flaxen tail and wrote. I wrote and wrote and wrote about that wonderful pony. All the times we'd had with him and how he affected our life, our children's lives, and what he had meant to us all. That Christmas I added pictures to my writings, put it all in binders, and gave a copy to each of the children.* That proved to be both beneficial therapy and an inspired gift.

## Ritual

The rituals surrounding death are many and varied and serve as important release valves in the process of grief. Phyllis was concerned that her vet would think her request for Yankee Doodle's tail was crazy, yet it's reminiscent of the Victorian tradition of keeping a lock of a dead loved-one's hair.

The traditional ritual of a service allows family and friends an opportunity to collectively express their grief and pay final tribute: *I used to ride an old school horse named Tommy all the time,* says

Adrian Arroyo. *Tommy was around forever, but then they had to put him to sleep. It was really sad. We had a nice little funeral, a burial ceremony, at the barn for him, and we all cried. A lot of the little kids had a hard time with his death because they'd just ridden Tommy, but I think saying goodbye that way helped everyone deal with it.*

Some rituals may be unorthodox, yet are no less valid or sincere. As his museum clearly indicates, Roy Rogers is a sentimental hoarder. He has every wristwatch he's ever owned plus thousands of items he'd collected long before fame and fortune placed a value on his life's artifacts. It was only natural for Roy to pay homage to his treasured Trigger by awarding him a place of honor among his life's keepsakes: *We moved up to Apple Valley, California, in 1965, June 27th, and at 5:00 a.m. on the third of July, I got a call from the ranch in Hidden Valley where we'd lived before,* Roy recounts. *I picked up the phone, and before anything was said, I said, "Old Trigger died, didn't he?" I just had a feeling... Danny said, "Just a few minutes ago." Danny had turned Trigger out after he'd fed him. He was feeding the other horses and he went and got a cup of coffee. Trigger was lying out there in the field but Danny thought he'd just laid down after he played around a little bit, so he went back out to finish feeding the horses. Then he said, "I went back out there again, and he was still lying there. So I thought maybe I'd better check him." He went out there and phht! (Roy's voice cracks) ...he was gone.*

*Trigger meant so much to me, I couldn't bear the thought of putting him in the ground and letting the worms take care of the situation. I had seen so many beautiful mountings in museums, so I called this friend of mine, a taxidermist, and all I had to do was tell him that old Trigger had passed away, and he went out and took care of everything. The next time I saw Trigger, he was mounted in our museum. I didn't have to go through any of the doing it myself.*

*I had a little situation happen here at the museum. A woman came up to me when I was answering questions people asked me about Trigger and she said, "How could you do that to poor old Trigger?" Now that stung me; it really hurt me. I looked right at her and asked, "Would you rather I'd put him in the ground and let the worms eat him up?" She said, "Oh, Gee, I never thought of that!" I said, "Well, next time you say something think a little bit about it." I'm happy I have him here. He's much better here than putting him in the ground.* When I saw Trigger, Buttermilk, and Bullet "living on" in the Rogers' museum I'd thought I'd have reservations, but I didn't—it was great to see them all again—it seemed fitting and right that they be there.

Yet another unusual equine tribute resulted from the age-old tradition of granting a last wish: *A lady called me up to do a phone consultation about her old horse, Rosebud, who had foundered and was in chronic pain,* explains Penelope Smith. *The horse couldn't even lie down. She was standing in one position. The lady knew it was time for the horse to be put down, but she wanted to know if there was anything Rosebud needed before the vet arrived the next day. This horse, who was such a good-humored horse even in the middle of all her pain, showed me a picture of herself wearing one of those little cone-type party hats and having a carrot cake. I thought, "Oh my God, how am I going to describe this silly picture to this sad lady?" I'm always honest even if the animals tell me things that are quite bizarre. So I described Rosebud's request of wearing a party hat and having a carrot cake. The woman started laughing and said, "Every birthday we celebrate in the barn, we put party hats on the animals and ourselves, and we have a carrot cake." Rosebud wanted a party on her death day. And she got it. The next day when the vet came, Rosebud lay down, which she hadn't been able to do for a while. Rosebud's party made me think she was a Buddhist, for they celebrate death as the special occasion of going back to your home—the spiritual realm. Everybody celebrates, joyously wishing the spirit home rather than concentrating on the sadness of a loss.*

Ritual, tradition, and horses share a great reverence to Native Americans: *I fully expect to meet my horses later on,* states Chris Hawkins. *I have coup sticks carved especially for every horse I've ever owned. An Indian coup stick has the horse's head carved on one end and the horse's hoof carved on the other end. Their mane is used as part of the coup stick. They have eagle feathers mounted on them for bravery and blue for far sight—to be able to see far and be aware of danger. The one for my silver Appaloosa, Tipper, is white with lightning streaks on the legs for speed. You're not allowed to use the coup stick until after the horse is dead. They are very sacred to us and are handled with great honor and love.*

Whether carving a coup stick or capturing a likeness on canvas, memorializing horses through art is a lasting ritual of tribute: *I did a portrait of the children of a riding family in Carolina, in which there was a little girl, who at the time was about ten years old,* reports Sam Savitt. *When she was twelve, she was killed in a riding accident. Her mother called me and asked me to come and do a painting of the ponies that she grew up with, though she wasn't riding a pony when she died. I asked the mother, "Doesn't this turn you off to riding—this happening?"*

*She said, "We're a riding family. We've always been riding. She was on a very good horse, but she really rode him off his feet."*

*Then she explained how it happened. It was an eventing meet and they'd held up the course because somebody had a fall. The girl didn't real-ize the clock was stopped, and thought she was losing time. So when they told her to go on, she went hell-bent-for-election, and at the last fence her horse was driven off his feet. He hit, turned over, and she was killed on impact. Her family felt this is the way it is—it happened—it does take a lot of courage sometimes. I did the portrait of her ponies, and it's a lovely little thing: two ponies in a stall with her monogrammed sheet lying on the stall floor. She named the painting "Claudia's Ponies."*

## Cycle of Life

The calm, accepting attitude of that equestrian family dem-onstrates a strength derived from the dichotomy of acknowledg-ing death as a part of life. Almost anyone who works with horses is exposed to that dichotomy: *Horses don't have histories, and they don't have futures; I don't believe that they think about tomorrow,* says Macella O'Neill. *When a horse is in pain and ready to die, they're not thinking about how they felt yesterday. They're just thinking of how they feel right now, and a lot of horses meet death with calm and dignity. They make it seem natural and reasonable. Even if they're ignorant of their own demise, they have a tremendous amount of acceptance and trust that are terrific lessons to learn.*

Dealing with equine euthanasia has helped Valerie Kanavy appreciate the gift of a quiet passing: *I was grateful my father went into a coma when he had cancer—that he died quickly and didn't suffer,* says Valerie. *Even though I miss him, I don't look on his death as a real separation. I know my father was with me in Holland* [at the World Equestrian Games]. *He's probably what really helped me win because he was up there, saying, "Hey, fix this for her, God." I really felt that.*

No longer with you, yet a part of you forever. There is great comfort in such thoughts, for each of us carries the personal gifts of shared experience, imparted knowledge, and deeper understand-ing bestowed by those we have been with and lost.

*Having horses in my life has given me opportunity to deal with death,* states Linda Tellington-Jones. *I've dealt with a lot, and I've come to see death as simply part of the seasons—just another phase of life. It's not the end, it's part of the seasons that roll over and come on again. By under-standing this, I have willingly been able to help horses through the process of death, to assist them through that gateway. Afterwards, I am able to acknowledge my grief and the pain I feel at the loss. I believe that experi-encing this process with horses opens spiritual doors for us, which make us deeper, more compassionate, more understanding humans who are able to deal with human death more effectively. Also, knowing that just because we're physically separated doesn't mean that memory doesn't abide with us—their spirit still remains.*

## Planning for the Inevitable

Aging is probably not the favorite subject of daydreams; yet a realistic life's design includes pondering and planning for those sun-set years. Many riders continue throwing a leg over a horse until the very end, while others—no longer riding—still insist on keep-ing horses in their lives: *If something should happen that I couldn't walk or ride anymore I would still like to watch the horses from my wheel chair*, states Carol Stratton. *Just wheel me out, put me in the middle of the pasture, and let them do their thing around me.*

*It's only been recently that I've stopped riding; I had a couple of falls, and realized it was time to quit*, admits Carol Grant. *But it's been like losing a part of myself. I still have my horse, Rosie. She was born here, I helped her into the world, and I'll always have her. Though there are days now I haven't felt good, my bones are sore, and yet I still have to tend this horse when I think, "Why don't I just get rid of her?" Then I go out to the barn and look at her—just look at her—and I know I'll have her until one of us dies. You see, with her I still have the memory of her mother, who was my horse; I have the memory of all her foals, and the memory of all the horses that came before her in my life. I've given instructions to my children that when I'm too old to live anymore, I want them to put me on a horse, and give it a good slap on the rump. That would be the happiest exit for me.*

Looking down the road to one's own demise is often put off until it's too late. Planning ahead for that fatal eventuality is not only prudent, but considerate of those we leave behind: *Now I'm sixty-four and have a heart condition*, reports Chris Hawkins. *Hey, how much longer have I got? But I'll tell you something, it doesn't bother me;*

*I don't sweat it at all. The only thing that I worry about is what's going to happen to my horses. So I made out a real good will. I am giving each one of my horses to someone special who I know will take care of it and keep it for the rest of its life. I've already made them swear upon the feather that they will never let them go, that they will be put down before they are let go to someone who'd take them down the road and hurt them. Each one of them, I made swear on the feather, because they're my babies. So I think it's going to work out all right. You won't find anyone in the world who loves a horse more than a Comanche—they're part of us. If there were no horses to love, there would be nothing for me. God deliver me from any heaven where there are no horses. I would not like that. I could not live that way. When I die, I'll ride over the moon on my Pegasus, Taj. I have all the confidence in the world that's what will happen....*

## Lessons Learned

The experience of losing equine partners in the course of life through advancement, sale, retirement, or death, allows us to confront and mollify loss by gaining the strength of acceptance, and recognizing the value of rebuilding to move on. Within that experience of loss is sown a growing appreciation of what we have in life: *In veterinary medicine we do a lot of euthanasia, so we cause death,* says Dr. Robert Miller. *Working with so many horses in life and death situations, I have become keenly aware of my own mortality. I have no illusions; I recognize that life is a very, very brief privilege, and I treasure it immensely.*

Questions raised while dealing with trauma or terminal illness help us sort out the emotional, financial, and ethical aspects of life, death, and euthanasia for those we love—man and beast. We are forced to consider quality of life as opposed to quantity, and ask under what circumstances might death be the kindest option. We learn that with the death of an animal or a human, ritual, tradition, tribute and tears all help to assuage the complex pain of grief.

*I used to think the more you had to deal with death, the less it would bother you,* says Buck Brannaman. *But instead of making me a little thicker-hided or less affected by it, it's made me more sensitive. Granted, I'm strong enough emotionally to handle a lot; my gosh, I've been through the mill quite a few times—I know it up, down, and sideways. So in that respect, I can bear a lot of emotional burden, but that burden hasn't made me less sensitive. I can tell you that. I take a lot of pride in being a man's man; but if you know what button to push, I'm the first one to admit, it doesn't take much to make me cry, either.*

No doubt many of us shed a tear at the news on July 6, 1998, that Roy Rogers had died at the age of eighty-seven. The sadness felt by his throngs of fans may be offset by the joyous reunion as Roy, back in the saddle on Trigger, with Robin in his lap, Debbie and Sandy hugging him from behind, rides Heaven's Happy Trails in glory with a song and a smile. How lucky we were to have grown up with him.

Ultimately, coming to accept death as an intrinsic part of life—whether perceived as an end or a transition—lends a sense of peace and solace to the subject of mortality. With that comes the strength to say goodbye and then to go on living with *HorsePower!*

# A WORLD APART

"One-twenty! I'll never make it now," trainer Mary Deringer Phelps silently chided herself as she wheeled the Suburban into the parking space. She was at Dallas-Fort Worth airport to pick up a woman she'd hired to judge the upcoming Willow Bend horse show. Since they'd never met before, they had decided to meet each other at the gate, but now it was so late that Mary was feeling anxious about missing their appointed connection. Grabbing her purse, Mary jumped out of the car and started race-striding towards the terminal. The flight monitor didn't ease her anxiety–not only was she running late, but the judge's plane had arrived fifteen minutes early!

Mary's mind started churning, "She's been waiting a half-hour now... she probably thought I forgot. She could be at a phone, or at baggage claim, or anywhere by now. I'd better keep an eye out on the way to the gate."

As she entered the wide concourse, the enormity of that task hit home–there were literally hundreds of newly-arrived strangers coming at her. She continued on towards the gate, scanning the crowds and wishing she had a photo or some description of the judge. All she knew for sure was that she was searching for a woman!

About halfway down the concourse Mary stopped—and without hesitation—walked up to a woman and asked, "Are you Gerry Friels?"

The startled woman replied, "Why, yes, I am. You must be Mary."

Mary sighed in relief, saying, "I am—welcome to Texas! Sorry I wasn't at the gate to meet you, but I know you understand about operating in 'horse-time'."

Gerry grinned and nodded her understanding.

As they turned toward the lobby, Gerry asked, "How did you recognize me?"

Mary shook her head in wonder, "I don't know... you just look like a horse person."

"I do? I'm not wearing my riding clothes... so what do 'horse people' look like?"

Mary thought a moment and replied, "They're confident, they have a certain bearing, they're tanned like English leather and they've usually got a smile on their face."

Both horsewomen laughed in recognition as they strode out into the brilliant Texas sunlight.

Although it is open to all willing to invest the time and effort to enter, the horse world is a world apart with its own language, its own proving grounds, its own risks, its own rewards and its own lessons. As a result, there is a defining demeanor evident in horse people which has been acknowledged throughout history—a subtle aura and attitude about true horsemen and -women that sets them apart. The very terms "knight," "cowboy," "wrangler," "caballero," "horseman," and "equestrienne" conjure up defining images of strength, quiet courage, a zest for life, compassion, physical confidence and self-assurance with just a touch of romance.

Mary's anecdote reinforces a conviction I've held since my youth: horse people are identifiably different. Perhaps it's the heat of horse fever that burns within them. Perhaps it's a reflection of their horse crazy commitment to the promised excitement of their next ride. Perhaps it's the confidence of *HorsePower!*

For horse people, *HorsePower!* is more than a concept or a book—it is that dynamic way of being which tests and strengthens the body, mind and spirit. Now that you are familiar with *HorsePower!,* you will be able to recognize its effects within your own personal experience. Look for it; be open to it; grow from it, and honor it. Then you, too, will be living with *HorsePower!*

# Glossary of Equine Terms

**aids:** Tools and techniques by which a rider directs a horse's movements.

**alpha mare:** The dominant adult female in a herd or band.

**American Saddlebred:** A breed developed in the United States for smooth gates and high leg action.

**anaphylactic shock:** An often severe and sometimes fatal systemic reaction to a serum as a result of previous exposure.

**Anglo-Arab:** A horse that is part Thoroughbred and part Arabian.

**anthropomorphism:** Assigning human traits or form to non-human beings.

**Appaloosa:** A breed with distinctive spotted markings developed by the Nez Percé tribe of the Northwest United States.

**artificial aids:** Devices such as reins, whip, spurs, that control a horse's action.

**band:** A small group of horses.

**barn sour:** A horse that is reluctant to leave the barn or shelter.

**bay:** A color type: brown body with black mane, tail, and black "points" up the legs.

**bearing reins:** Leather restraints that control the set of a carriage horse's head.

**bight:** The extra length of rein from the rider's hand to the end buckles.

**bolter:** A horse that runs off at high speed for no apparent reason.

**bowed tendon:** An injury to the hard fibrous tissue in the leg.

**boxed:** Kept in a stall.

**break:** Taming and training a horse to obediently accept tack and riders.

**breastplate:** Straps across a horse's chest that prevent the saddle from sliding back.

**bridle path:** 1) Shaved area of the mane just behind the ears to allow for the bridle to rest on the poll. 2) A riding trail.

**canter:** A three-beat gait.

**cantle:** The raised back of a saddle.

**catch colt:** Offspring of horses that were not purposefully mated.

**catch rider:** A rider hired to show others' horses at competitive events.

**cavaletti:** A series of ground poles or small jumps used for training rhythmic gaits or jumping.

**cecum:** Cul de sac where large intestine begins.

**Centered Riding:** Riding technique developed by Sally Swift.

**chef d'équipe:** Team manager.

**Clydesdale:** Scottish breed of draft horse.

**cold-blooded:** Refers to larger, more docile working breeds of horses from Northern European colder climates, such as the draft horse breeds.

**colic:** A generic name for gastrointestinal disorders such as gas, impaction (obstruction), twisted intestines, etc. in horses which may cause discomfort or death.

**colt:** A weaned male horse less than six years old.

**conformation:** The skeletal and muscular structure of a horse.

**Congress:** The Ohio Quarter Horse show, one of the largest in the United States.

**cribbing:** A bad habit that some horses get. It clamps its teeth on a wood rail or stable door and sucks in air.

**crest release:** The rider moves his hands up the neck of his horse to allow for the horse's natural head action when jumping.

**crow hopping:** A series of small bucks.

**curry:** The action of cleaning a horse by rubbing its coat to loosen dirt and debris.

**currycomb:** A metal or rubber brush used to clean a horse.

**dam:** A horse's mother.

**diagonal:** 1) The action of the opposing fore and hind legs of a horse moving simultaneously. 2) An imaginary line going diagonally across the length of an arena.

**dink:** Rodeo term for a spiritless or worthless horse (or bull) on which a rodeo rider will not have a competitive ride to place in the money.

**diurnal:** Animals that are active during the day.

**dressage:** (dres–sahj) French term referring to a particular type of advanced training of horses in a ring, also known as "ballet on horseback."

**EIA:** Equine Infectious Anemia, an untreatable blood disorder caused by a virus transmitted by large biting insects (*EQUUS* March 1997 p. 12).

**equitation:** The art of riding. In horse shows, equitation classes judge the rider's position and control of the horse.

**equinology:** A term invented by the author to indicate the specialized study of horse behavior.

**eventing:** Also referred to as three-day eventing or combined training. A horse trial consisting of separate events of dressage, cross-country, and stadium jumping.

**feral:** A released domestic animal and its descendants that have reverted to living in a wild state.

**filly:** A young female horse under three years of age .

**fit:** A horse in top condition.

**five-gaited:** A horse with two additional gaits: the "rack" and "slow gait" as well as walk, trot, and canter.

**flake:** Referring to a single thin portion of baled hay, there are about a dozen flakes to a bale.

**flying change:** Changing from one lead to the other while continuing to canter.

**foal:** A baby horse from the time of birth to weaning.

**founder:** Internal deformity of the foot, resulting from rotation of the coffin bone due to simultaneous detachment from the hoof wall and pull by the deep flexor tendon: (*EQUUS* 233 March 1997 p. 11).

**frame:** Refers to the manner in which a horse carries itself in motion.

**front up:** The action of saddle seat horses to elevate their front ends and lower their hind ends.

**gait:** The pace and sequence of travel such as: walk, trot, canter, gallop, rack, pace.

**galloping boots:** Protective gear put on a horse's legs to prevent injury while running.

**gaskin:** A middle area of the hind leg.

**gelding:** A male horse that has been surgically neutered.

**get the gate:** Slang term referring to being eliminated from class competition.

**girth:** The strap that encircles a horse behind its front legs to hold a saddle in place.

**ground tied:** A horse trained to stay when the reins are dropped to the ground.

**gymkhana:** A field day of equestrian games and competitions.

**habit:** Formal riding attire.

**hack:** A ride for pleasure or exercise.

**half-halt:** A technique to slow a horse's pace or regain its attention.

**half-seat:** The rider lifts his weight up out of the saddle.

**hand:** The unit of measurement of equine height. One hand equals four inches.

**Hanoverian:** A German breed of horse.

**harness driver:** A cart driver, specifically for racing, trotting, or pacing Standardbreds.

**haute école:** French for "high school." Refers to advanced dressage techniques.

**hazard:** Obstacle in competitive driving competition.

**headstall:** The top of the bridle that rests on a horse's poll.

**herd:** A group of horses normally comprised of mares, foals, colts, fillies and a dominant stallion.

**hippotherapy:** Therapeutic programs carried out on horseback.

**horsemanship, horsemastership:** Being skilled in training, care, and riding of a horse.

**horsenality:** A term invented by the author to indicate distinctive traits of individual horses.

**horse trial:** A shortened version of eventing competition.

**hotblood:** A fiery temperament; Thoroughbreds and Arabians are considered hotblooded breeds.

**imprint training:** Human handling and training of a foal taking place immediately after birth.

**jigging:** The action of an impatient horse taking short prancing steps.

**leads, right and left:** When cantering, a horse reaches further forward with one front leg. Turning in the direction of that "leading" leg offers greater balance: i.e. turning right with the right leg leading, or left while on the "left lead."

**lead change:** Switching from one lead to the other.

**liberty horse:** A horse trained to perform free of all physical contact and restraints.

**Lippizaner:** Austrian breed of gray horse used in dressage and haute école.

**longe:** Working a horse on a thirty-foot long line traveling in a circle around the trainer.

**mare:** A female horse of four years or more.

**marathon:** A long distance driving competition.

**Moshe Feldenkrais:** Developer of a system of gentle movements and manipulations that awaken new brain cells (in humans and horses) and activate unused neural pathways to help develop body coordination.

**monocular vision:** The ability of horses to use each eye independent of the other.

**Morgan:** A versatile breed of horse developed in Vermont.

**natural aids:** Directing a horse's movements by use of a rider's hands, legs, and weight.

**navicular:** A degenerative disease of the navicular bone in the foot of a horse.

**near side:** The left side of a horse—the side nearest a mounting rider.

**nocturnal:** Animals that are active at night.

**noseband:** A leather band that is part of a bridle.

**off side:** The right side of a horse.

**on the bit:** A horse is on the bit when it submits to its rider by moving freely forward with its whole body into a relaxed poll, jaw, and neck.

**on the muscle:** Referring to an anxious horse that is alert and ready to run.

**overface:** Forcing a horse to do something it is not yet ready for, either in training or ability.

**overgirth:** Large strap that is placed over the saddle to hold it in position.

**over-reach:** The action of a horse's hind foot striking its front foot by overstriding.

**packer:** A well-schooled older horse that performs dependably over fences.

**parasympathetic system:** Automatic bodily function such as breathing and blinking.

**passage:** A slow, cadenced trot with a moment of suspension before each foot touches down.

**piaffe:** A dressage movement requiring trotting in place.

**prancing on the forehand:** A horse that has the majority of its weight on its front end.

**point to point:** A race or competition over fences from one landmark to another, usually held on a race course.

**poll:** The flexible top of the horse's head where it joins the neck.

**project horse:** A horse purchased to be trained then sold for profit.

**pull-on bell boots:** Protective gear to protect a horse's hooves and ankles.

**pulse monitor:** Device to measure a horse's heart rate.

**Quarter Horse:** A horse breed developed in the United States that got its name for being fastest over a quarter-mile track.

**quirt:** A short riding whip.

**recover:** When a horse's vital signs return to a normal rate after strenuous exercise.

**remount:** Supply of fresh horses.

**rising trot:** The rider rises out of the saddle every other beat of the trot—also called "posting."

**Roman ride:** Riding two horses simultaneously by straddling both with one foot on each back.

**reefing:** Jerking on the reins so that the bit hurts the horse's mouth.

**schooling:** Teaching a horse flatwork or jumping; general training.

**Selle Français:** A French breed of horse.

**show circuit:** An organized set of competitions that relate to particular breeds or types of performance.

**sire:** A horse's father.

**sitting trot:** The rider remains in the saddle for all beats of the trot.

**snubbing post:** A support to which a young horse is tied until it is accustomed to being restrained.

**span:** A pair of animals used together in driving.

**Spanish Riding School:** Specialists in haute école dressage training of Lippizaners.

**stakes horse:** A horse with the ability to regularly compete in monied events—usually a racing term.

**stallion:** A male horse that can be used for breeding.

**Standardbred:** American breed of harness racer—either trotter or pacer.

**stifle:** The joint connecting the hind leg to the body of a horse.

**stone bruise:** Injury to the sole of a horse's foot caused by impact.

**stopped out:** In a jumping contest a horse that refuses to jump three times is eliminated and said to have "stopped out."

**stride:** The distance between one foot leaving the ground and where it is put down again.

**strong:** A term referring to a horse that always wants to run.

**suspensory:** A tendon in the lower leg.

**tack:** Equipment used on the horse for riding such as a saddle, bridle, saddle pad.

**tack up:** To saddle and bridle a horse.

**Tennessee Walker:** A breed developed for a smooth, fast walk for overseeing large plantations.

**Tevis Cup:** The 100 mile endurance race in the Sierra mountains of California.

**Thoroughbred:** A breed developed for racing.

**three-gaited:** A horse that walks, trots, and canters.

**tie-down:** A leather strap attached to the noseband and breastplate to restrict head throwing.

**trick ride:** Performing unusual feats and gymnastics on horseback.

**trot:** A two-beat gait in which the legs move in diagonal pairs.

**trotting poles:** Cavaletti or poles placed on the ground to train rhythmic gaits.

**twitch:** A restraining device that squeezes a horse's muzzle.

**warmblood:** The offspring of a cross between a hotblood (Eastern or Oriental breed) and a coldblood (Northern European horse from a cold climate) horse.

**wean:** To separate a foal from a mare so that it no longer nurses.

**weaving:** A bad habit some horses get. It swings its head side to side while standing still—usually an indication of boredom or distress.

**withers:** The top of a horse's shoulder.

**yearling:** A colt or filly between one and two years of age.

Some definitions are from the glossary of THE COMPLETE BOOK OF HORSES & PONIES by Margaret Cabell Self

# Bibliography

"AHC Study Finds More Horses, Owners." *Equus* 233 March 1997: 77.

American Horse Council, *Horse Industry Directory.* Horse Industry Statistics: 4.

Auerbach, Ann Hagedorn. *Wild Ride.* New York: Henry Holt and Company, 1994.

Chenevix-Trench, Charles. *A History of Horsemanship.* Garden City: New York: Doubleday & Company, Inc, 1970.

Churchill, Winston. *My Early Life, A Roving Commission.* New York: Charles Scribner's Sons, 1930.

Dorrance, Tom and Milly Hunt Porter, Ed. *True Unity.* Fresno: Give-It-A-Go Enterprises, 1987.

"Events & Athletes: Equestrian." *XXVI Olympiad—Atlanta 1996: Official Souvenir Program.* 1996.

Grandin, Temple. *Thinking in Pictures.* New York: Vintage Books, 1996.

Harris, Moira C. "The 'Horsey Set' Suffers a Setback." *Horse Illustrated* May 1996: 2.

Hart, Stephen. *The Language of Animals.* New York: Henry Holt and Company, Inc., 1996.

Helm, Mike. *A Breed Apart.* New York: Henry Holt and Company, Inc., 1991.

Hillenbrand, Laura. "Leading the Blind." *Equus* 229 November 1996: 74.

Huyler, John S. *The Stamp of the School: Reminiscences of the Thacher School 1949-1992.* Seattle: Special Child Publications, 1994.

Jaffer, Nancy. "Michael Matz: Giving Riding a Leg Up." *Spur* March/April 1997: 32.

Jeschko, Kurt and Harald Lange. *The Horse Today—& Tomorrow?* New York: Arco Publishing Company, Inc., 1972.

Josephy, Jr., Alvin M. *500 Nations.* New York: Alfred A. Knopf, 1994: 362.

Kilby, Emily. "Restoring a Tarnished Image." *Equus* November 1993: 40.

Mahan, Larry, "*HorseWorld*" episode #04-92, Tri-Crown Productions 1/14/92.

McBane, Susan and Helen Douglas-Cooper. *Horse Facts.* New York: Dorset Press, 1991.

Montana, Gladiola. *Never Ask a Man the Size of His Spread.* Salt Lake City: Gibbs Smith, Publisher, 1993.

Morel, Mary Kay. "A Leap of Faith." *Horse Illustrated* September 1996: 45.

Morris, Desmond. *HorseWatching.* New York: Crown Publishers, Inc., 1989.

*Random House Webster's College Dictionary.* New York: Random House, 1991.

*Random House Historical Dictionary of Slang.* Volume 1, New York: Random House, 1994.

Roberts, Monty. *The Man Who Listens to Horses.* London: Random House (UK) Limited, 1996.

Rogers, Roy and Dale Evans with Jane and Michael Stern. *Happy Trails: Our Life Story.* New York: Simon & Schuster, 1994.

Sappington, M.S., Ph.D., Brenda Forsythe. "Horse Sense." *Horse Illustrated* January 1998 22 (1): 10.

Saslow, Dr. Carol A. "Helping Your Horse to Generalize." *Horse Illustrated* February 1994: 20.

Savoie, Jane. *That Winning Feeling! A New Approach to Riding Using Psychocybernetics.* No. Pomfret, Vermont: Trafalgar Square Publishing, 1992.

Savoie, Jane. *That Winning Feeling! Audiotape 1: Choose Your Future.* No. Pomfret, Vermont: Trafalgar Square Publishing, 1993.

Self, Margaret Cabell. *The Complete Book of Horses & Ponies.* New York: McGraw-Hill Book Company, 1973.

Steinkraus, William, Ed. *The U.S. Equestrian Team Book of Riding.* New York: Simon and Schuster, 1976.

Tellington-Jones, Linda with Ursula Bruns, *An Introduction to the Tellington-Jones Equine Awareness Method.* Ossining, NY: Breakthrough Publications, 1985.

Timney, PhD, Brian, "What Horses See." *Equus* 246 April 1998: 36.

Thomas, Heather Smith. *The Wild Horse Controversy.* South Brunswick and New York: A. S. Barnes and Company, 1979.

Vernon, Arthur. *The History and Romance of the Horse.* New York: Dover Publications, 1946.

# Suggested Reading and Viewing

Brannaman, Buck, *Groundwork,* book or video, (800) 269–3647.

Budiansky, Stephen, *The Nature of Horses.* New York: The Free Press, 1997.

Cooper, Diana Star, *Night After Night.* Washington, DC: Island Press, 1994.

Crabtree, Helen, *Saddle Seat Equitation.* New York: Doubleday, 1976, 1982.

Crabtree, Helen, *Hold Your Horses, Saddle & Bridle Magazine,* St. Louis, MO, 1997, (800) 878–8768.

Doolittle, Bev, *The Art of Bev Doolittle.* Trumbull, CT: Greenwich Workshop, 1990.

Doolittle, Bev, *New Magic.* New York: Bantam Books, 1995.

Hassler, Jill Keiser, *Beyond The Mirrors.* Quarryville, PA: Goals Unlimited Press, PA, 1988.

Hassler, Jill Keiser, *In Search of Your Image.* Quarryville, PA: Goals Unlimited Press.

Hearne, Vicki, *Animal Happiness.* New York: Harper Collins, 1994.

Hunt, Ray, *Think Harmony with Horses.* Pioneer Publishing Co., 1991.

Huyler, Jack, Video tapes: *A Gymkhana Training Film and Tips on Riding Speed Events,* available from the Thacher School, 5025 Thacher Rd. Ojai, CA 93023.

Josey, Martha, *Running to Win.* Karnack, TX: Josey Enterprises, Inc., 1985.

Kursinski, Anne, with Miranda Lorraine, *Anne Kursinski's Riding Clinic: A Step-By-Step Course For Winning in the Hunter & Jumper Rings.* New York: Doubleday, 1995.

Lawrence, Dr. Elizabeth, *His Very Silence Speaks.* Detroit: Wayne State University Press, 1989.

Lawrence, Dr. Elizabeth, *Hoofbeats and Society.* Bloomington: Indiana University Press, 1985.

Lawrence, Dr. Elizabeth, *Rodeo: An Anthropologist Looks at the Wild and the Tame.* Chicago: University of Chicago Press, 1984.

Lyons, John, with Sinclair Browning, *Lyons On Horses.* New York: Doubleday, 1991.

Lyons, John, Symposiums, books, videos, tapes: PO Box 479, Parachute, Co 81635, (970) 285-9797.

Masson, Jeffrey Moussaieff and Susan McCarthy, *When Elephants Weep.* New York: A Delta Book, 1995.

McCormick, Adele von Rüst, Ph.D. and Marlena Deborah McCormick, Ph.D., *Horse Sense and the Human Heart.* Deerfield Beach, FL: Health Communications, Inc. 1997.

McElroy, Susan Chernak, *Animals as Teachers & Healers.* New York: Ballantine Books, 1996.

Miller, Dr. Robert, *Imprint Training of the Newborn Foal.* Colorado Springs: Western Horseman Books, (800) 874-6774.

Miller, Dr. Robert, *Health Problems of the Horse.* Colorado Springs: Western Horseman Books, (800) 874-6774.

Miller, Dr. Robert, Videos: *Influencing the Horse's Mind, Control of the Horse, and Early Learning,* available from Video Velocity, (800) 284-3362.

Plumb, J. Michael, *Michael Plumb's Horse Journal,* P.O. Box 420234, Palm Coast, FL 321142, (800) 829-9145.

Roberts Monty, Training tapes available from Flag is Up Farms, Solvang, CA: (888) 826-6689.

Rogers, Dale Evans, *Angel Unaware.* Revell, 1991.

Rogers, Roy and Dale Evans, with Carlton Showers, *Happy Trails.* New York: Simon & Schuster, 1994.

Savitt, Sam, has written, co-authored, and illustrated too many books to list here. His subjects vary from horse stories such as his award-winning *Wild Horse Running,* to horse health, *How To Take Care of Your Horse Until the Vet Comes,* to art: *Draw Horses with Sam Savitt.*

Savoie, Jane, *Cross-Train Your Horse, Book I: Simple Dressage for Every Horse, Every Sport;* and *More Cross-Training. Book II: Build a Better Performance Horse with Dressage.* No. Pomfret, VT: Trafalgar Square Publishing, 1998, (800) 423-4525.

Savoie, Jane, Audio Tapes: *That Winning Feeling! Cassette I: Choose Your Future. Cassette II: Relaxation and Imaging Skills,* No. Pomfret, VT: Trafalgar Square Publishing, 1993, (800) 423-4525.

Savoie, Jane, Video Tapes: *The Half Halt Demystified! Tape I: Learning the Half Halt. Tape II: Putting Your Horse on the Bit.* No. Pomfret, VT: Trafalgar Square Publishing, 1993, (800) 423-4525.

Shrake, Richard, *Resistance Free Training.* Ossining, NY: Breakthrough Publications, 1993.

Shrake, Richard, Video tapes. Sunriver, OR: A Winning Way Ltd., (800) 635-8861.

Smiling Pinto Station, equestrian books and video tapes (800) 284 3362.

Smith, Penelope, *Animal Talk, Animals...Our Return to Wholeness.* Pt. Reyes, CA: Pegasus Publications, (800) 356-9315.

Smith, Penelope, Audio tapes: *Animal Death: A Spiritual Journey; Healing Power of Animal Communication; The Interspecies Telepathic Connection Series.* Pt. Reyes, CA: Pegasus Publications, (800) 356-9315.

Smith, Penelope, Video tapes: *Telepathic Communication With Animals.* Pt. Reyes, CA: Pegasus Publications, (800) 356-9315.

Steinkraus, William, *Reflections on Riding & Jumping.* No. Pomfret, VT: Trafalgar Square Publishing, 1997, (800) 423-4525.

Swift, Sally, *Centered Riding,* New York: St. Martin's/Marek, 1985, (800) 423-4525.

Tellington-Jones, Linda with Sybil Taylor, *Getting In TTouch.* No. Pomfret, VT: Trafalgar Square Publishing, 1997, (800) 423-4525; and The Tellington TTouch, from TTeam Training, PO Box 3793, Santa Fe, NM 87501, (505) 455-2945.

Tellington-Jones, Linda with Andrea Pabel, *Let's Ride!* No. Pomfret, VT: Trafalgar Square Publishing, 1997, (800) 423-4525.

Tellington-Jones, Linda, Video Tapes: *The TTouch of Magic for Horses, The TTouch of Magic for Dogs, The TTouch of Magic for Cats,* plus many other horse training videos including TTouch for dressage horses. TTeam Training, Santa Fe, NM 87501, (505) 455-2945.

Thompson, Diana, *The Whole Horse Journal* PO Box 425, Santa Rosa, CA 95402, (707) 542-4646.

Wanless, Mary, *For the Good of the Horse.* No. Pomfret, VT: Trafalgar Square Publishing, 1997, (800) 423-4525.

# Photo Credits

# Index